Hey Ranger 2

Hey Ranger 2

More True Tales of
Humor & Misadventure
from the Great Outdoors

Jim Burnett

TAYLOR TRADE PUBLISHING
Lanham • Boulder • New York • Toronto • Plymouth, UK

This Taylor Trade Publishing paperback edition of *Hey Ranger 2* is an original
publication. It is published by arrangement with the author.

Published by Taylor Trade Publishing
An imprint of The Rowman & Littlefield Publishing Group, Inc.
4501 Forbes Boulevard, Suite 200, Lanham, Maryland 20706

Estover Road, Plymouth PL6 7PY, United Kingdom

Distributed by NATIONAL BOOK NETWORK

Library of Congress Cataloging-in-Publication Data

Burnett, Jim.
    Hey ranger 2 : more true tales of humor & misadventure from the great outdoors /
Jim Burnett.
    p. cm.
    Includes bibliographical references.
    ISBN-13: 978-1-58979-329-3 (pbk. : alk. paper)
    ISBN-10: 1-58979-329-3 (pbk. : alk. paper)
    1. National parks and reserves—United States—Anecdotes. 2. Outdoor life—
United States—Anecdotes. 3. Accidents—United States—Anecdotes. 4. National
parks and reserves—United States—Humor. 5. Outdoor life—United States—
Humor. 6. Accidents—United States—Humor. 7. Burnett, Jim—Anecdotes.
8. Park rangers—United States—Biography—Anecdotes. 9. United States—
Description and travel—Anecdotes. I. Title. II. Title: Hey ranger two.

E160.B775 2007
333.78'30973—dc22
                                                            2006100995

Contents

Introduction

At this moment all across America and around the world, people are involved in an incredible variety of activities in the Great Outdoors. Whether it's a picnic or stroll in a park close to home, a weekend of camping or boating, a backcountry expedition to a remote wilderness area, or any of a host of other outdoor pursuits, spending some time close to nature seems like a fun and healthy idea. After all, what could *possibly* go wrong on a nice outing to a park or other recreation area?

As the stories on the following pages confirm, the answer is—probably more than you could ever imagine!

Perhaps you—or someone you know—has taken such a trip, one that just didn't work out *quite* the way it was planned. If that's the case, you're in good company. Last year there were about 273 million visits to America's national parks alone, not to mention countless excursions to other federal, state, and local public lands. When that many people come into close contact with Mother Nature, it's inevitable that some of those adventures will take an unexpected turn.

Once the excitement is over, many of those situations have a humorous side, and in their aftermath park rangers have been saying for years, "Somebody *really* ought to write a book!" During three decades as a ranger at eight national parks all across the U.S., I came in contact with literally thousands of everyday Americans in an amazing variety of situations, and some of these encounters were shared in *Hey Ranger! True Tales of Humor and Misadventure from America's National Parks.* That book was published in 2005, and its wonderful reception has led to this sequel, which contains additional entertaining stories from national parks and other recreation areas around the country and beyond—even as far away as Australia.

For the benefit of those of you who haven't read the previous *Hey Ranger!* a little explanation of the title is in order. Rangers all over the world are frequently greeted by the phrase "Hey Ranger!" but the *way* those two little words are spoken can convey an amazing variety of meanings. Depending upon the circumstances, those can range from a simple "Hi, how are you?" to a frantic "Help, come quick!" Sometimes there's a definite tone of surprise, which translates into "Oops, I sure didn't expect to see *you* here!" In many cases, what is said or happens next can turn a ranger's day from a routine to a memorable one, and you'll find some amusing and sometimes incredible examples recorded in the following pages.

The job of a park ranger can be both challenging and deadly serious at times, and outdoor mishaps occasionally have dire consequences. It's not my intention to minimize those realities, but this subject has already been well covered by a number of other writers. In both the original *Hey Ranger!* and in this sequel, I've chosen to take a totally different approach and look at the lighter side of life in the parks.

This book is written in an informal, conversational style, and each chapter is its own stand-alone story, so you can read it a bit at a time, whenever you're ready for an entertaining break from your daily routine. Some of the characters in these true tales have narrow escapes, but everybody survives in the end, so the result is fun, family-friendly reading that everyone from veteran outdoorsmen to armchair travelers can enjoy.

Since these *are* true stories, many of the names in this book have been changed in deference to both the guilty and the innocent. A number of readers of my first book and my fellow rangers responded to an invitation to submit their own favorite anecdotes for this sequel, and in those cases their real names have been used to give credit where it's certainly due—unless they preferred to remain anonymous.

Some of you may have occasionally envied the experiences of the men and women who get to work and perhaps live in a park. After all, who wouldn't enjoy a career at some of the most scenic and historic locations in America? At first glance it looks pretty inviting: spend your days floating the river, hiking the trails, talking to visitors, or patrolling the campground. Like any other profession, however, there's a lot more to rangering than first meets the eye, and these stories also include some behind-the-scenes glimpses at a few humorous aspects of the job.

For sake of simplicity, I've used the word *park* throughout the book to refer to the whole range of public parks and recreation areas, regardless of which agency operates a site or whether it's at the federal, state, or local level. If you were to consult a list of all of the official designations for those areas, you'd quickly find that it's a veritable jungle out there, so I'll just make it easy for you and we'll avoid getting lost in that maze of titles.

The writer Charles Dickens noted, "Accidents will occur in the best regulated families." Accidents will also sometimes occur on the "best regulated" outdoor trips, but that's often the way it is with misadventures in the Great Outdoors—they seem to have a way of sneaking up on you, usually at very inconvenient times.

The cover of this book aptly illustrates that mishaps can also result from actions as well as accidents. "Look before you leap" is useful advice only if the individual involved is wise enough to conclude that leaping may not be the best idea after all! As you'll discover on the following pages, some people seem determined to confirm an observation by the eighteenth-century author Charles de Montesquieu: "When God endowed human beings with brains, He did not intend to guarantee them."

I trust you'll find some entertaining and informative insights throughout this book, and in between the smiles discover a few useful tips to help you avoid having one of those "accidents."

Thus prepared, you can join ranks with a former vice president of our country who is reputed to have remarked, "We are ready for an unforeseen event that may or may not occur."

So get out and enjoy a visit to a park or other recreation area—but try to be sure that none of your "unforeseen events" result in a "Hey Ranger!" moment that could earn you a spot in a sequel to *this* book.

Happy reading!

It Seemed Like a Good Idea at the Time

Grand Teton National Park in northwestern Wyoming is one of those "crown-jewel" parks that has something for almost everyone: rugged mountain grandeur that defies description, hiking trails and scenic drives, rushing rivers and crystal blue lakes, world-class mountaineering and places to spend the night that run the gamut from primitive backcountry camping to luxurious lodges.

The park hosts about 2.5 million visitors a year, most of them during the summer season, so it's not surprising that at least a few of those folks unintentionally provided some good material for this book. They did so simply by getting themselves into situations that looked a lot different once the smoke had cleared than they did in the heat of the moment. That was literally the case on one summer evening for the family in the following story.

Many visitors to parks like Grand Teton have some preconceived ideas about activities that just naturally seem to go with the setting. Perhaps it's cooking a meal—or at least toasting a marshmallow—over a campfire, or seeing a particular species of wild animal. For some folks from warmer climates, just the thought that it's going to be chilly enough to justify a cozy fire on a midsummer night sounds mighty appealing. As a native of Texas, I can understand why there's great satisfaction in being able to return home in July to sweltering one-

Grand Teton National Park in Wyoming includes some of the most spectacular mountain scenery in the country, with plenty of opportunities for both fun and miscues in the Great Outdoors. (National Park Service)

hundred-plus degree temperatures and report gleefully to one's neighbors, "It was downright *cold* up there at night!"

Perhaps all those factors came into play when a man, his wife, and two teenage daughters checked into one of the tent cabins operated by a park concessioner at Colter Bay in Grand Teton National Park. These accommodations are constructed of a combination of log and canvas walls and a canvas roof, and are equipped with a potbellied stove to provide a source of warmth—along with a little wilderness ambience—when needed.

On the night in question, the mid-July weather had been unseasonably warm, and the family didn't go to bed until 11:30 P.M. Despite the mild temperature and the late hour, Dad decided to light a fire in the ol' potbellied stove before retiring for the night. For purposes of this story, I'll refer to this gentleman as Gustaf in honor of Gustaf Pasch, the man credited with inventing the safety match in 1844.

Gustaf soon discovered that there is both an art *and* a science to starting a blaze in one of those not-so-modern heating appliances. The sixteenth-century writer John Heywood noted, "There is no fire without some smoke," but more than one modern camper has succeeded in generating an abundance of smoke but very little fire. This was apparently the case in that tent cabin in the Tetons, since several attempts by Gustaf to kindle a blaze using wood and paper were unsuccessful. I don't know if he had any accessories available to aid in his efforts, but ironically several modern products would have been off-limits if he had heeded their seemingly contradictory warning labels.

Gustaf might have been tempted, for example, to try a butane-fueled fireplace lighter, a device described as "having an extended nozzle, typically four to eight inches long, from which the flame is emitted, and typically used to light charcoal and gas grills and fireplaces." Seems like a potentially useful tool for starting a wood fire, and a lot easier than striking countless matches, but a leading brand of those lighters carries the dire warning, "Do not use near fire, flame, or sparks." Hmmm. . . . Well, how about a popular brand of man-made fire logs? They promise to be "easy to light, clean burning," and provide "up to four hours of relaxing flames." Uh-oh, the label also notes in bold, red print: "Caution: Risk of fire." That seeming oxymoron was actually timely advice in this case, since those products aren't intended for use in a wood-burning stove.

When all else fails, surely one could resort to some old-fashioned matches, but one brand carries the warning, "Caution: Contents may catch fire." Goodness, we can't have *that* result from matches, can we? Whatever incendiary aids Gustaf had available, it is likely that the late hour contributed to some serious impatience as his fire-starting efforts continued to fizzle instead of sizzle. It's been said that desperate times call for desperate measures, and necessity may be the mother of invention, but I'd propose that desperation can also lead to the Mother of All Mistakes.

That must have been the case in a classic "it seemed like a good idea at the time" situation, so our intrepid woodsman removed the lid on the top of the obstinate stove and poured some Coleman fuel into the opening—and onto the failed but still faintly smoldering fire.

For benefit of any readers who aren't outdoors types, Coleman fuel is a form of highly refined gasoline intended *solely* for use in the tanks of camping stoves, lanterns, and similar carefully engineered appliances. Conspicuously absent from the list of approved uses for this very flammable substance is "fire starter for potbellied stoves," and the man obviously either failed to read or chose to ignore the warning statements the manufacturer has dutifully included in abundance on each container.

The park's report didn't mention how much fuel was poured into the wood-burning stove, but this is a case of even a *little* dab will more than do you, and as soon as the volatile liquid was added, the smoldering fire immediately burst into flames. While starting a fire was the desired result, I'm confident that Gustaf intended that any combustion be limited to the confines of the stove. Unfortunately, that was not the case, and the suddenly enthusiastic fire quickly spread to the tent walls and ceiling.

The good news is that our leading man suffered only minor injuries, and the family safely evacuated the burning structure. The park fire brigade was summoned, nearby campers assisted in dousing the flames with extinguishers, and the professional firefighters soon arrived to complete the job. As confirmation that foresight actually does pay, the canvas on these tent cabins had been treated with a flame-resistant coating, which ensured that the entire structure did not ignite and burn.

Even so, significant damage resulted, and the family also lost their clothing, camping gear, and bicycles in the fire. I hope the teenagers in the group were old enough that they didn't face the dreaded "What I did on my summer vacation" essay upon their return to school for the fall term. On second thought, this little example of how *not* to do it would probably put them in contention for the grand prize in that exercise.

This next story involved a bizarre example of "fire in the hole" instead of out of the stove, and I share it with a little trepidation, lest I introduce someone to a concept that was previously unknown to any of my readers. However, this event was widely reported in the media, so I'll include it with a warning that the following activity is definitely a no-no in any national park, and a questionable idea anyplace else simply on the grounds of safety.

On a Saturday morning in a recent October, employees at Joshua Tree National Park in California received reports of a disturbance in the group campsites at Indian Grove Campground.

Rangers responded to the area, and during the ensuing investigation confiscated seven homemade cannons that were being used to shoot potatoes.

Yes, I'm talking about your basic spuds, originally made famous in places like Ireland and Idaho. This is definitely a bizarre twist on Longfellow's famous line, "I shot an arrow into the air: It fell to earth I know not where." I'd offer the suggestion that firing *anything* into the air without knowing exactly where it's going to land is not a great idea, but this is especially true in an area such as a public park.

When all was said and done, in addition to the artillery pieces, rangers had confiscated parts for additional cannons and several five-pound bags of potatoes. This produce was presumably intended for launching but was thankfully spared that fate. The campsite where this activity occurred was occupied by a Boy Scout troop, and their leader was issued a citation and warnings for a variety of offenses. This is not intended to be a putdown of scouts or their leaders in general, most of whom do a great job. In this case, though, I had to wonder if they were trying to develop a new merit badge—for a combination of marksmanship and cooking.

I must have led a sheltered life, because prior to reading this report, I confess I was unfamiliar with the concept of using potatoes as artillery rounds. However, a little research determined that this activity has something of a cultlike following. I also read about people who have lost fingers and sustained a variety of other serious injuries while engaged in potato cannoneering, and buildings as far as two blocks away from the cannon have been damaged when struck by potato rounds. That doesn't strike *me* as a desirable outcome.

So if you still insist on trying this, your first step is to find a nice big piece of private property out in the middle of nowhere, then get the owner's permission, and make sure your medical, life, and liability insurance are up to date. I suspect, however, that somewhere in the fine print of those policies is wording that may exclude coverage for such activities. Whatever you do, keep soaring spuds out of public places like parks.

We're all familiar with the old cliché about it raining cats and dogs, and with Chicken Little's cry that "the sky is falling." However, scattered potato showers is definitely a new—and unwelcome—twist if you happen to be on the receiving end of thudding spuds, and this situation certainly adds a new angle to the familiar question, "Would you like fries with that?"

Knowing "when to say when" and recognizing that it's time to call off an activity is a key to having a safe outdoor adventure, a principle aptly illustrated by a story from Utah's Capitol Reef National Park. This is spectacular desert terrain with magnificent rock formations, but like anywhere in the desert, it is also serious flash flood country. A good rule of thumb anywhere, including the desert, is never to drive (or wade) into flooded streams, even if you think the water isn't very deep. The power of running water is simply greater than most people realize, and muddy flood waters can hide drop-offs or other obstructions in what you expect to be a road.

It was early August, and intense storm activity over the previous several days had caused significant flash flooding in the park. In the event you aren't familiar with some western lingo, I'll explain that the normally dry stream beds in this part of the world are often called *washes*. You can ponder the application of the term *wash* to an area normally bereft of any hint of moisture. Perhaps this is akin to the fact that here in the U.S. we drive on parkways and park on driveways.

A couple from Germany was visiting the area in a rented Grand Cherokee and encountered a wash along the Burr Trail Road that actually held water. In a classic "sure wish we hadn't done that" moment, they attempted to drive their vehicle across the flowing water. Perhaps, like many of their counterparts in the U.S., they had seen too many of those TV commercials with SUVs being driven in some highly questionable locations or conditions that seem to defy gravity or a host of other natural laws.

I suspect that somewhere on the bottom of that TV screen there is a brief disclaimer in fine print that says something like, "These are professionals, don't try this at home," "Simulated conditions, not intended to represent actual use," or some similar comment required by the company lawyers. Disclaimers notwithstanding, the impression received by some viewers is, "Don't worry, this baby can go *anywhere!*" I'll refrain from suggesting that this is exactly the message intended by the people who produce those commercials.

As the unfortunate couple at Capitol Reef quickly learned, "it'll go anywhere" is not always the case in the real world, and their vehicle was immediately swept off the road by the force of the water. You can mark this down as true 100 percent of the time: You don't *ever* want to be washed down a wash, either inside or outside of a vehicle. Thankfully, the SUV remained upright as it floated and bounced downstream, although the passenger-side window shattered as the vehicle rocked back and forth on its trip. This allowed some muddy water to slosh into the truck, which I'm sure greatly contributed to the confidence and comfort of the occupants.

The couple stayed in the Jeep as the chocolate-colored water continued to rise and nearly reached window level before, thankfully, it began to drop. I can only imagine their relief when the vehicle finally stopped moving down the wash and the water continued to fall. Perhaps their ensuing optimism stemmed from the fact that they were from Europe, and therefore had a lot more faith in the quality of modern vehicles than I do. For whatever reason, the report states

Originally a cattle trail, the historic Burr Trail Road runs through parts of the rugged backcountry in Utah's Capitol Reef National Park. It is not suitable for all types of vehicles, so inquire locally before making this spectacular drive. (Phil Stoffer, USGS)

that they remained sitting inside their Jeep for the next half-hour, hoping that they could eventually restart the engine and simply drive away.

Maybe the driver was thinking something like, "Hey, this rig is supposed to be *really* tough, and the engine is probably just a little wet. We'll wait here for a bit until it dries out, and then surely it will crank right up." Mere speculation on my part, hindsight is always twenty-twenty, and perhaps there was still more water flowing down the wash than the report suggests. In retrospect, however, they probably wished they had abandoned ship and found a spot on higher ground to wait for help, because before long, a *second* surge of flood water came down the wash.

Unable to open the vehicle's doors, the pair eventually had to climb out through the broken window and then managed to wade to the bank. Amazingly, neither was injured, and they were subsequently found by another group of visitors, who gave them a ride to park headquarters.

Park staff located the Cherokee about a mile downstream from the point where it had originally been swept off the road. The passenger compartment was nearly filled with muddy water, so I'd say the report's description of the SUV as "totaled" was not an exaggeration. I gather that by this time neither the driver nor the rescuers were giving any thought to trying to start the vehicle.

At the conclusion of the park's report, rangers were working with the rental agency on a plan to remove the SUV from the park's backcountry. I'm sure those folks who answer the toll-free numbers for the help desks of car rental companies could write their own book of weird tales, but I suspect this call was one that got referred at least one level up the supervisory chain, with the introductory comment, "Uh, boss, you aren't going to like *this* one. . . ."

Neither the boss nor the bystanders were thrilled with the outcome of our next story, which also involved water in another desert park. This group wanted to get away from it all—or *almost* all. They were on a private (as opposed to commercial) river trip through Cataract Canyon in Utah's Canyonlands National Park, one of the truly classic stretches of serious white water anywhere in the country, and apparently they concluded that their outdoor adventure just wouldn't be complete without the special delivery of one particular item.

According to boaters on a separate commercial river trip in the area, at 11 A.M. on a mid-June morning a low-flying small plane suddenly appeared within the depths of the canyon. In honor of a pair of famous aviation pioneers, I'll just refer to the pilot and his passenger as Wilbur and Orville. The aircraft made three passes through the canyon, the last two at elevations estimated at thirty-five to fifty feet above the river. This was not received with great enthusiasm by the sixty-six people on the commercial trip, who felt they were being "buzzed" by the plane.

Although the commercial group did not witness the actual incident, on the third pass the single-engine airplane suddenly crashed into the river and sank within fifteen minutes. Wilbur later stated that the accident occurred when the aircraft developed an engine problem and he tried to switch fuel tanks. That's a procedure that would seem to require at least brief and full attention to detail, and one ideally to be avoided while flying at a very low altitude through a canyon.

Wilbur and Orville were fortunately able to crawl out of the plane and were rescued by their friends from the private river trip. Both sustained scrapes and bruises, and Orville suffered a broken collarbone. The injured men were treated by an Emergency Medical Technician in the private group and then transferred to a larger, faster-moving boat that was part of a second commercial trip. It carried the pair downstream to a point where they could be moved to a still faster private speed boat.

That craft delivered them to Hite, at the upper end of Lake Powell, where there is a small airstrip. At about 5 P.M., six hours after their unplanned swim began, Wilbur and Orville were loaded onto a small commercial plane that had been hired to fly them to a hospital in Grand Junction, Colorado.

The report didn't mention the cost of these various shuttle services, nor the value of the crashed airplane or the expenses incurred in its removal, but I'm sure the bottom line was a considerable sum. Perhaps you're wondering why the Cessna was buzzing through the canyon in the first place. I'm glad you asked.

By prearrangement with the private river group, the occupants of the plane had dropped a container of ice cream, attached to a life jacket, to the boaters! I guess for some folks, a day in the "wilderness" just isn't complete without their favorite dessert.

The French philosopher Voltaire, who wrote during the eighteenth century, observed that "Ice cream is exquisite. What a pity it isn't illegal." While consuming ice cream is thankfully still legal, delivering it in the manner described above definitely isn't. The report was unfortunately silent on one key piece of information: What flavor of ice cream could *possibly* be worth all that trouble? I certainly don't know, but based on the outcome of this fiasco, I'd suggest that an appropriate guess would be "Rocky Road."

Ignorance Is Not Bliss

One of the interesting aspects of a ranger's job is dealing with questions from park visitors. The moment you put on that uniform, you're assumed by many people to be an expert in virtually *any* subject even remotely connected to the park, the earth, or even the solar system. Oliver Goldsmith once wrote, "Ask me no questions, I'll tell you no fibs," but "ask me no questions" is not a request rangers are allowed to make—at least not while they're on duty. Rangers also aren't supposed to tell fibs in response to visitor's inquiries, although in some cases the temptation can be pretty strong! After you've read the following examples you'll probably understand why that's the case.

Questions come in just about as many varieties as visitors, and they include the daily dozen ("Where's the restroom, is it going to rain today, how far to the nearest McDonalds . . . ?"), the sincere seeker ("What kind of bird, or tree, or flower, or . . . is that?"), and the inane inquiry. It's this last group that can pose a major test of tact and diplomacy. It can sometimes be difficult keeping a straight face when confronted with a question that causes the ranger to wonder, "Is he (or she) really *serious*, or is this one a joke?" More often than not, the question seems to be asked with good intentions, which suggests that one or more of the following are true:

1. a significant percentage of park visitors really are in a totally alien environment once they leave the city or the suburbs, so they simply don't know any better;
2. this person decided to give his brain a vacation, too, so he left it at home during his trip;

3. the American educational system is in far more serious trouble than even the pundits in the media would have us believe.

Many of the following questions have been a part of ranger lore for years and others are relative newcomers. Some were asked of me personally, and a few were sent by Considerate Contributors in response to my invitation to submit material for this book. Where necessary, I'll provide a little background so you can understand the context of the question.

Mesa Verde National Park in southwestern Colorado contains numerous examples of world-class cliff dwellings and other archeological treasures. Several of the best sites require at least a short hike from the parking lot, prompting rangers at that park to be asked more than once, "Why did the Indians build the ruins so *far* from the road?" (One would think they'd have been more considerate of the tourists who would come to see what was left of their homes hundreds of years later.)

Mesa Verde National Park in Colorado contains more than 4,000 known archeological sites and over 600 cliff dwellings. These visitors are taking a tour of the largest ruin, now known as Cliff Palace. (Phil Stoffer, USGS)

The staff at Mesa Verde also has to endure the inquiry, "Why did the Indians only build *ruins*? Did they run out of money before they finished?" (Those ancient structures were built long before Europeans arrived in North America, so at least we know the answer to that question isn't, "It was a government funded project, and Congress didn't appropriate enough money to finish the building.")

Carlsbad Caverns National Park in New Mexico is to caves what the National Gallery is to art. There are plenty of caves in the world that boast magnificent or unique formations and others that lay claim to many miles of passageways, but for the combination of beauty, size, and easy access for the average visitor, it's tough to beat the underground wonders of Carlsbad.

Located within the boundaries of the same park are both Carlsbad Caverns and Lechuguilla Cave. Between the two, the park offers a nice variety of tours, from paved walking trails that wind through tastefully lighted rooms, to completely wild, undeveloped routes that require expert spelunking skills and a permit or a trained guide to explore.

Reports will occasionally surface in the media about another major find of a new area of the caverns, especially at Lechuguilla Cave. It's those news stories that probably account for some of the following

Look but don't touch! Carlsbad Caverns National Park in New Mexico offers the chance to easily enjoy some of the most beautiful cave formations in the world. (National Park Service)

questions inflicted on rangers at that park and undoubtedly at other areas that have caves:

"How much of the cave hasn't been discovered yet?" and a closely related inquiry, "What's *in* the undiscovered part of the cave?" (Rangers are very talented at what they do, but the answers to these questions require extrasensory perception or other prophetic abilities that are not part of their job description.)

Those inquiries can probably be placed in the "I just didn't think about what I was asking" category, but I do have to wonder about, "How much of the cave is *under*ground?"

Caves that still have actively growing formations tend to be damp, since those stalactites "hanging" from the ceiling and the stalagmites "growing" from the floor of the cave are formed by mineral deposits dissolved in water that seeps down through the layers of rock above. This is presumably the basis for the inquiry, "Why don't you fix all the drips and leaks in here?"

Many parks have entrance stations, where visitors pay the required fee to—guess what—enter the park. The employees who staff those facilities are some of the unsung heroes of the National Park Service. They are almost always the first contact visitors have with any official representative of the park, and the work requires both stamina and patience.

One of the dubious "fringe benefits" of working in an entrance station is the chance to hear—and try to answer—some classic questions. Among them is a trio of closely related inquiries: "Where am I, and how did I get here?" "Where am I and why am I here?" and "I need to know how to get back to where I came from."

Apparently these employees are presumed by some visitors to have psychic powers, and I'm sure it takes admirable restraint to avoid suggesting to the occasional grouch that the employee would not only be glad to tell the person how to get back where he came from, but also to help him do so as quickly as possible.

A spin-off to the various entrance station inquiries is the occasional visitor who stops a ranger or other employee and says he's finished his visit but can't find the way back out of the park. In some cases, this question comes within sight of the entrance station, which is duly pointed out by the park staff member.

"No, you don't understand," is the visitor's reply. "I'm not looking for the entrance; I'm trying to find the *exit*." (It's a challenge to find a polite way to suggest he try the outgoing lane on the opposite side of the entrance station.)

Every park also has its own set of site-specific, traditional questions. A major landmark at Yosemite National Park in California is a spectacular cliff face named Half Dome, so I guess the question "What happened to the *other* half of Half Dome?" is inevitable. Some people apparently assume the natural features in the park were installed there just for the purpose of entertaining park visitors. That's the only reason I can imagine why anyone would ask at Yellowstone National Park, "Do the geysers erupt at night?"

Perhaps that's related to the old philosophical question about whether a tree falling in the forest makes any sound if there's no one there to hear it fall. If it's dark and there's no one to see the geyser erupt, why should it bother?

One of the great scenic drives in the world is the Going-to-the-Sun Road in Glacier National Park, which crosses the Continental Divide at Logan Pass at an elevation of 6,646 feet. Even at midday in the summer it's usually pleasantly cool—and sometimes downright chilly—at that altitude in Montana, but I actually had one visitor ask me why it didn't get *warmer* as they neared the summit. Their reasoning—honest now—was that they thought it should be getting hotter as they approached the pass since the road was taking them closer to the sun!

The companion question to the previous one sometimes occurs at Grand Canyon National Park, where it's roughly a vertical mile from the top of the canyon's South Rim to the Colorado River in the bottom of the famous gorge. Some visitors are under the mistaken impression that the temperature gets cooler as you descend into the canyon. I can only guess that these folks are applying the analogy of entering a cave, where the temperature (at least in the summer) is normally cooler inside than outside the cavern.

The obvious problem with comparing this or any other canyon to a cave is the fact that one key component is missing in the case of a canyon—the ceiling. Perhaps these are the same folks mentioned previously who wondered how much of the cave is underground.

Just for the record, temperatures almost always rise as you descend into a deep canyon, although there are always exceptions, such as shady areas near a waterfall. The serious summer heat within places like the Grand Canyon is a major contributor to the number of search and rescue missions, and a common mistake for canyon hikers is the failure to carry—and consume—enough water and other suitable liquids. For some tips on safe hiking in any climate, see the "Useful Links" page on the Internet at www.heyranger.com.

Yosemite National Park includes incomparable scenery all year long. Just don't worry about what happened to the "other half" of the huge rock named Half Dome. (National Park Service)

After the publication of my first book, I had the opportunity to do several live radio interviews, including National Public Radio's "Talk of the Nation." Part of that show included questions phoned in by listeners, so much of the fun was that I (and the program host) were never sure what was coming next.

One of my favorites was a question that comes in several variations, depending upon what part of the country you're in. The caller was a former seasonal park ranger at Rocky Mountain National Park, who noted that she had been asked on a number of occasions, "At what elevation do the *moose* turn into *elk*?"

I was strongly tempted to comment, "It depends upon which side of the Continental Divide you're on," but remembering that I was on

Moose are fun to watch but can be ill-tempered, so photograph them from a safe distance. Despite occasional questions to the contrary, they never turn into elk, regardless of the elevation at which you may find them. (National Park Service)

live national radio on a reputable network, I decided against it. After all, someone, somewhere, would probably hear that response from a retired park ranger and take me seriously!

Geography and basic scientific principles apparently pose challenges for some folks, as almost any ranger who has worked at a park along a seacoast can probably attest. I consulted several reputable textbooks and dictionaries to be sure things haven't changed in the years since I took that general science class, and those sources all agree that the terms *altitude* and *elevation* normally refer to the height above sea level, with sea level representing "0" on the scale.

Since that's the case, it's interesting to hear someone sitting in a boat on the ocean ask, "What elevation are we at right here?" If you're in places like Alaska where you can see impressive mountains right from the ocean, perhaps that gives the illusion that the elevation of the *water* must be higher as well.

I'll concede that the tide rises and falls by several feet during the course of the day and that if you want to split hairs you can get into discussions about terms such as *mean sea level*, so we'll cut these folks at least a *little* slack. If the reason for the question was concern about whether they'd get a nosebleed from the altitude, or if they need to

Elk are found in many parts of the country. Sometimes mistaken for deer, adults such as this bull and cow are larger than Bambi and his relatives. (U.S. Army Corps of Engineers)

check with their cardiologist about whether they're going to need supplemental oxygen, I don't think they had cause for concern, at least as long as they stayed on board the boat.

Now, don't you wish you had the chance to answer such great questions on *your* job? Maybe you already do, so start taking notes for your own book!

The metric system used in most of the rest of the world does create some confusion in a few areas. When I worked at Glacier National Park in northwestern Montana, our best radio reception was often from stations across the border in Canada. That was obviously the case for tourists as well as local residents, and visitors from further south weren't accustomed to hearing the weather forecast refer to temperatures using the Celsius (C) rather than our more familiar Fahrenheit (F) scale. This was standard stuff in Canada, so just as in the U.S., the weatherman simply tossed out the numbers and didn't normally bother to mention that these degrees were of the Celsius variety.

I did a mental double take a few times myself when we first moved there, so it's only fair to give you a quick refresher course in the difference between the two systems. The freezing point for fresh water is 32°F but 0°C. A comfortable summertime high of 75°F would be about

24°C, and a nice, brisk evening of 45°F would read about 7° on the Celsius scale.

Those differences would explain the dismay I'd occasionally hear expressed by visitors to that park after they'd heard a weather report on their car radio from a Canadian station.

"Hey Ranger! We were planning to camp out tonight, and we knew it would get colder up here in the mountains than it does back home. We were looking forward to getting away from the summer heat, but we just heard the weather forecast on the radio, and they said the low tonight is supposed to be only 5°. We didn't come prepared for it to get *that* cold up here! All the motels in the area are full. Do you know where we could buy some extra blankets or sleeping bags?"

These visitors were invariably relieved to learn that the coming night should be pleasantly chilly but not unreasonably frigid, and that furthermore there was no secret government cover-up about a return of the Great Ice Age. Now that you've read this chapter, you'll know that there's no cause for concern on that point—unless you notice that above an altitude of 5,000 feet anywhere in the lower 48 states the grizzly bears are turning into polar bears.

Does the River Run Downstream?

Forming part of the border between Pennsylvania and New Jersey, the Delaware River is one of the most popular locations for float trips in the northeastern United States. Forty miles of the river flow through the Delaware Water Gap National Recreation Area, and since portions of the park are within about seventy miles of New York City, the area can be a little busy at times. A Tuesday in late September probably seemed like a great day for a canoe trip on the Delaware River for a couple we'll call Jack and Jill, for reasons that will become apparent later. They'd miss the weekend crowds and enjoy some pleasant fall weather.

Jack and Jill rented a canoe from a local outfitter for a one-day outing on the Delaware and headed to a location called Smithfield Beach to start their adventure. Their destination—a spot called Kittatinny Point—was only six miles downstream, and under typical conditions their trip would require about three hours. The canoe rental company employee arranged to meet them later that afternoon at Kittatinny Point and shuttle them back to their car.

Their destination had an additional advantage as a place to end a voyage on the Delaware River, especially for boaters who were not familiar with the territory. Information on the park's website states, "Passing under the Interstate 80 bridge, canoers should paddle towards

Canoeing is a great way to enjoy beautiful rivers and lakes. Choose a trip appropriate for your skill level—and always be sure you know which direction is *down*stream! (U.S. Army Corps of Engineers)

the left (New Jersey) bank to reach the canoe beach at Kittatinny Point."

An interstate highway bridge would qualify as a major landmark for virtually anyone and, therefore, make it pretty hard to paddle accidentally past their goal. On any river trip, overshooting a takeout point can have consequences ranging from inconvenient to catastrophic, depending upon what lies downstream and how far it is to the next spot where boaters can safely end their trip.

Jack and Jill probably had in mind a quiet, relaxing day, drifting lazily down the river and enjoying some early fall color as they were carried gently along by the current. They'd paddle a little along the way but wouldn't work up a serious sweat. The Delaware River doesn't really have anything that would qualify as major rapids, but some occasional riffles might add just a little touch of excitement to the trip.

Our couple embarked on their mini-adventure, but after six hours of steady paddling, Jack and Jill had managed to cover only about three miles of river. Based on their available information, they'd already journeyed for twice as long as expected, but anything even remotely resembling the landmark I-80 bridge had not appeared. I suspect that by then, they had decided that this canoeing business was a lot harder than it looked on those TV shows touting "fun and easy outdoor getaways within a day's drive of home." What could possibly have gone wrong?

Jill later said, "When we reached the fourth set of rapids and the water was *still* going the 'wrong' way, we decided *we* had probably been going the wrong way." Perhaps they figured that the *first* three sets of rapids had been a little confused, and the situation would change if they just hung in there a little longer.

Quite a few years back, a fellow named Newton came up with the concept of something called gravity. Among the implications of this law of physics is the fact that water in a free-flowing, natural state will *always* run downhill, leading to a corollary of Newton's law: The river always runs *downstream*. Perhaps Jack and Jill both happened to be absent when that topic was covered in science class, which just goes to show it's always good to ask for the makeup assignment if you miss any days of school.

A commonly accepted definition of the term *canoeing* is "to travel by canoe down a river." The absence of a strong current in the river may have caused some confusion, but after launching their canoe, Jack and Jill had obviously made just one mistake. However, it was a biggie: they headed *up*stream instead of downstream.

Given their intended destination for the day, this is akin to driving from New York to Miami by way of Toronto, and it illustrates another definition of the word *gravity*. If you're headed the opposite direction than you intend on a canoe or any other kind of trip, the gravity of your situation will eventually become apparent. How quickly that revelation occurs will be a major factor in determining whether you look back on this day with a grin or a grimace.

This is probably a good spot to offer some free Rangerly Advice, although I realize that for many people this goes against the grain of the Independent American Spirit, especially as it applies to travel. This seems to be especially hard for those of us who are included among the male gender, but it's really pretty painless: When navigation is in doubt, just stop and ask for directions.

In the case of Jack and Jill, a variation of that principle applies: Get some basic information from a reliable source before heading out in a canoe, kayak, inner tube, boat, or any other aquatic conveyance on unfamiliar waters. I'd say the odds are extremely high that the canoe company employee could have provided one very important detail, supplemented if necessary with hand motions: downstream is *thataway*. Lacking that essential data, this trip was definitely destined from the outset to qualify as a Preventable Melancholy Situation. Finally accepting their error, the couple decided to turn around and paddled back downstream for another ninety minutes. At least the going got a lot easier.

By this time, daylight was fading, so Jack and Jill made at least one good decision, and wisely concluded they should pull over to the shore and wait for morning. Stopping where you are and waiting for help is *always* the right call on any trip to the Great Outdoors if you're faced with impending darkness, haven't the slightest clue where you are, and therefore have no idea how far it is to your destination.

Ironically, in this particular case, our couple didn't realize that they were only about a hundred yards upstream from the point where they had started, over seven hours earlier! The Proper Authorities were notified when the pair didn't arrive at their takeout point, rangers Mike Zirwas and Jennifer Kavanaugh began a search, and the missing boaters were found in pitch darkness and in good shape. While another Jack and Jill intentionally went up a hill, our duo mistakenly went up a river with the best of intentions but the worst of directions. I hope they completed their adventure a little wiser about the fact that rivers really *do* run *down*stream.

There are a lot of rivers where there's usually enough current to make it pretty obvious which way the river is running. Among those is the Buffalo National River, one of the premier places in the U.S. for a canoe trip. Located in the Ozarks of northern Arkansas, this park includes 135 of the river's 153 miles. One of the most popular sections of the Buffalo River is a seven-and-a-half-mile day trip between Buffalo Point and Rush Landing, named for the site of a mining rush back in the late 1800s.

Most of the year this is a great choice for families and novices—just enough current and a few minor rapids to make it interesting but nothing that requires much skill, unless the river is running high due to recent rainfall. There is, however, one key point that all of the canoe rental companies emphasize to their customers—*don't* miss the takeout point at Rush Landing. Unlike Jack and Jill's intended destination on the Delaware, I'm happy to report for the sake of the scenery that there is not an interstate highway crossing the Buffalo River at that point to use as a landmark. If Rush Landing happens to be deserted when you arrive, you have to be paying at least a little attention to avoid overshooting that spot.

Immediately beyond Rush, the river takes a sharp bend and forms an "S" curve at the point where Clabber Creek enters the Buffalo from the left-hand bank. Over the years this tributary has carried lots of rocks into the channel of the Buffalo, creating Clabber Creek Shoal, the only really challenging rapid on the lower portion of the river. At this location there's no question that the river runs downstream!

If the water level is high enough, it is possible—with skill and a little daring—to travel back upstream through these rapids in a flat-bottomed johnboat powered by an outboard motor. Just don't plan to *paddle* back upriver at this spot in a canoe.

In his *Buffalo River Handbook*, author Ken Smith describes this spot as "the wildest rapids of the lower river. . . . Where Clabber Creek enters from the left at the end of Rush Creek Hole, the shoal spills off to the right and then sharply to the left. The first hazard is getting swept into the right bank; immediately afterward the danger is being swamped in big Haystack waves."

This is clearly not a desirable stretch of river for anyone other than experienced boaters. Oh, there's just one other little detail: once you pass Rush Landing and go through Clabber Creek Shoal, you enter the Lower Buffalo Wilderness Area. It's then about twenty-four miles to the next maintained road and takeout point, where the Buffalo empties into the White River. Missing the takeout at Rush would convert an easy day trip into an unplanned expedition that usually takes at least two full days by canoe. I'll let you guess what percentage of casual canoeists are prepared for *that* trip.

The park staff has tried to prevent such errors by putting up a sign marking Rush Landing and doing its best to ensure that canoe outfitters educate their customers on this important point. The rental companies themselves are motivated to do so, since they aren't thrilled with the prospect of having to make a very long drive to retrieve their canoes from the White River. Even so, unplanned adventures sometimes occur.

On the day in this story, a group of a dozen people in six canoes left Buffalo Point, headed for Rush. The couple in the lead canoe failed to make the scheduled stop at the landing and continued on through the rapids at Clabber Creek, despite yells from their friends to stop.

The remainder of the group had beached safely at Rush and waited for a few minutes to see if their companions would somehow manage to return. Due to the sharp bend in the river at the rapids and the thick trees and brush on the shoreline, it's not possible from the landing to see what's happening downstream below the rapids, so the fate of the lead canoe and its occupants was unknown.

After some time had passed, with no sign or sound from the hapless pair, the rest of the party held a powwow. Loyalty overcame discretion, and a decision was made to send a *second* canoe with two people downstream to check on the missing couple. It's important to know that everyone in the group was in the beginner canoeist category, so in retrospect it wasn't exactly clear what the intended "rescuers" hoped to accomplish. Nonetheless, two volunteers stepped forward and launched their craft into the Great Unknown.

Several more minutes passed, and despite considerable yelling and hopeful listening from the Rush contingent, there was no reply from the downstream quartet. The remaining party now consisted of eight people and four canoes. Another strategy session was held, and . . . drum roll, please.

The decision was—since two canoes and four people had disappeared downstream without a trace, and since none of the remainder of the group had any skills whatsoever in dealing with such situations, why not launch *another* canoe and send two *more* people into this watery black hole and see if *they* can solve the problem? This apparently seemed like a good idea at the time, so away went another pair. At least the numbers were now even, with half the group safely ashore at Rush Landing and the other half somewhere downstream in the Land of Mystery.

In his famous work *Leaves of Grass*, Walt Whitman wrote, "Conquering, holding, daring, venturing as we go the unknown ways, 'Pioneers! O pioneers.'" I don't know if this group of canoeists felt like pioneers, but any "conquering" was being done by the river and "holding" was probably limited to holding *on* for dear life once their canoes started through the rapids. I will concede they were "daring" and will tactfully withhold any comments about the wisdom of that trait in this situation. Finally, they certainly did venture into "unknown ways" and places.

Long after this little adventure had ended, I've pondered the rationale of the group. One theory is that there may be a primeval urge in mankind, similar to the one that caused the people in some ancient cultures to toss unlucky maidens into the mouth of a volcano in an effort to appease their fire gods. In the case of the canoe group, perhaps they thought if they just sent enough people over the brink, the river would finally be satisfied and toss all of them back upstream again!

Fortunately the remaining six people finally concluded that it "might be a good idea to call the rangers." This was one of those fortuitous occasions when help was actually in the right place at the right time, and no sooner had a good decision been made by the group than—almost as if by magic—the cavalry arrived.

A fellow ranger named Mike Holmes and I were on boat patrol on the Buffalo, and as we approached Rush we saw a group of people on the bank. As soon as they spotted us we heard the familiar cry, "Hey Ranger!" Based on the vigor of the accompanying arm-waving and jumping up and down by these folks, we rated this situation as at least a "moderate" on the Impending Crisis Scale.

We pulled our boat to the bank, and it didn't take long to get the full story. Fortunately we were conducting that patrol in a flat-bottomed johnboat with an outboard motor, rather than in a canoe, so we at least had a good chance of making a return trip to Rush after checking on the missing boaters. After safely navigating the rapids, it didn't take us long to start spotting canoes and their previous passengers scattered up and down the riverbank. All had taken an unplanned swim but were fortunately wearing their life jackets and had made it safely to shore.

Within half an hour, we had the people and their possessions rounded up and back in one spot not too far downstream from Clabber Creek. For at least one day, these hapless boaters seemed to feel they had received some tangible value from those contributions they make to Uncle Sam every year on April 15. It was already obvious to everyone that any attempt to paddle back upstream through the rapids was out of the question, and we explained that the idea of towing the canoes back to Rush, one at a time behind our johnboat, wasn't really feasible either.

At least one of the group already knew that it was over twenty miles down to the White River, and when he shared this cheering prospect with his buddies, a somber gloom settled over the crowd. At that point, it was easy for a ranger to become a hero simply by knowing his territory.

Although it wasn't visible from the bank due to the vegetation, a little distance inland from the river in this area are traces of an old, abandoned road. This route was used decades earlier by wagon freighters during the mining boom years at Rush, as they hauled zinc ore down to the White River and returned with supplies. Not far downstream from Rush, what remains of the road is often blocked by huge piles of driftwood deposited by periodic floods. However, unless the river is unusually high and flooding the old road, it's possible to use this route just below Clabber Creek to bypass the rapids on foot and return to Rush.

It was simply a matter of knowing where to find the path, haul the canoes back to the crossing over Clabber Creek, wade that stream, and then portage the boats a short distance back down the road to Rush Landing. When compared to a twenty-plus-mile, multinight paddle, this option was a really easy sell to our group, and within an hour, everybody was safely back at Rush and eventually headed on their way home.

There are some good lessons to be learned from these stories for anyone planning a river trip anywhere, anytime, but they are especially applicable for any "pioneers" venturing into The Great Unknown: Don't rush into anything until you know where you're headed, be sure you can recognize your destination when you've arrived, and, above all, remember—the river *always* runs downstream!

Stalking the Wild Beast

National parks and similar sites can provide some outstanding opportunities for nature photography. Whether it's sunsets or snow-capped peaks, wildflowers or wild animals, planning, patience, and often just plain ol' good luck can provide a chance for a prizewinning shot—or a least one good enough to inflict on your family and friends when you get back home.

The technology may change over the years, but the dreaded offer still arises from time to time: "Hey, let me show you the pictures (or movies, slides, video, or DVD) of our vacation!" Sorry, how to get out of *that* one politely is beyond the scope of this book.

The best you can do is hope that the images in question are going to be shown on a large screen rather than in a scrapbook or a pile of photos passed from hand to hand. If you've lucked out and gotten the on-screen version (anything from ancient slides to a modern DVD), give this line a try: "You know, I bet the color would be a *lot* clearer if we turned out *all* the lights in the room."

If there's more than one of you in the captive audience, discreetly select one as the Designated Commenter ("oh, ah, wow, I can't believe *you* took that picture . . .") and the rest of you can at least get a nap once the lights are turned off. Important disclaimer: If you're prone to snoring even during a short nap, you should volunteer to be the Designated Commenter (DC). If you tend to sleep soundly, it would also be wise to sit close to the DC, so he or she can give you an unobtrusive poke in the ribs just before the lights come back up at the end of the show.

By the way, don't confuse the job of Designated *Commenter* with that of the Designated *Commentator*. The latter is always self-appointed and is the person (or sometimes a couple) who offered to show you those photos in the first place and provide the detailed commentary on their trip. I'll try to make an important contribution to society and suggest that if you just happen to have some great pictures of your last trip (or two or three), please be slow to offer to share those with others unless you are absolutely, positively certain that they *really* want to see them!

If you find yourself a captive for a photo-sharing session, perhaps you'll be in luck and have a friend who actually *is* a gifted photographer, and everyone can enjoy the travelogue. Along with scenery, wild animals rank high on the list of favorite outdoor photo subjects, and for good reason. In areas where they are legally protected from hunting and other disturbance, many birds and animals gradually lose their fear of humans and can be approached much more closely than in other locations.

This, of course, creates its own set of challenges, and I'll keep the sermon short. Despite appearances to the contrary, parks are not petting zoos, animals that live there *are* still wild, and they can certainly be dangerous. Just follow two basic rules: Keep a safe distance, and never, ever offer food to a bird or animal to try to lure it closer for a good photo. Check with rangers about appropriate distances, because

Way too close for comfort! Elk are tempting subjects for photos, but these large animals are surprisingly agile and can be very dangerous if approached too closely. (National Park Service)

some parks, such as Yellowstone, have regulations about how far people must remain from wildlife for safety reasons.

Modern cameras with telephoto and zoom lenses do make it possible to get photos that weren't an option even a few years ago. If you don't have a lens with enough power to get that wildlife photo from a safe distance, buy a commercial shot or postcard at the visitor center.

Longer ago than I'll admit I was a youngster on a family vacation to the Great Smoky Mountains National Park, in the days when roadside bears were commonplace. Back in those olden times, many people's photos were taken with a simple box camera—no adjustments necessary or possible. You just looked through the viewfinder and clicked the button. The closest equivalent today would be those inexpensive, one-time-use cameras.

The problem with those basic cameras was that what you saw through that tiny viewfinder was akin to the image in the passenger-side mirror on your car, except the cameras didn't come with that familiar warning, "Objects in mirror are closer than they appear." What you saw through that camera appeared to be quite distant, perhaps somewhere in the next county, even though you really might be only a few feet away.

A great way to watch wildlife safely. This ranger is getting a spotting scope lined up so a group of visitors can enjoy a better view. (National Park Service)

Hey Ranger 2

Late one afternoon on my visit to the Smoky Mountains, a shout was heard in the campground: "Here comes a bear!" Sure enough, an adult black bear was casually ambling through the adjoining campsite, and lots of Kodak moments were being snapped by a small crowd of onlookers. One middle-aged man knelt down directly in the animal's path, but a reasonably prudent distance away. He brought his camera up to one eye, closed the other eye, poised his trigger finger over the shutter button, and then waited, and waited, and . . . .

Perhaps the man was inexperienced with the camera, or maybe he was simply excited and forgot that a vast gulf existed between the real world and what he saw through that viewfinder. Soon a couple of people standing nearby began shouting advice to the photographer that it was time to relocate, but our shutterbug was either deaf or determined. Finally, a semihysterical woman, presumably a relative of the photographer, screamed at the man to "run!"

Incidentally, "run" is *not* good advice in any encounter with a bear in the wild, but our character was apparently finally satisfied that he had an adequate photo and decided it was time to move along. I hope he got his shot before he lowered the camera, opened both eyes, and found himself only a couple of yards from his subject!

I'll never know whether it was quick reflexes, classic clumsiness, or just blind luck, but without even rising to his feet the man managed to lunge horizontally a very impressive distance as the bear ambled past. The photographer's agile move was deserving of consideration for a future Olympics gymnastic routine, where both the Russian judge and I would award him at least a 9.5 on a 10-point scale. The good news was that the photographer apparently didn't have a Snickers bar or other tasty items stuffed in a pocket, and the animal simply ignored him and continued on toward the nearest garbage can. Sometimes it's simply better to be lucky than smart.

Other quests for photographs can have a different kind of surprise. Candid Contributor Pat Ballengee of Catheys Valley, California, shared the following story to prove that you can't always believe your ears:

> In the early 1980s I visited Grand Teton National Park on a three-month journey west. I traveled with two cats in a full-size van, camping along the way. My feline companions were house cats, and road travel was something they didn't love, but they adjusted. Charlie was the more adventurous of the two. He didn't mind a leash, and his deep, groan-like voice, characteristic of the Siamese, would holler continually during our entire walk.

One day we stopped at an empty parking area that provided a hiking trail alongside Jenny Lake, and Charlie was aching for some new scenery. The trail was narrow, winding, and wooded, and one side afforded lovely views of the lake and Tetons beyond. Along the opposite side of the trail, both up ahead and behind, the foliage was thick and obscured visibility.

Charlie dove into that walk having a lot of energy to work off. His loud, long, groaning meows broke the still silence of the lakeside trail as we began our hike. Back in the parking lot, a couple arrived to take some photos. I heard their faint voices behind us, and walking a cat is very slow exercise, so I was waiting for the people to get closer so I could gather up Charlie and make room for them to pass.

Time went by, but the other people weren't catching up with us. Charlie and I walked on, and they *still* weren't catching up. I continued to hear the same faint voices, but I noticed they were now like whispers, rather than faraway voices. All at once I heard an outbreak of laughter directly next to us behind the thick foliage. The couple had heard the sounds from Charlie and had been stalking quietly through the bushes in the hopes of seeing the "big cat" making all that noise! The man's camera had been poised to catch the wild animal on film before it bounded away!

Sometimes the mere suggestion that wild animals may be found in the area forms the basis for a great story. Candid Contributor Linda Kennedy from Belgrade Lakes, Maine, shared a wildlife tale that confirms that some people who have spent their lives in urban America simply have little or no experience with the natural world. Linda and an acquaintance were headed to a rural area of northern Maine for a weekend retreat. Their drive took them down a two-lane highway through a remote area, and as they were riding along, Linda's passenger noticed a sign that read "Moose crossing next 15 miles."

An adult moose is a very large animal, and hitting one with a vehicle can be a serious situation for both the moose and the occupants of the car. As a result, the Appropriate Authorities had posted the sign to warn motorists to be especially alert along that particular stretch of highway. To draw extra attention to the notice, the sign in question was even fitted with blinking lights.

Linda's city-dwelling passenger was quite curious about the sign and couldn't figure out how the light would blink if a moose were about to cross the highway. Linda describes herself as something of a comedian, so she mentioned in a matter-of-fact tone that the moose had all gone to road-crossing school and had learned to push a button to acti-

Mountain lions are majestic animals that are rarely seen by humans. They're also potentially dangerous, so if you're in "lion country" inquire about what to do—and not do—if you encounter one. (National Park Service)

vate the warning lights, just as people do for pedestrian crosswalks in the city.

The scary part of this story is that the lady actually believed this tale, and she talked about it during the whole weekend. Linda says she finally had to come clean on the ride home, thereby saving her guest from a potentially embarrassing situation in the future.

Some encounters with wildlife have the potential to be painful if not deadly and they don't all involve bears, moose, or other large animals. An example occurred during one of the highlights of my ranger career—the opportunity to run the Colorado River through the Grand Canyon. In case that term isn't familiar to you, I'm not suggesting that either I or any other rangers (good as they are) can run or walk on water. This "river running" was aboard a large inflatable raft during a ten-day trip that covered most of the length of the canyon—225 river miles beginning at Lee's Ferry, just downstream from Glen Canyon Dam, and ending at a spot in the lower end of the canyon named Diamond Creek.

In those days the park normally made about two river patrols a month through the length of the canyon. In addition to the ten days actually spent on the river, each trip required time to buy supplies, load a small mountain of gear, and haul it by truck on a lengthy drive to the put-in point at Lee's Ferry. At the end of the trip, most of those steps had to be repeated in reverse when equipment was cleaned, repaired, and repacked for the next voyage.

It was a pretty demanding schedule for the one Boatman, as the river ranger was called, so a seasonal (temporary) employee was designated as the "Assistant Boatman," whom I'll refer to from this point on as simply the "AB." This individual's primary tasks were to load the boat in the morning, unload it in the evening, handle the cooking, dishwashing, and other camp chores, and perform any and all "other duties as assigned." This allowed the Boatman to concentrate on safely navigating a challenging stretch of river, where running the rapids required skill, concentration, split-second decisions, and sometimes a bit of daring. It may sound like—and is—a great job, but it also comes with considerable responsibility, especially if you're transporting other people on your boat.

During my first summer at the Grand Canyon, a special river trip was planned in late July. In addition to the usual "patrol" purposes of this expedition, it also included transporting six scientists who were conducting a variety of research projects in the depths of the canyon. Good scientific data is important if any park is to make sound decisions about managing its natural resources, so these projects were important to both the NPS and the individual researchers.

Shortly before this trip was scheduled to depart, the AB resigned, and I was given the opportunity to fill in for this one trip while a long-term replacement was hired. The job was just as advertised, but in addition to a great experience it came with one significant fringe benefit: The Boatman and his assistant got to sleep on the boat each night, while everyone else picked out a spot on the beach.

Camp was made each night on a sandbar along the bank of the river, and depending upon their preferences for accommodations, our passengers either rolled out a sleeping bag, pitched a small tent, inflated an air mattress, or all of the above. Due to the warm weather, more sleeping was done on top of rather than inside sleeping bags, and that's what made the boat such a great spot.

Sleeping on the partially beached raft was similar to the combination of a giant waterbed and the mother of all air mattresses. It was also cooler than on the sandbar, but there just wasn't room for everybody on the trip to share this suite.

I didn't fully appreciate the benefits of this arrangement until one morning about halfway through the trip. Everyone was starting to stir from his bed and look for that first cup of campfire coffee, thoughtfully prepared by the early-rising AB. One of our researchers preferred to sleep a little further away from the rest of the group, and as he started to roll up his sleeping bag, he alertly spotted an unusual pattern in the sand. Upon closer examination, he noticed that these markings appeared to be tiny tracks, which ran across the soft sand to the edge of his sleeping spot, disappeared, and then resumed on the opposite side of the place where he had spent the night.

A great thing about this group was that no matter how obscure the question, if it involved the natural world someone in the party probably knew the answer. Scientists are by nature curious individuals, and when our alert observer commented about this interesting phenomenon, a crowd gathered around to see what could be learned.

One among our number was by trade an entomologist, or insect expert, and he immediately solved the mystery.

"Hey, look at that," he exclaimed. "That's really amazing!" Turning to the man who had spent the night in that spot, he commented, "Good thing you're a sound sleeper."

"Why's that?" asked his companion.

"Know what those tracks are?"

"Well, no." This man's specialty was fish, which don't leave many footprints in the sand.

"Scorpion," replied the bug guy in a matter-of-fact tone. "They're nocturnal, so they're only active after dark. Looks like that little rascal took a stroll across the beach during the night, marched right across your body, back down the other side, and kept on going."

A somber silence descended upon the rest of the group, as they all pondered their own nearby sleeping spots on the ground. Our resident expert in things that scurry in the night sensed the discomfort and sought to reassure his comrades.

"Scorpions rarely bother people unless they're stepped on or feel threatened, and besides, only one species in this area has venom that's really dangerous to humans. Otherwise, a sting isn't much worse than a wasp's, unless you happen to be allergic to the venom." Glancing over at the man who'd had an unknown close encounter of the creepy kind, he concluded cheerfully, "It's good you didn't swat at him in your sleep, though."

Thus supposedly reassured, the crew went back to the business of breaking camp. A good rule of thumb anytime, but especially if you're camping, is always to shake out your shoes, boots, and other items of clothing before putting them on. The same advice applies to a sleeping bag or other covers before crawling in for a snooze. The purpose of that shaking is to dislodge any nonhuman life forms that may have taken up residence in those locations before you insert one of your body parts into the same space.

I couldn't help but observe that there seemed to be a renewed vigor in such precautionary measures for the balance of the trip. It was a bit like the situation at times in parts of California and other earthquake territory—there was a *whole* lot of shakin' going on. There must have been some further review of sleeping arrangements by the group as well, since I noticed that a couple of members who had previously opted for sleeping under the stars decided there were advantages to pitching their small tents after all—and keeping those screened doors zipped tightly shut at night.

Later in my career an assignment to the Big Thicket National Preserve in southeast Texas provided a much different environment and a whole new cast of characters in the wild beast category. Often described as the "Biological Crossroads of North America," this relatively new park does contain an amazing variety of plants, animals, birds, and other life forms. Even I was surprised at the degree of diversity found in the park one day when I was driving down a narrow, dusty, unpaved lane leading to a remote area of the park.

The road twisted and turned back and forth through a thick forest, and the route had obviously been determined by the "path of least resistance school of engineering." This approach is often used in rural areas for roads developed by local residents instead of the Official Authorities, and it has the advantage of keeping any design and engineering costs to an absolute minimum. It simply involves dodging the bigger trees and making enough trips over the same route with sturdy vehicles until what passes for a road eventually develops.

Riding with me in my government pickup truck was an individual from New York City who was on his first trip to anywhere west of New Jersey, and he was taking in the variety of new sights with great interest. As we rounded a sharp bend in the road, I suddenly slammed on the brakes to avoid hitting a large, rangy cow that was wandering down the road in front of us.

I started to tap on the horn of my truck to encourage the bovine commuter to yield the right-of-way when my passenger whispered loudly, "Wait, don't scare it off!" Only then did I notice that he was hurriedly removing his camera from its case and rolling down the passenger side window, obviously preparing to lean out and take a photo.

"Well, okay," I thought to myself. "He's probably never even *seen* a cow before, at least not in any form other than beef by the pound in his local grocery store, so even this scrawny specimen is a pretty big deal for him. After all, what could be more typically 'Texas' than a picture of a cow?" I waited patiently until my passenger fired off several shots with his camera but was totally unprepared for what came next.

"Hey," my guest almost shouted with glee, "I've never seen an *elk* before, and I sure didn't expect to spot one here in East Texas."

You know what? Neither did I!

5

Stetsons in the City

Many people have a fairly romanticized view of the life and work of national park rangers. The title often conjures up images of sweeping scenic vistas, a cozy cabin on the shore of a mountain lake, and lots of peace and quiet. The reality is, of course, that such assignments are few and far between, many rangers work in smaller parks east of the Mississippi River, and peace and quiet are rare commodities for almost any ranger's job. The typical day for many park employees begins with a commute to work from a home in suburbia.

Back in the early 1970s, the National Park System was undergoing an era of expansion. A number of new sites were being added, including national recreation areas in urban locations such as New York City and San Francisco. The theory of top NPS management at the time was that since the majority of park visitors were now coming from cities rather than rural areas, and we were venturing into uncharted waters in operating a whole new category of urban parks, all newly hired permanent rangers should have an initial assignment in one of those areas.

The outcome of this experience was supposed to be greater understanding of why some people say and do rather unexpected things when they visit parks, especially those in more remote locations. I don't know how well that experiment worked overall, but my six months of living in the Washington, D.C., area did help me appreciate the chance to spend much of my career away from a big city.

Considering the available options, I actually fared pretty well in my assignment to Greenbelt Park, in the Maryland suburbs of our nation's capital. Located near the intersection of the Beltway and the Baltimore-Washington Parkway, the park's 1,175 mostly wooded acres include a campground, hiking trails, and picnic areas. Greenbelt is part of what is called National Capital Parks, the Park Service organizational level that also manages sites such as the Washington Monument, Lincoln Memorial, Ford's Theater, and other landmarks in the D.C. metropolitan area.

My wife Velma and I arrived at Greenbelt shortly after Thanksgiving, and we were soon moved into our government-owned, two-bedroom

Most park rangers don't work in the wilderness. The Washington Monument is one of many national park sites located in urban areas. (National Park Service)

mobile home, which was planted squarely in the center of the campground. It was a bit snug, but the rent we paid to Uncle Sam was reasonable by local standards, and the surrounding "neighborhood" (i.e., campground) was a lot more pleasant than a big-city apartment complex.

The purpose of having a ranger actually live *in* the campground was to have a staff member close at hand in case of after-hours emergencies. Because we arrived during the winter, things were pretty quiet for the first several months. This turned out to be a benefit we didn't fully appreciate until spring and the return of campers in larger numbers.

On our first night in our new home, however, I had reason to wonder if our relative "bargain" in lodging was going to prove to be a case of "you get what you pay for." We had been busy unpacking boxes, so it was about midnight when we finally turned in for some much-needed rest. We quickly found out that there were *some* drawbacks to living in a trailer in the woods, even in the middle of the Washington, D.C., metropolitan area.

I had just started to drift off to sleep when I realized that I was being dragged—very reluctantly—back from dreamland by an unusual noise. Perhaps you've experienced a similar sensation. It's your first night in an unfamiliar place, you're tired after a really long day, and suddenly you're lying in bed in the dark trying to identify a strange sound. You consider the possibilities: maybe it's the refrigerator humming, or the floors creaking, or the plumbing burping. . . . In this case, it seemed a little more ominous, because on the scale of potentially worrisome noises, this fell somewhere between "scratching" and "gnawing."

I lay there for a few moments, listening carefully, thinking that *surely* I had just imagined it, wishing that it would go away, and most of all hoping that my beloved bride was already sound asleep and hadn't heard it too. I lay absolutely still, barely breathing, trying not to disturb her, and listened carefully. There it was again—scratch, scratch, gnaw. . . .

"Did you hear that?" Velma was obviously wide awake, too, so it was clearly time to go do my husbandly duty.

"Yeah, I'm sure it's nothing to worry about," I replied hopefully. "I'll go have a look."

I climbed out of bed, groped for the light switch in the unfamiliar room, and headed down the hall in the direction of the sound—which, of course, promptly stopped. A halfhearted search failed to find anything amiss, and I returned to bed.

"What was it?" Velma asked.

"I don't know. I didn't see anything, so it's probably no big deal."

Yeah, right!

The light had been off for about four seconds when the sound began again.

Okay, okay! This time I was determined not to get into an up-and-down-all-night game, so I started a systematic search of the trailer. Since the noise stopped when I turned on the lights, I dug out a flashlight, covered the lens with my hand to reduce the beam to a faint glimmer, and moved stealthily from room to room in the near darkness until I narrowed the source to the bathroom.

It took a little while longer to pinpoint the problem to the inside of the linen closet. A growing pile of tiny bits of foam ceiling tile caused me to look up, and behold—a small jagged hole appeared in the illumination from my flashlight.

I turned out the light, stood still for a couple of minutes, and was rewarded with the pitter-patter of miniature feet on the ceiling above my head. Yes, it was December, but not the 24th, and these were definitely not the hooves of tiny reindeer on my roof. When the gnawing resumed I flipped on the flashlight and got a quick glimpse of two beady little eyes before the mouse scampered away again.

Well, what we had here was a Distinctly Melancholy Situation. It was now about 1 A.M. on an early December morn, a cold, steady drizzle was falling, and since I was new to town I had absolutely no idea what stores offering anti-mouse warfare items might be open at that hour. Our existing supply of such essentials among our household goods, packed or unpacked, was basically zip. I know that necessity is reputed to be the mother of invention, but desperation also works pretty well, so I'll share a tip that saved what was left of the night at least once for me.

After taking a quick inventory of possible defensive measures in our new abode, and finding little to work with, I decided to give it my best and probably only shot. I got into position just outside the open closet door, turned off the light, and waited for the attempted break-in to resume. I gave him (her?) time to get well into the process of enlarging the hole, checked the grip on my weapon and sprang into position—firing a long burst from the aerosol can of deodorant directly into the teeth of the invading army.

This was met with a satisfying scramble of activity in the overhead space, followed by the sound of retreating footsteps, so I fired several more salvos through the now vacant hole just for good measure.

Somewhat to my amazement—and relief—this seemed to discourage the rascal, so I stuffed the end of a rag into the hole and returned to bed. I wonder what the spouse and any offspring of the deodorized mouse thought when it returned from its foray, reeking with the evidence of a close escape from chemical warfare. Perhaps I had discovered a new WMD (**W**eapon of **M**ouse **D**eterrence).

The following day we took some more traditional measures, including plugging up all of the likely points of entry we could find around the outside of the trailer. Now better prepared to repel boarders, we managed to avoid any additional attempted break-ins by furry freeloaders. Welcome to life in urban America!

Despite this somewhat rocky start, after a little over five years of living in various apartment complexes during my stint in the army and then graduate school, Velma and I were looking forward to having a "place of our own" for a few months—even if it was a trailer in the woods. At least there weren't other tenants overhead and on either side of us.

When milder weather arrived, so did the campers. They soon made up for the lack of full-time neighbors, and I got my first lessons in "campground management." I had grown up camping in parks, so I had a really positive impression about campers. Almost all of them are friendly and helpful, and fun to be around. That's still the case, but I quickly found out that life is sometimes a little different when you're the guy who appears to be responsible for running the place—and who is therefore supposed to have all the answers.

Don't get me wrong: I still think that most campers are wonderful people and great to be around. It's just that *sometimes* when you live and work in a campground full-time, you'd prefer not to be in continuous contact with folks 24 hours a day, 7 days a week.

There is apparently a rule duly recorded somewhere in the cosmos that at least 10 percent of the owners of travel trailers or motor homes absolutely should not, under any circumstances, check the fuel level in their RV's propane tank before they leave home for the first trip of the year. I came to that conclusion after answering about 274 knocks on our front door during the month of April, normally between the hours of 9 P.M. and midnight.

The campers usually realized that their propane tank was empty once they were completely set up in their site and tried to light the hot water heater or cook a bedtime snack. We also got a few inquiries right about sunup, when it was time for the early risers to cook breakfast down in the ol' motor home. The conversations all followed the same general pattern.

"Hey ranger, do you know where we can get some propane? We thought we had some in our tank from last summer, but it must have leaked out over the winter, or something."

The answer was "yes," I did know, since after the first couple of late-night inquiries I had completed a comprehensive survey of every propane outlet within about a twenty-five mile radius, along with their hours of operation. I even made up some maps and written directions to the ones closest to the park. Unfortunately, none of the locations anywhere in the vicinity were open late at night—or before sunup. Most people accepted that news philosophically, but a few were a little more determined.

One guy noticed by the dawn's very early light that we had a couple of upright propane tanks chained to a post next to our mobile home. They provided fuel for the kitchen stove, hot water heater, and central heat. This resourceful citizen was not above asking if he could "just hook up my little bitty tank to your big one," so he could "get enough gas to make it through the weekend."

The Grand Champion, however, was the lady who arrived at our front door in her bathrobe and hair curlers early one morning and wanted to know if she could come in, take a shower, and do her hair since they were out of propane and therefore had no hot water. Her reasoning was that they planned to take the White House tour later that morning and she needed to look her best, just in case they happened to run into the president.

I was able to politely decline both requests and all in all, Greenbelt Park was a good introduction to life both in the campground and in the big city. I would have ample opportunity to put all of that training to good use later in my career, because like most other rangers, I had plenty of dealings with both mice and men in the years to come.

Marina Mania

F ew recreational activities known to mankind offer more potential for both fun and mayhem than boating. I freely admit that this is a strictly personal opinion, based on extensive firsthand observation and experience during years of work at parks where water-based recreation was a primary activity. I'm willing to concede that there are plenty of other candidates for this dubious distinction, including the vast array of activities such as skiing and snowboarding that people do on snow and ice. However, since the subject of this chapter is boating, I'll stick with my first vote. Read on and see if you agree.

An easy way to test my theory is to find a busy boat ramp or marina and spend a few hours there on a busy weekend, just hanging around and watching the action. Better yet, pick the first really nice weekend of the season in your area, when novice boat owners are likely to be headed out on the water for the very first time. If you decide to make such an excursion, take along a video camera if you have one. You've got a good chance of capturing some potential prizewinning footage for *America's Funniest Home Videos*.

Let me hasten to add that some boating mishaps can have serious consequences, and I'm not trying to make light of those situations, or to make fun of anyone who might have a less-than-happy experience on the water. Fortunately, everyone involved survives the majority of boating miscues, hopefully a little wiser for the experience. I trust the following stories will help some of you avoid a similar misadventure.

Most boating blunders occur because some new boaters simply don't take the time to get some basic instruction before setting out on their maiden voyage. Unlike cars, trucks, airplanes, and similar modes of transportation that weigh thousands of pounds and can go very fast, no license or training is required in most locations to buy, rent, or borrow a boat and head for the nearest water to find out what it will do.

It's been said about travel that "getting there is half the fun." A corollary when it comes to boating is that getting a boat off the trailer and into the water quickly and easily is often *more* than half the work—but not necessarily quite that much fun. My previous book included several examples of such challenges in a chapter called "Back It Up Right Here," and I won't repeat any of that information. This is a subject ripe with possibilities, so here are a couple of other examples to prove that Murphy is alive and well on the boat ramps and waterways of the world.

For the benefit of those of you who aren't boaters, I'll explain that a boat or launch ramp is simply a road of sorts, preferably paved, that slopes down into a body of water. In the best of all possible situations, it allows the mariner and an assistant to back a vehicle, towing a trailer that carries a boat, down to the edge of the water. At that point they slide the boat off the trailer into the river, lake, or sea, secure the vessel to the nearby bank or dock, and the driver moves the vehicle and trailer to a nearby parking lot. The driver then strolls back to the waiting boat for a fun day on the water. Nothing to it, right? Well, maybe . . . .

Backing a boat trailer, either loaded or empty, down a steep slope is an acquired skill, and while practice makes perfect, the *lack* of practice makes for a perfect mess. I'd humbly suggest for the uninitiated that the place to learn is *not* a crowded boat ramp on a busy weekend. Find a large, empty parking lot somewhere close to home and get a friend with experience in the art of trailer backing to give you some tips. You'll save yourself and everybody else trying to use that boat ramp a lot of time and frustration—and possibly avoid finding yourself in a less than flattering role on someone's videotape!

On several occasions, I saw an unusual approach to the backing-up challenge. The person in question had attached a trailer hitch to both the back *and* front of his tow vehicle. The hitch on the back was used to tow the boat and trailer down the highway to the vicinity of the ramp. At that point, the trailer was unhitched, the vehicle turned around, and the trailer was reattached to the hitch on the *front* of the vehicle.

This approach put the boat ahead of the tow vehicle as it was driven down the ramp, so the driver didn't have to look over his shoulder or use the mirrors to see what the trailer was doing. This technique seemed to be most popular with owners of small motor homes, which usually don't offer the driver any visibility out a back window. I suppose you could say they were "fronting down" instead of "backing up" their trailer. It definitely looked weird, but some people seemed to find it easier.

Now, some of you who have experienced the nightmare of jack-knifed trailers while trying to back one up are probably thinking, "Wow, why didn't *I* think of that?" Well, like any other innovation, I feel obligated to mention that this approach *does* have its pitfalls.

In the traditional, rear-bumper-hitch approach, it's sometimes necessary to back the tow vehicle far enough down the ramp that part of the rear wheels of the car or truck are actually in the water. This is a situation where a few inches, give or take, can make a big difference. Caution is required not to back *too* far into the water in the effort to allow the boat to slide or be pushed off the trailer easily. If things get out of hand, the result may be a wet trunk—definitely not desirable, but it could be worse.

Now, picture the opposite scenario, with the *front* of the vehicle attached to the trailer. Very few vehicles have the engine mounted in the rear, so going nose-first toward the edge of the water presents the distinct possibility of a series of unfortunate events. If carried to their ultimate conclusion, those events can qualify as a Definitely Melancholy Situation.

Someday a genius will solve the energy crisis by inventing a vehicle engine that runs on water, but the reality is that current versions don't. Back in the *real* old days, vehicles had a manual "choke," a knob the driver pulled or pushed to adjust the air and gasoline mixture in the engine. Too much gas resulted in the engine being "flooded," a problem that could usually be resolved by readjusting the choke and then letting enough time pass for the excess gas to evaporate from the carburetor before attempting to restart the motor.

I can attest from personal observation (but thankfully not personal experience) that driving a vehicle nose-first too far into the water will also result in the engine being flooded, but in a seriously different context than in the old manual choke days.

One driver of a small motor home and his buddy proved that point in a scenario that definitely fits in the "but it seemed like a good idea at the time" category. I arrived on the scene at Lake Mead National Recreation Area just in time to see the result, but too late to prevent what to everyone else in the area was clearly a very bad idea, right from the get-go.

This gentleman was a proponent of the "front-first" approach and had successfully managed to launch his boat despite unusually low water levels at the ramp. These conditions meant that the water increased in depth very gradually, which required that boat trailers had to be driven further out into the river than normal to get enough water under the hull to float the boat.

That was not quite as big a problem for the traditional, back 'em up launchers, but this nose-first maverick ended up with both the front *and* rear wheels of his little motor home in the shallow water before he got the boat off the trailer. When it came time to back up and park his rig, he just didn't have enough traction or horsepower to return to dry land. According to witnesses, he was just spinning his wheels and going nowhere fast, as water spurted and bubbled around the vehicle's exhaust pipe.

Our leading man in this unfolding drama was still at the point where a successful ending was possible, but his options were rapidly narrowing. Unfortunately, he was determined to resolve his problem without admitting that a little help, such as a towrope attached to a second vehicle, would be useful.

To make the story a little more personal, this gentleman needs a name. If I had an attorney, he or she would undoubtedly advise me to avoid using the real names of people who might feel I am presenting them in an unflattering light. To that end, I'll assign an alias to this individual, and in view of the situation and his determination, the famous quotation "Don't give up the ship" comes to mind.

While this rallying cry is often attributed to Commodore Perry at the Battle of Lake Erie in 1813, it can be traced back at least to 1776, where those same words were reportedly uttered by Captain James Mugford, a true hero of the American Revolution. In honor of that brave mariner I'll adopt his last name for our equally determined, if not necessarily heroic, motor home driver.

Mugford at least tried to size up his problem and came to the conclusion that solving his stalemate would be easier if he removed the boat trailer from the front of his motor home. This was actually a pretty good idea, since it meant he had less weight to drag back up the incline of the ramp. After pulling their previously launched boat over to the nearby shore, Mugford and his friend waded out into the water, unhitched the trailer, and managed to drag and roll it back to dry land.

Now, without the restraining influence of the boat trailer/anchor, *surely* the vehicle could be backed safety up to Terra Firma. Alas, according to my reliable eyewitnesses, this was not to be, and the little engine that couldn't once again failed to deliver the goods.

Opportunity did knock twice, and it was still possible to simply poll the audience and see if some helpful bystander with a sturdy tow-rope and a Bubba Truck would give him the needed extra oomph. Failing that, he could almost certainly secure help from the adjacent marina staff, even if it cost him a few bucks.

True to his historic namesake, however, Mugford was determined to see this through on his own. I tried in the aftermath to reconstruct his reasoning, which seemed to follow these steps:

1. The water that held his vehicle captive was pretty shallow, and based on the difficulty of floating their boat off the trailer it must not be much deeper twenty feet from shore.

2. If the water wasn't very deep and he couldn't back up, why didn't he just go *forward*, make a U-turn, and drive right back up the hill?

Apparently destined to confirm that truth is sometimes stranger than fiction, that's just what Mugford decided to do. I arrived at the top of the launch ramp just as our hero and his mighty motor home had almost reached the top of the "∩" in their maneuver. Already past the point of no return, he learned several critical pieces of information:

1. His vehicle didn't exactly turn on a dime (or a quarter), so the arc of the "U" turn took it much further out into the water than he anticipated.

2. If you are determined to try this maneuver, it *does* matter whether you make your turn to the left or to the right. In this case, the end of the exhaust pipe for the vehicle was located on the right-hand (passenger) side. If Mugford had turned to the right, the exhaust discharge would have at least stayed closest to shore, where the water was a little shallower. Unfortunately, he zigged when he should have zagged, and turned to the left.

3. Although the water near the shore was inconveniently shallow, that situation did not prevail for an unlimited distance.

4. If they are driven in water of sufficient depth for a long enough period of time, the engines of about 99.999 percent of vehicles will eventually stall, especially if very much of either the engine or the end of the exhaust pipe is completely underwater. When that occurs, the outcome invariably qualifies as a Certified Melancholy Situation.

Mugford, his friend, and their vehicle were all safely returned to dry land in due time, although when last seen his vehicle was being towed to a distant repair shop—nose first. I dutifully completed the necessary paperwork, a copy of which was provided to Mugford at his request. I wondered for some time if he filed a claim with his insurance company, and what kind of response that elicited. Now that I think of it, if an insurance adjuster somewhere hasn't written his or her *own* version of this book, I'm willing to bet there is more than ample material provided by the Mugfords of this world.

This situation might have been avoided altogether if it had been easier to launch the boat without driving the tow vehicle so far into the water. To that end, our famous American ingenuity has risen to the challenge and manufacturers have developed a vast array of boat trailer designs and accessories to make launching a boat as painless as possible.

One of the problems common to launching a boat is that there's too much friction between the bottom of the boat and the trailer to allow the boat to easily relinquish its perch and slide smoothly into the water without protest. To help solve this problem, some boat trailers are equipped with rollers to make this parting of boat and trailer easier.

There are many designs of trailers and rollers, but some of the most sophisticated use a type of lever action that actually raises the bottom of the boat completely free from the main support beams of the trailer. When elevated to this position, the boat is resting only on the surface of the rollers, which then do what rollers are supposed to do: roll. If the boat and trailer are parked on a slope, and the boat isn't otherwise secured to the trailer, the boat simply rolls downhill off the trailer and slides right into the water. Pretty nifty solution.

As is always the case with any technology, however, there is room for operator error. I confirmed the truth of that one day when I got word of a "problem" at the boat ramp. I arrived to spot a vehicle and empty trailer parked about halfway down the ramp—not in itself an unusual situation. Just downhill from the trailer, a small crowd had gathered around a nice, bright yellow boat, about twenty-four feet in length. This situation *was* unusual, since the boat was sitting firmly on the asphalt of the ramp, at least fifteen feet from the water.

It didn't take long to sort this one out, and the situation proves that sometimes you can have *too* much help for a simple job. The erstwhile boaters had arrived at the ramp and had both gone to work readying their craft for launching. One man ensured the drain plug was in place (good idea) while another removed the tie-down straps that secured the rear of the boat to the trailer.

The first man then disconnected the heavy steel winch cable that secures the bow (front) of the boat to the trailer. Hmmm. This last step was a bit premature, since the boat was still quite a distance from the water. However, it was probably not a deal killer because this was a pretty heavy boat, and the combination of its sheer weight and that wonderful scientific principle called friction would probably hold it on the trailer.

Then the turning point arrived. What we had in this situation was a classic failure to communicate, since one man got a little overanxious to swing that handle and activate those magical rollers. This was the first trip for the boat, the trailer, and the proud new owner, and the captain and crew had been eagerly anticipating how easy those highly touted lever-action rollers would make it to unload their boat.

Once the lever was pivoted into action and the rollers lifted the boat to the "ready" position, the answer proved to be—very easy indeed!

Those heavy-duty rubber rollers performed just as advertised, but under the circumstances this was *not* a case of "let the good times roll." According to an eyewitness, there was enough downhill slope on the boat ramp that even a modest shove on the boat wasn't needed to let another law of nature called gravity overcome friction. Faster than you could say, "Houston, we have liftoff," a launch was underway.

Well, perhaps a little modification of that term is appropriate. What was actually underway was a very efficient unloading, but since *launch* in the case of a boat implies the involvement of water, that announcement requires revision to another famous line, "Houston, we have a problem!" Several thousand pounds of brand-new boat sitting on a launch ramp some distance from the water qualifies as both a problem and a Peculiarly Melancholy Situation.

It took considerable work and a little ingenuity by the driver of a heavy-duty wrecker to get the boat back on its trailer with minimal additional wear and tear on that nice, shiny fiberglass hull. Fortunately no one was hurt and, to everyone's amazement, damage to the boat appeared to be fairly minimal.

For quite some time thereafter, there was an unusual yellow smudge on the black asphalt on the launch ramp, a skid mark of sorts left behind by that boat. It prompted a quizzical look and occasional question by more than one boater who used that area for several weeks, providing the regular visitors to that site multiple opportunities to retell what quickly became a local legend.

During the process of gathering information for the inevitable United States Government Case Incident Report, I tried to reconstruct the thought process that got this pair into their predicament. Frankly, I didn't have much success, but perhaps it's a good example of the merits of the principle, "When in doubt, read the instructions." Then again, maybe it was simply a case of being in too much of a hurry to start having fun, proving the wisdom of Caesar Augustus's advice from long, long ago to "Make haste slowly."

Haste is rarely desirable during the process of launching *or* landing a boat, and further confirmation is provided in the following story, shared by Gordon R. Smith from Salt Lake City, Utah. Mr. Smith is a veteran "ham" radio operator and part of a group of volunteers that provides radio communications during an annual event on the Colorado and Green Rivers in Utah called the "Friendship Cruise."

Mr. Smith also graciously provided the following photograph, which was taken some years ago at a launch area on the Colorado River

A classic boat ramp "oops" situation. A few feet can make a big difference when you're backing a vehicle into the water to launch or retrieve a boat. (Gordon Smith)

just outside Canyonlands National Park known variously as MGM Bottom, Potash Boat Ramp, or Potash Boat Dock.

Since this is one of the few places along the entire 180-mile Friendship Cruise route where it is possible to drive a vehicle to the bank of either the Green or Colorado Rivers, the boat ramp at MGM Bottom serves as a radio communications site, a put-in and take-out point for boaters, and a staging area for other support personnel for the event, including a fuel truck to provide gasoline for boaters.

In Las Vegas there is a posh hotel and casino known as the MGM Grand. Lest anyone confuse those two locations with similar names, there is a lot of grand scenery but not much else at MGM Bottom. There is, however, a paved boat ramp at that spot, contrary to the conclusion you might be tempted to draw from the picture.

The driver of the truck in the photo was using that ramp, but the river level was high and the man either failed to hear or ignored several warnings from people on the bank, such as "Uh, I think that's far enough." Mugford apparently has a number of relatives, and it's a good thing there were volunteers on shore with the large fuel truck to help tow this driver's pickup back to dry land, because it's a bit of a drive for a wrecker if you have to summon one to MGM Bottom.

Mr. Smith reports that this paved ramp also tends to get covered with mud, so when the water is up, it doesn't look much different from the surrounding bank. This was the situation when the photo was taken, and such conditions can create challenges for boaters who are returning to land as well as those trying to put a boat in the water.

One handicap of motorized boats is that the noise of the engine makes it a little hard to hear other sounds, including comments from nearby people on the shore or in other boats. As a result, here's a good rule of thumb for anyone using a motorized craft: If people nearby seem to be trying to get your attention, perhaps there's a reason other than the fact that they are just being friendly. If conditions permit, it might be a good idea to idle or shut down the boat engine briefly and see what the commotion is all about.

As proof of that suggestion, Mr. Smith reports that the following was a common shouted exchange between the people on shore and incoming boaters approaching the mud-covered, and therefore "invisible," paved boat ramp at MGM Bottom:

Us (shore crew): "It's concrete here."
Them (boat crew): "What?"

Us: "IT'S CONCRETE HERE!"

Them: "I can't hear you."

Us (Louder): "**IT'S** . . ."

Boat: Crunch!

Us: "Never mind."

At that point, the situation at MGM Bottom probably looked (and felt) anything *but* grand to the arriving boaters, and that paved boat ramp hidden under the muddy water proved once again that things aren't always as they appear in the Great Outdoors. My parting admonition about boat ramps is to be alert to attempted warnings from bystanders. All unsolicited advice is not necessarily good advice, but if you don't at least weigh your options, your name may end up being Mugford—or Mud.

Monumental Mix-ups

In an earlier chapter, "Ignorance Is Not Bliss," I included a few examples of crazy questions about the Great Outdoors. Improbable inquiries aren't limited to the natural wonders in parks; historical areas get their fair share as well. While I'm confident that *you* would never ask such questions, other visitors certainly take up the slack. With apologies in advance to history teachers and serious students of our nation's heritage, the following are some classic examples of inquiries made of rangers in several historical parks. In many cases I'll give a little explanatory information following these queries so you can amaze your friends the next time you play one of those games that require knowledge of truly obscure facts.

"Were any of the scenes from the movie *Gettysburg* filmed during the actual battle?" (This would have been a bit difficult, since Thomas Edison didn't develop the motion picture camera until 1891, almost thirty years after the battle was fought.)

"Which side had control of the Pentagon during the Civil War?" (Despite rumors to the contrary, Abraham Lincoln did *not* deliver the Gettysburg Address from the press briefing room at the Pentagon. According to the Department of Defense, construction on the world's largest office building began on September 11, 1941, a rather ironic date in terms of recent historical events, and not quite four score and seven years after the major events at Gettysburg.)

Battlefields around the country include thousands of monuments and memorials. This is the North Carolina Monument at Gettysburg National Military Park. (National Park Service)

This next one has been asked so many times that it provided the basis for the title of a book by a legitimate historian. The question—and the title: *How Come They Always Had the Battles in National Parks?* (Boy, I bet the visitors in the picnic area and campground were seriously annoyed by all of that shooting, yelling, and other commotion!) The subject of battles and national parks (or national battlefields and a host of other names for these sites) brings us to the interesting question of monuments. That term may conjure up a variety of pictures in your mind, from the 555-foot-tall Washington Monument in our nation's capital to a small marker in a cemetery, or something in between.

Perhaps no other event in our nation's history can top the Civil War in terms of promoting the building of monuments. Erected after the end of the war, these memorials honor personnel from entire states, various military units, and even individual soldiers. They come in all shapes and sizes, in styles ranging from the grandiose to the modest, and in numbers that occasionally make me marvel that there is any unused granite remaining in North America. Lest you think I exaggerate, here are a couple of examples: Vicksburg National Military Park contains 1,325 historic monuments and markers, and Gettysburg has over 1,400 such items.

Those areas are only two of the 144 units of the U.S. National Park System that are classified as either a National Battlefield, National Battlefield Park, National Military Park, National Battlefield Site, National Historical Park, National Historic Site, or International Historic Site. I'll leave it to your imagination to estimate how many monuments must exist in all of those locations, not to mention the additional areas under the control of state or local agencies or private organizations.

Don't get me wrong—these memorials to the sacrifices of brave men and women from both the North and South are a good reminder for present generations about a pivotal event in our nation's history. At some battlefields, however, it's almost hard to see the ground for the granite. It must have become a matter of honor at times for one group not to be outdone by another in the contest to see which could erect the most imposing tribute to their heroes.

One of the reasons battlefields were preserved as parks was to protect them from disappearing under the spreading tide of suburbia. I absolutely agree that it would be a tragedy if a site like Gettysburg were to become simply another shopping center or subdivision. However, with modern development crowding the boundaries of many such sites and commemorative monuments dotting the landscape of most parks, some visitors are understandably a bit confused as they gaze across the landscape and try to picture in their mind's eye the historic struggles that occurred there over 150 years ago.

With that perspective, the presence of all those monuments prompts a host of classic questions, including the following samples:

"Did the soldiers hide behind the monuments during the battle to keep from getting shot?"

"How long did it take to repair the monuments after the battle?" (There must have been a lot of bullet holes or damage from all that cannon fire.)

Other visitors duly note the fine condition of these memorials and wonder, "Where did they store the monuments during the battle so

Living History Demonstrations, such as this one at Petersburg National Battlefield in Virginia, help bring stories from our nation's past alive for park visitors. (National Park Service)

they wouldn't be damaged?" (I hope at least one of the approaching armies was considerate enough to send word ahead and give the appropriate authorities time to move those monuments to a safe spot.)

A fun and effective way for people of all ages to learn about the past is through what is often called "Living History" demonstrations. These activities involve park employees or volunteers who dress in costume appropriate for the time being depicted and then go about a variety of day-to-day activities from that period.

In addition to those directly associated with parks, there are a number of excellent Living History programs operated by private organizations—Colonial Williamsburg in Virginia is a prime example. There are also groups of volunteer historical reenactors around the country whose members donate their time and often furnish their own uniforms and equipment to put on demonstrations lasting from a few hours to several days. The best of these groups go to great lengths to ensure historical accuracy at their events.

On his website, "The Civil War Fife and Drum Page," Paul Boccadoro includes some questions visitors have asked historical reenactors at various events. He generously shared the following examples, and I'll add some occasional commentary for purposes of clarification—or a little fun.

Join me at a historical battlefield on an imaginary stroll through a Civil War era encampment of men, women, and children. They're cooking over open fires, wearing uniforms or other clothing typical of the period, and spending the night sleeping on the ground. Horses are tethered at one edge of the camp, replicas of historic weapons are stacked next to a cannon, and the pungent smell of wood smoke drifts between rows of canvas tents. It probably won't be long before you'll overhear questions such as these directed to the reenactors:

"Hey mister, did you fight in the Civil War?" (Be sure you speak up if you ask this one, since if he really did, he's about to celebrate his 165th birthday and is probably rather hard of hearing.)

Another visitor stops near a fire where a pig is being slowly roasted on a spit over the glowing coals, carefully tended by a character who seems to have stepped right off the screen in the movie *Gettysburg*. The tourist takes in the scene, focuses his gaze on the pig, and then asks in all seriousness, "Is that thing actually made of *wax*?" (Gosh, I hope not, because if so, it's going to be melting really soon over that hot fire.)

Those uniforms from long ago are typically very warm, and even reenactors get thirsty. You won't spot any cans of cola, at least in plain view, but you'll almost certainly spot a number of canteens and buckets. That prompted one person to ask, "Is that *real* water in your canteen?"

"How much is this wooden lantern, there's no price on it. . . . Oh! I thought this was a yard sale." (You should have been here earlier, before the *really* good stuff was sold.)

"They actually had rope back then?" (Yeah, but the color choices were pretty boring.)

And last but certainly not least, "How do you get all the flags to fly in the same direction?" (This is a military camp, folks, and we run a *really* tight ship here, so even the wind toes the line.)

In addition to questions from visitors, a touch of humor can also be found in some historical documents. A good example is found at Apostle Islands National Lakeshore in Wisconsin, which according to the official *National Parks Index* includes "twenty-one picturesque islands and a 12-mile strip of mainland shoreline along the south shore of Lake Superior." Among the park's features are "sandstone cliffs, sea caves, pristine beaches, old-growth forest, commercial fish camps, and six historic light stations." Definitely a neat spot, worthy of a visit.

One of those historic light stations is the Sand Island Lighthouse, and two volumes from the keeper's logs are preserved in the National

Archives. Excerpts from those logs, along with some comments by the park staff, are posted on the park's website (www.nps.gov/apis/), which notes, "The log entries for a few years at the turn of the century offer us an extraordinary glimpse into the lives of a lighthouse keeper, his wife, and their island neighbors. In the pages of the log, the modern reader will find shipwrecks and near-disasters, humor and pathos, flashes of anger and loneliness . . . interspersed among the mundane details of a long-vanished way of life."

An entry for Friday, June 16, 1899, includes information about one of those mundane details of life—a successful day of fishing—as well as a little humor. I'll preface this quote with apologies to any readers who are associated with the practice of law.

"At 2:15 p.m. Keeper went to East Bay and got mail, got home at 4:30 p.m. and went out and lifted hookes—got 4 trout and 4 lawyers."

All of those modern jokes comparing lawyers to sharks might explain how the keeper landed four of the former on his fishhooks, but a better explanation for his notation is included in the commentary on the park's website: "A relative of the cod, the 'lawyer' is more properly called the American burbot (*Lota lota*). The burbot is said to be flavorful and nutritious, but has never been a popular food fish and thus had little commercial value. Several explanations have been offered for the nickname, none complimentary to the legal profession." Apparently lawyers didn't get much more respect in 1899 than they sometimes do today!

The lighthouse keeper also recorded an interesting description of the running aground of a steamer not far from his post during a thick fog. Fortunately no lives were lost, and the ship was eventually pulled safely back into deeper water. The keeper's log entry on July 13, 1899, succinctly explained the reason for this mishap: "Cause of casualty, compass deranged."

This sounds entirely plausible to me, because even in recent years I've known of people who succeeded in getting thoroughly lost on a perfectly clear day on water or on dry land, all because they were absolutely convinced that their compass was giving completely inaccurate readings. As a result, they followed their instincts rather than the compass and ended up way off course, although that begs the question about whether the compass or the human "navigator" was the one who was deranged.

As an official representative of the government, that light keeper's report and explanation hopefully saved a lot of time and expense in an

The Devils Island Lighthouse is one of six historic light stations in Apostle Islands National Lakeshore (Wisconsin) and the setting for a story in this chapter. (National Park Service)

investigation of the ship-grounding incident, and perhaps he was onto something after all with his "deranged compass" theory. The next sentence in his report notes that another nearby lighthouse was "not visible, fog thick." The name of *that* beacon? The Devils Island Light.

Deranged compasses and Devils Island? Sounds more like the Bermuda Triangle than the Great Lakes!

The assumed presence of historical documents such as those lighthouse logs sometimes leads people to visit historical sites looking for specific bits of information. While the already overworked park staff does what it can to be helpful, there simply isn't enough time for them to delve into detailed individual research on topics such as family histories. Occasionally, however, these requests can provide amusing insights into just how much attention some people paid back in their American History class.

I had one such conversation with a nice older couple who were visiting Colonial National Historical Park in Virginia. In order for the lady to gain admission into a historical organization, she needed to prove that one of her direct ancestors had fought in the American Revolution. Her husband was doing his best to help and showed me a stack of papers listing basic facts about some of her family members who lived back in the 1700s.

Since we're talking about the American Revolution in this story, I'll call this gentleman George, in honor of one of our country's founding fathers. George shuffled through his papers, found a page listing vital statistics for several individuals, and pointed to one of the names.

"I'm ninety percent sure this is the one we're looking for. Do you know of any books that might include proof of his military service?" With obvious pride, he added, "I'm almost certain he fought with Washington right up until the end of the war."

I looked at the information briefly, and then suggested that the *next* relative on his list might be a better choice. George looked surprised and asked why.

Mustering my best attempt at a diplomatic tone, I pointed out that according to George's papers, the man he had in mind had died in 1774, whereas the second person on his page had lived until 1789. My hopes for one of those "Ah-ha" moments for George didn't materialize, and instead his response was a somewhat defensive "So?"

All across America at that very moment, scientists probably puzzled over an unexplained blip on seismograph needles that recorded a minor earth tremor in a place not previously known to have any underlying fault lines. Unknown to the seismologists, the cause was simply George's dear departed history teacher turning over in her grave.

I always tried, especially in my role as a friendly and faithful servant of the people, to avoid embarrassing anyone in front of a spouse, child, or other family member. My last hope in this case was for his wife Martha to catch my hint, jump into the conversation, and save the day. Unfortunately, a quick glance in her direction revealed that she looked just as confused as her husband.

George had painted all three of us into the proverbial corner, so I dug down a little deeper into my reserves of tact and said as gently as I could, "Well, the American Revolution didn't *begin* until 1776, so if this gentleman actually died in *1774*, maybe the *other* relative would be a better candidate for your research."

Thankfully, the light finally did come on for George, and better yet, his spouse was a model of decorum and appeared to ignore this entire conversation. They went on their way after thanking me for helping narrow down their search. If I had know about it at the time, maybe I would have suggested they begin their research with a quick reading of *How Come They Always Had the Battles in National Parks?*

I mentioned above that park staff members normally just don't have the time to help much with individual research, but a major, multiyear cooperative effort by the NPS and a number of groups and volunteers has provided a great resource for genealogists and others interested in the Civil War. If you're part of that group, be sure to investigate the "Civil War Soldiers and Sailors System" (CWSS) by doing a search for those words on the Internet.

George isn't the only one among us who has a hard time keeping historical events in their proper sequence, and as evidence I offer a story from Fort Point National Historic Site in California. Fort Point is one of those hidden gems that many people miss during a visit to San Francisco, but it has both some fascinating history and spectacular views. Constructed between 1853 and 1861 to prevent entrance of a hostile fleet into San Francisco Bay, the brick fort is the only one of its kind on the West Coast.

Fast forward to 1933, when construction began on the Golden Gate Bridge. Some accounts say that initial plans for the bridge called for Fort Point to be demolished, but, thankfully, the span was redesigned to allow for preservation of the historic fort. That decision also provided the opportunity for a question overheard at a ranger talk at Fort Point and submitted for your reading pleasure by Kathryn Grogman from Los Angeles, California.

Perhaps the unnamed visitor asking this question had missed some of the facts about the age of the fort, or assumed that the Golden Gate Bridge predated the Civil War. In either case, the question of the week during the ranger's talk was, "Why did they build a fort *underneath* the Golden Gate Bridge?"

Unlike the chicken and the egg, the sequence of events for the fort and bridge is thoroughly documented, but I'm willing to bet that inquiry has come up more than once. I trust that in our current era rangers successfully bite their tongues and avoid giving what would admittedly be a great reply: "It's part of the Homeland Security system."

A deluge of well-meaning but sometimes wacky questions can be prompted by a recent event or, even more often, by the release of a movie or TV show. This occurred at Jamestown after the production of an animated motion picture about Pocahontas by a major Hollywood studio in 1995. For the next year or so, the beleaguered staff at that site had their patience sorely tested by the same movie-inspired inquiries, over and over and . . . .

Here's your quick crash review of essential American history to help you put these questions in perspective. Jamestown, located in what we now call Virginia, was the site of the first permanent English settlement in North America. In May 1607, English adventurers selected Jamestown Island as the place to build their fort. Just for the record, this was thirteen years before passengers aboard the Mayflower landed in Massachusetts at a place they named Plymouth. If you're paying attention and are reasonably adept at basic math, you'll note that the four hundredth anniversary of the settlement of Jamestown, a truly notable event in our nation, occurs in 2007.

Jamestown is now part of Colonial National Historical Park, which also includes Yorktown Battlefield, the location of the last significant battle of the American Revolution in October 1781. A scenic twenty-three-mile drive named the Colonial Parkway connects those two sites, which rather ironically mark the beginning and the end of English colonial America only a few miles apart. In keeping with the title of this chapter, I'll note that Jamestown boasts its own monument, the 103-foot granite Tercentenary Monument, erected by the government in 1907 to mark the three hundredth anniversary of the site.

Among the key players in the early history of Jamestown were some names we all studied in school, including Pocahontas and Captain John Smith. When Hollywood came calling in the 1990s with plans for a movie about Pocahontas, the park staff had hopes that the resulting film would help tell this story in a way that would capture the interest of a new generation.

Well, capture interest it did, but in Hollywood it's all about entertainment, and artistic license was alive and well when the film hit the wide screens all across the country. Keep in mind that Jamestown is located on a flat, swampy island barely above sea level in southeastern Virginia. The mix of tidal marshes and wooded areas gives the island a special beauty of its own, but the terrain has about as much elevation variation as a slightly warped tabletop.

As a result, the film's depiction of dramatic cliffs and waterfalls resulted in some confused and occasionally even belligerent visitors to the actual site, who understandably had a very hard time locating those nonexistent natural features they'd seen in the movie. I was working at this park during those years, and one visitor actually accused me of keeping the location of the waterfalls secret, so the park employees could have those scenic wonders all to themselves!

Some of you reading these words probably thought at one time or another that you'd enjoy working as a park ranger, or at least felt a tinge of envy for those who are lucky enough to spend their working years at a historic icon such as Jamestown. If that's the case, put on your imaginary ranger uniform and take a stroll with me right on the same island where Pocahontas herself once walked.

It's a very warm and steamy summer afternoon in 1995 and you're tempted to take off that trademark, flat-brimmed Stetson hat and fan your damp brow, but that would be bad form, because here comes a nice family with a question for the ranger. A quick glance at their red, sweaty faces confirms that mom, dad, and their six-year-old have spent quite a while roaming the grounds, and it's obvious that they have a question. Well, probably several questions.

Dad is clearly frustrated and glances down at his young daughter. "Hey, there's a park ranger. Why don't you ask *her* your question, because she'll *certainly* know the answer."

Well, smile and brace yourself, because you can make a pretty good guess about what's coming next.

"Mrs. Ranger," implores the little girl, "we've been looking all *over*, and we can't find the talking tree *anywhere!*"

It's true that the real Jamestown *does* have a lot of trees, but none of them are Grandmother Willow, who in the movie was a centuries-old mystical spirit who lived in a very ancient tree. When the Hollywood Pocahontas needed some good advice or just an encouraging word, this talking tree was just the place to go.

While you're pondering an appropriate answer, your little visitor tosses in a follow-up: "And by the way, we *also* haven't seen the talking raccoon."

There's probably a logical answer to that one, but not one you could use with a first-grader. I'll have to confess that I didn't get around to seeing the movie, but according to reliable sources, in one scene this famous and talented raccoon hides atop a moose. Other than possibly a few occupants of zoos, moose have not been residents of coastal Virginia anytime during recorded history, preferring instead more northerly locales. That probably explains why this particular raccoon is now missing in action.

As soon as filming of the movie was finished, the movie moose undoubtedly headed back for a place with a climate that was much more moose-friendly than the Mid-Atlantic coast, and the talking raccoon must have gone along for the ride. Uh-oh, here comes another group, so I'll just leave you with this family to answer their daughter's questions. As an aspiring ranger, I'm sure you're up to the task. Meanwhile, I suspect the latest arrivals will have a question or two about the mystery of the missing waterfall.

Perhaps it's hiding behind the monument.

The Bear Facts—and a Little Fun

I have absolutely no scientific basis for the following opinion, which (I hope) indicates that our elected officials have not spent any tax dollars on a government-funded study of this subject. However, I *have* conducted a totally nonrandom survey of a small number of friends and relatives, which means that I asked this question of the first twenty or so acquaintances I encountered after this thought occurred to me. Based on the results I've read of some expensive taxpayer-supported research, I strongly suspect that my data is just as good as those higher-priced spreads.

You can, if you would like, participate in this study right now, simply by answering the following question. It's not necessary to send me your vote, since I've already tallied the results, which will be provided shortly. Here's the question:

"Which large animal do you most associate with national parks?"

The winning response is (the envelope please) . . . "bears." The runner-up was bison, also frequently but incorrectly called "buffalo," thanks mainly to the influence of the entertainment industry. The outcome of this survey came as considerable relief to me, since bears happen to be the subject of this chapter.

There is probably some evidence to back up the results of my survey. Those of you who use computers and the Internet are familiar with the use of a "search engine," which diligently combs through the world of cyberspace and provides a list of sites on the Internet that contain any word or phrase you choose to enter.

Just for curiosity's sake I typed in the word *Bears* and within 0.08 seconds was rewarded with "about 247,000,000" results. Most of those "hits" actually had to do with the noun *bear* and referred to the animal rather than the verb form of that same word, as in "bear with me." As proof that the Internet can open up a whole new world of information about virtually any subject, including bears, I offer the following examples of some news headlines I found during a recent search of the web, along with a little personal commentary:

"Sharks Too Much for Bears." I *have* seen bears spend some time in the water, either in search of a meal such as a tasty fish or simply having fun. However, until I saw this headline, I wasn't aware that bears were inclined to venture very far into the ocean. Bears are pretty tough critters, so this information supports the idea that you don't want to mess around with those sharks. Maybe the movie *Jaws* wasn't so far-fetched after all.

"Bears Too Strong for Lions." I guess if they just stay on dry land, the bruins don't have much to fear, even from the supposed King of the Beasts. This is all the more reason that we mere humans need to give bears (or lions) a wide berth.

"Eagles Tame Bears." These majestic birds are obviously no match for bears when it comes to size and sheer power, but apparently speed, mobility, and the ability to fly out of reach of those teeth and claws tip the scales in favor of one of our national symbols.

"Bears Can't Handle the Heat." Well, I'm not surprised. If you had to wear one of those heavy fur coats around all the time, I bet you wouldn't fare too well in hot weather either. There's a very good reason you shouldn't waste your time looking for bruins in the desert.

And finally, "Bears Fall in London." This shouldn't be unexpected, since a big city is way out of the comfort zone even for animals as smart and adaptable as bears. At least London doesn't have much in the nature of cliffs or canyons, so I can only hope the bears mentioned in this headline simply tripped over a curb and weren't injured.

Although all of the above headlines are 100 percent accurate and legitimate, they actually refer to the outcome of basketball games by a team in Great Britain called the "Genesis Brighton Bears Basketball Club." They're shared here courtesy of Sam Hale, who writes the headlines for stories posted on the team's website (www.brightonbears .com/).

As long as I'm venturing out on unscientific limbs, I'll also offer the opinion that few wild animals are more misunderstood, more misrepresented in the media, or evoke as many different emotions in people as do bears. Stop and think about it for just a minute. In our culture most of us first encounter bears at a very early age. We have bears in classic stories ("Goldilocks and the Three Bears," "Winnie the Pooh," and "Paddington" to name just a few); cartoon characters (Yogi Bear); numerous sports team mascots; and countless soft and cuddly toy versions of these bruins and their various cousins.

Since this is a book about the Great Outdoors, let's not overlook the longest running and one of the most successful public service advertising campaigns in U.S. history—Smokey Bear. (No, I didn't get the name wrong. According to the definitive source of information on the subject, www.smokeybear.com, "Smokey's correct, full name is Smokey Bear. In the popular song 'Smokey the Bear,' written in 1952 by Steve Nelson and Jack Rollins, a 'the' was added to his name to keep the song's rhythm intact. This small change has caused confusion among Smokey fans ever since.")

Madison Avenue has obviously recognized the mystique and enduring appeal of these animals. In just the past several months I've seen television commercials and magazine ads using bears to hype goods and services including vehicles, foods and beverages, insurance, and a host of personal care products. It's no wonder that modern visitors to our parks are sometimes confused about how they should act around bears.

That uncertainty has even extended all the way to Washington and at least one of our former elected officials. Back in the early 1970s, I read a newspaper story about a congressman from a large eastern city that I shall tactfully leave unnamed, who was demanding a congressional investigation of an important issue. The subject of his ire? A report from one of his constituents who had just returned home from a trip to the Wild West and observed that bears were actually running around *loose* in Yellowstone National Park! What could those rangers have been thinking to allow such a thing?

In a defense of sorts of our anonymous congressperson, his reaction is unfortunately not uncommon. As evidence, I offer a story submitted by Candid Contributor Bill Hayer from Bellevue, Washington, who spent eleven summers in Yellowstone National Park working for the park concessionaire. Concessionaires are private companies that operate the hotels, restaurants, gift shops, and other commercial facilities under a contract with the National Park Service. Like park rangers, many of the concession employees come into frequent contact with the public and accumulate their own share of park stories as they either overhear conversations or are asked questions by visitors.

During the summer of 1987, Bill was working as a waiter at Old Faithful and had a table of guests whose comments confirmed that some visitors to parks such as Yellowstone are simply in a totally alien environment. Everyone at the table was fully convinced that the animals in the park such as the "buffalo" (actually bison) were not "real," but were actually electronic, mechanical statues like the animated figures of birds and animals at Disneyland. They believed that sensors in these make-believe animals caused them to go into motion whenever people got near them!

Such stories go a long way toward explaining the sometimes bizarre and even dangerous behavior some people exhibit around wild animals in parks. If there's any small consolation in the above tale, it's that perhaps at least these people would be less inclined to try to feed an animated statue.

Although I hope bears will always have the freedom to roam in our parks, and people will be able to enjoy seeing them in their natural environment, there's no question that allowing people and bears to share the same real estate does pose some challenges for park management. A good bit of time and money is spent on "bear management programs," which in fact focus primarily on managing the activities of people so bears can continue to behave as wild animals rather than actors in those television commercials.

This approach is necessary because bears (**B**ruins **E**arnestly **A**voiding **R**egulatory **S**ystems) are very smart critters. Given the opportunity, they will quickly learn to hang around people and survive on unhealthy goodies provided by humans rather than find their own meal out in Real Nature. Bears and any other wild animals who have lost their fear of people and come to associate humans with food *will* become a problem.

Most "bear problems" can be traced either to edibles or images, the latter being attempts by people to get too close to the wild animals in their quest for a good photo. Hollywood did flirt with reality in the name of at least one movie, *The Bad News Bears*, because getting up close and personal with one of these animals can definitely result in some bad news for the human involved.

Even the National Park Service and other agencies managing public lands have undergone a progression of attitudes about how to deal with bears. Just a few decades ago, park campgrounds and picnic areas had open trash cans that provided a veritable bruin buffet, and it was considered "normal" to see bears wandering through campsites and

The bear in this photo from the past may look cute, but begging for handouts from motorists or breaking into cars to get a snack is bad news for bruins and visitors alike. (National Park Service)

rummaging through garbage cans at all hours of the day and night. Although some current visitors are disappointed that bears are not seen as frequently in close proximity to people as they were in years past, the present situation is definitely better for both people and bears.

Okay, end of the background material, and back to some fun stories. There are enough tales about bears in parks to fill lots of books, and plenty of them have already been recorded for posterity by other authors. I'll share just a couple from my own experience and one that's among the classics of park lore.

The following story has been told and retold, probably in various forms, by rangers at Yellowstone, and it occurred before more stringent measures were employed to reduce the number of bears hanging around campgrounds. I include it as an example of how a bad situation can only get worse when park visitors try to solve bear problems on their own.

A man had just walked out the door of a snack bar in the park with his hands full of tasty morsels when he noticed a bear headed in his direction. The man panicked, dropped his food, and began to climb the nearest tree. The animal, seizing a golden opportunity, headed over to this unexpected offering and began to enjoy a free meal.

At this point other visitors arrived on the scene in their vehicle and decided to scare away the bear. A woman grabbed a pot and pan, got out of her truck, and started rattling and banging the utensils with great vigor. The startled bear stopped eating and headed for the nearest tree.

Unfortunately, it was the *same* tree where the man who was the original owner of the goodies had already taken refuge.

As the bear began to climb the tree the man climbed even higher. The woman continued to shake and bang the metal pans, which simply encouraged the beleaguered bruin to climb further up the tree. It would be interesting to know what the man was thinking; this Escalating Melancholy Situation would probably be an example of being caught between the devil and the tall green tree.

Fortunately, a park ranger arrived on the scene and was able to convince the lady to stop creating all that racket and leave the area. Once peace was restored and everyone had pulled back a reasonable distance, the bear came down from the tree and departed. According to this Yellowstone legend, it took the ranger a much longer period of time to talk the man into returning to the ground.

I've heard and read plenty of stories about people taking refuge in trees from bears and of bears climbing a tree to escape humans. In the summer of 2006 newspapers around the country carried a story about a housecat that treed a bear in a New Jersey backyard. However, the preceding story from Yellowstone is the only one I've personally heard about both a bear and a person climbing the *same* tree, at least if the bear was not intentionally in pursuit of the human.

Back in the days before serious efforts were made to keep bears out of campgrounds, I was a youngster on a camping trip with my family in the Great Smoky Mountains National Park.

Just before dark one evening, a lone motorcyclist pulled into the vacant campsite directly across the road from my family's camp. This was apparently going to be a one-night stand, the weather looked good, and the new arrival was either short on camping gear or just decided to keep things simple. It didn't take long to make camp, which consisted of unrolling his sleeping bag on top of the picnic table in preparation for a night's sleep under the stars.

Even back in those days, rangers made noble efforts to warn campers to store food properly in places where it would be inaccessible to foraging animals. Nonetheless, it was not unusual for people to leave ice chests, cooking gear, or even groceries out in the open. Perhaps thinking it was a good idea to keep such items off the ground, a popular location to store them was on the picnic table provided in each campsite.

Just for the record, this action has absolutely no value in protecting the goodies from any wild creatures ranging in size from ants to bears. The animals themselves probably appreciate people who leave the food on the picnic table, since this may reduce the effects of moisture from the ground and help keep the potato chips crisper for the midnight snackers. Denizens of the wild are a quick study when it comes to locating an easy meal, and opportunists such as raccoons and bears know to check out those picnic tables for any keen cuisine as they make their nightly rounds through the buffet line we humans call a campground.

Darkness had settled over the valley like a soft blanket, campfires had died down to a few glowing embers, and except for the peaceful sound of a gentle breeze in the treetops, the night was quiet and campers were peacefully snoozing away, snug in their beds. The silence was deceiving, because the area was far from devoid of activity. Join me for a minute in an imaginary conversation taking place along the road looping through the area.

A pair of black bears has stopped to compare notes, and the younger one gives his report. Waiting a respectful distance off to one side are a large raccoon and a trio of skunks. They know there will be plenty to go around and there's no sense trying to compete with the big boys.

"The people in sites 3 and 18 left boxes of food right out on the picnic table and the campers in #21 thought they'd be smart and put the groceries *inside* their tent," begins the smaller bear. "There are ice chests on the ground at sites 7, 11, and 15. Number 7 smells like fish, but the cooler in #15 is a lot bigger. Oh, *here's* a weird one for you. There's a human sleeping on top of the picnic table in #23. I didn't take time to stop and see if he's hiding anything in his sleeping bag."

Bear number two ponders this information. "I know I always get first choice since I'm the oldest, but this time I'll let you pick. Which one do you want?"

Taken by surprise, bruin number one wavers for a moment or two. "Gosh, that fish at #7 smelled great, but there could be a *bunch* more stuff in that larger cooler in #15. I could hear some people talking in that tent, so I didn't check it out up close."

The senior bear growls a little impatiently. "Well, what's it going to be? 7 or 15? Meal or no meal?"

Once a decision has been made, the deli bar is open and the critters go to work. Eventually, the obvious items are claimed, but there is still one question to answer. You've seen this one coming, and sure enough, the serenity of a pleasant summer night was suddenly shattered by a classic example of a blood-curdling scream.

In such situations, the combination of curiosity, anxiety, and the instinct for self-preservation is enough to bestir most people from their beds, and the area was almost instantly alive with activity. The air was filled with the sound of tent zippers being hastily opened and the banging of doors on trailers. Flashlight beams stabbed wildly back and forth in the darkness in search of clues about the crisis, and a few brave souls even ventured out into the night to see what was amiss.

The initial scream had subsided to animated conversation, and it didn't take long to hone in on the campsite with the motorcyclist. In the absence of an obvious threat, a small crowd began to form, and the story soon circulated among the gathering throng.

Not surprisingly, the man asleep on the picnic table had suddenly awakened to the combination of a distinctly unpleasant odor and a gust of warm air, both of which originated in the breath of a bear who was sniffing around the man's face. Just so you can claim bonus points for educational value simply by reading this book, I'll confirm for you that based on my somewhat limited experience, wild bears *do* in fact have a serious case of very bad breath.

I attribute this to the fact that bears are classified as omnivorous, which means that they will eat virtually anything, including most of the stuff we humans toss into the garbage can. This diet, combined with the observation that I've yet to see a bruin use either a toothbrush or mouthwash, produces the infamous bear breath. Now that I've brought this point into the public forum, don't be surprised if you see a TV commercial featuring a bear using one of those products to resolve this issue.

Incidentally, my personal experience with bear breath is thankfully not based on close encounters with free-ranging bruins. From time to time, rangers find it necessary to capture a bear that has been causing

You may not like dandelions in your lawn, but they make a great snack for bears! (Melinda Webster, National Park Service)

a problem in areas such as campgrounds and transport the miscreant to a remote area, where it will (hopefully) revert to more natural habits. During the course of such relocations, the bear is usually safely confined in a live trap, which amounts to a small cage on wheels, and dozing peacefully under the influence of a temporary sedative. This allows rangers to work safely in close proximity to the animal—and to get an unavoidable whiff or two of bear breath.

While in custody, the captive bear is weighed, measured, and sometimes fitted with a radio-tracking collar, a numbered and brightly colored ear tag, or some similar form of identification. This allows easy recognition of repeat offenders and is much more effective than the approach used for their human counterparts, a mug shot. It takes a trained eye to distinguish one bear from another, especially if the only glimpse the eyewitness had was of the south end of a northbound bear as it headed off into the woods with a camper's supper.

Back in the story in the campground, the animal was simply checking out this stop on his or her nightly rounds, looking for whatever tasty morsel might be found on the picnic table. Fortunately, the motorcyclist didn't qualify and hadn't stored any foodstuffs in his sleeping bag, and the bruin made a hasty departure when it was rudely greeted by this unexpected occupant of the snack bar.

For some reason, the idea of an idyllic night in the Great Outdoors seemed to have lost some of its appeal for this gentleman. Even before his neighbors had returned to their own sleeping bags, he had broken camp, jumped onto his cycle, started the engine, and roared off into the night. It would be interesting to know how far he rode before stopping again, and whether or not he ever gave camping another try. I suspect that for the rest of his life, he had a slightly different reaction than most of the rest of us whenever he heard the song "Smokey the Bear."

And the Winner Is . . .

Our national parks are wonderful places to visit, and I don't want to give you the impression from the following stories that they have become overrun with crime. However, the reality is that not everyone is in the park just to enjoy the scenery, and some Rangerly Advice is to take at least the same precautions in a park as you would in any city. Keep your vehicle locked, secure your valuables, and don't take candy from strangers (or give it to the animals).

Having said that, I hope you'll get out and visit your parks, have a good time, and enjoy the following proof that crime still doesn't pay. Just for fun, I'll give out a few awards in this chapter for some especially outstanding examples of—well—plain ol' dumb crooks, plus one for extra creativity by the good guys.

At about 2 A.M. on a June morning, a ranger on the Blue Ridge Parkway in North Carolina responded to a report of a motor vehicle accident. He determined that there had been a rollover accident involving a Land Rover, but the driver was nowhere to be found. The ranger's investigation at the scene discovered drug paraphernalia inside the vehicle, which upped the ante for this situation from your basic accident report to something potentially much more interesting.

The ranger was subsequently contacted by an officer at the Wautauga County Sheriff's Office, who advised that they had the dri-

The Blue Ridge Parkway winds for 470 scenic miles through the mountains of Virginia and North Carolina. Enjoy the views and a leisurely drive; if you're in a hurry, better stick to the Interstate. (National Park Service)

ver of the abandoned Land Rover in their custody. He had walked to the administration building of a nearby town to report the accident and had knocked on a door to try to locate someone so he could do his duty. That was certainly the proper thing to do and besides, he would need an official report to file an insurance claim to get his vehicle repaired.

There's a long-running television game show where contestants are asked to choose whether they want the prize that's hidden behind door number one or door number two. One of the items is more valuable than the other, and depending upon what they see when their choice is revealed, they may be delighted or disappointed. In the matter at hand from the Blue Ridge Parkway, the driver-turned-hiker had to choose *which* door at the city administration building to knock upon to make his accident report. In his situation the outcome was more a case of *surprise* than prize, since the door he selected happened to be that of the on-duty magistrate.

When the judge answered the door, he detected a strong odor of alcohol on the man he found standing outside and called the sheriff's office. The individual admitted to drinking and driving, submitted to an intoxilizer test, and was subsequently issued citations for DUI and drug possession. Perhaps this lends some credence to the saying that no good deed goes unpunished, but there's also obviously confirmation about where the use of drugs and alcohol can lead you. I'll award this man a diploma from the School of Hardly Wise Knocks.

While the above incident clearly rates pretty high on the Oops-O-Meter, one would think that a fondness for chocolate chip cookies would be pretty harmless. What's more, every dentist in the country would likely applaud one trait of the character in this next story, who was apparently dedicated to flossing his teeth after enjoying those tasty cookies. *Surely* flossing after eating would qualify as a good deed.

There is, of course, a little more to this story, which unfolded in early February at Indiana Dunes National Lakeshore. A ranger stopped to chat with a visitor at the park's Inland Marsh parking area, and the citizen then set out on a hike while the ranger went on to check a nearby area. When the ranger returned to the first parking lot about ten minutes later, he noticed that a window in the visitor's car had been broken.

The ranger also noticed that a gray van was leaving the area and alertly recalled that this van was similar in description to a vehicle believed to be associated with numerous car break-ins during the past three years. Rangers stopped the vehicle and detained the driver while another ranger contacted the original hiker, who until that point was unaware of the damage to his car. A check of the victim's vehicle produced a list of missing items, which were subsequently found in the suspect's van. The stolen property in question? A box of chocolate chip cookies and several tooth flossers.

While the theft of those items may sound pretty insignificant, I'm sure the owner of the vehicle from whence they came was less than pleased with the broken window on his car. In a great example of the principle that one good thing leads to another, further inventory of the van's contents turned up other items that connected the driver to additional vehicle break-ins. During their investigation, rangers determined that the van's driver had an extensive criminal history of over two dozen arrests for previous misdeeds.

Park Law Enforcement Specialist Joni Jones gets bonus points for a creative suggested headline for the report of this incident: "Sweet Tooth and Good Oral Hygiene Are Suspect's Downfall." However, my award for the Grand Prize in Creative Crime Headlines goes to Bill Hallainen, longtime editor of the NPS "Morning Report" with his title, "Thief Gets Just Desserts."

Sometimes an encounter with a malefactor will help add to the ranger mystique in the local area, which is never a bad thing—at least from the ranger's standpoint. One of my assignments was to the Big Thicket National Preserve in southeast Texas, in the early years of that park. One summer afternoon another ranger and I were wrapping up the day's work and heading back to town from one of the more remote sections of that area. We were driving down an unpaved road and were nearing the park boundary when we spotted a man walking down the road in front of us.

Well, he was *trying* to walk, but from his uneven gait and less than straightforward progress toward his destination, it was apparent that he either had a medical problem or was under the influence of something on a no-no list. Like all good rangers, we were concerned for his welfare and first wanted to ensure that this wasn't a medical emergency.

We pulled up behind the man in our government pickup, stopped, and got out to check on the situation. The fact that he didn't even hear our truck approach was one clue to this guy's condition, but as the two of us walked into his line of vision, the situation changed abruptly. We recognized the man as a resident of the nearby rural area, someone with whom we had had previous experience in similar circumstances.

It was immediately obvious from both word and deed that this gentleman had absolutely no interest in any help from these representatives of the United States Government—or any other Proper Authorities. With apologies in advance to all those outstanding citizens who share this name, for the sake of the story I'll just refer to our newfound companion as Billy. In addition to some pretty straightforward verbal feedback, Billy confirmed his intentions to part company with us by walking—as best he could—off the road into the adjoining wooded area.

Even our brief conversation had provided adequate opportunity to confirm that this was not a medical issue, but rather a situation involving the overly generous use of an intoxicating beverage. This diagnosis did not require a high level of discernment on our part, since a distinctive aroma could be detected on Billy's breath and person, even at a distance of several feet. Just to clinch the deal, at the time of our contact Billy was holding an open pull-top can of a popular brand of such beverages. When requested to give us the container in question, Billy not only declined to do so, but apparently felt a pressing need to ensure that not a *single* drop of the contents was spilled.

He accomplished this feat by covering the opening in the top of the can with his thumb, and did so with such vigor that he managed to push the end of the thumb through the hole and down into the can itself. Billy had pretty large fingers, and I was intrigued to learn that it was actually possible to wedge an adult-sized thumb into that small opening with such apparent ease. I have thankfully never had that experience myself, but I suspect for most people this action would register fairly high on the "Ouch-O-Meter." The fact that Billy seemed totally oblivious to any discomfort provided further confirmation of his condition.

Well, now we were faced with a classic dilemma. The man obviously posed enough threat to his own welfare, and possibly to others he might encounter if he wandered back into the road, that we couldn't simply ignore the situation. Given Billy's less than cooperative attitude, we could either take him immediately into custody, which at a minimum would require a wrestling match, or seek a less confrontational solution.

After walking about twenty feet into the woods, Billy made a gradual turn back to his original direction of travel, parallel to the road, and resumed his hike. His progress was hampered by the fact that he had to make frequent minor course corrections to dodge trees in his path, but he was doing his best to make haste and escape his potential captors.

The trees at least provided frequent and convenient handholds, although the use of his left hand was somewhat hampered by the aluminum can still attached to his thumb. My partner and I walked alongside for a short distance, hoping to talk Billy into a more cooperative attitude. Nothing doing in that department, but it was pretty clear that Billy wasn't going to be able to maintain his present pace for very long.

Deciding that discretion was the better part of valor, my fellow ranger and I returned to our truck, contacted headquarters via our two-way radio, and requested that someone there attempt to phone Billy's residence, which was only a couple of miles away. Since we were driving a pickup truck, we were not in a good position to haul an uncooperative individual anywhere, much less to the nearest calaboose, which was close to an hour's drive away. In our remote area it would also be a very long wait for backup from local authorities who would have a vehicle properly equipped for that task.

While we were waiting on the outcome of the phone call, we simply started our truck, put it in first gear, and crept along the road, keeping pace with our erstwhile hiker. Intent on making his escape, Billy was apparently completely oblivious to the fact that we were following alongside in our vehicle. Sometimes things actually do work out the way you hope, and we soon received a radio call that a couple of Billy's family members were en route to give us a hand. Shortly thereafter, in a case of perfect timing, Billy finally embraced one last tree with a bear hug and slid ever so slowly to a sitting position.

We parked our truck and walked back over to Billy, who by that time was considerably more cooperative. As they say in these parts, he was just plain tuckered out from his attempted jog in the woods, and he looked up at us in absolute amazement. It took a while for him to catch his breath, but he finally managed to gasp out a question.

"How'd you boys manage to keep *up* with me? Shoot, you ain't even *breathin'* hard!"

We were saved the need to conjure up an appropriate answer by the timely arrival of Billy's brother and cousin, and he was more than willing to accept a ride back to the house with his family. The relatives were both apologetic about the situation and appreciative of our willingness to simply hand Billy over to them for safekeeping.

Most of all, however, they were amazed at his thumb-in-the-can situation, which they found to be hilarious. I suspect his predicament provided the basis for a family tale that would be oft-repeated for years to come. We decided to leave the problem of thumb extrication in their hands, but the best part of the story for us was Billy's admonition to his family members as they were preparing to drive away.

"Don't ever try to outrun them rangers. You *just* can't do it. Those boys are in *some* kinda good shape!" For at least one of our local residents, a legend had been born, and Billy is the winner of my "Thumbs Down" award.

Some people will apparently go to special lengths to attract attention to their illegal activities, thereby invoking a well-established principle for law enforcement officers known as the JDLR (**J**ust **D**on't **L**ook **R**ight) rule. On a February morning in the Big Cypress National Preserve in Florida, a ranger stopped a Jeep Cherokee that was not only being driven in a closed area but that also had two women riding on the roof. This would rate at least a B+ on the JDLR scale. The report didn't provide their explanation for this activity, but perhaps the SUV didn't have a sunroof and they just wanted to enjoy that famous Florida sunshine.

The two women and the driver of the vehicle were identified as juveniles from Naples, Florida, and thanks to the miracle of modern communications and good computer technology, the ranger soon discovered that the license plate on the Jeep was from another vehicle.

This information is guaranteed to induce a law enforcement officer to engage in further investigation, which soon revealed that the vehicle had been reported stolen.

Not content with the fact that they were already in deep tapioca, the trio provided conflicting accounts and false information about the stolen vehicle and other aspects of their situation. In addition to a variety of federal violations relating to the off-road vehicle operation and providing false information, this merry band faced charges of grand theft auto and probation violations from local authorities. Perhaps someday in the future they'll actually buy, rather than steal, a vehicle, and when they do, maybe they'll finally get that sunroof.

This next story is another good example of skewed logic. I refer to the erroneous belief in some circles that if you're guilty of some nefarious deed and your capture by the long arm of the law appears to be imminent, it's a good idea to try to dispose of any incriminating evidence that might be in your possession. While you're at it, you might as well ditch any form of identification being carried on or about your person.

I'll call this the John Doe Delusion, which is the mistaken belief that if the authorities can't identify you, they can't charge you. On the contrary, the inability of someone caught in the act of a no-no to produce a credible form of identification simply raises the level of suspicion that there's more here than meets the eye.

In the case in question, the neighboring sheriff's department at Colonial National Historical Park in Virginia had just broadcast a "BOLO" (Be on the Lookout) for a stolen car. Lo and behold, it wasn't long before Ranger Bob Whiteman spotted that very vehicle on the road in front of him. Being a prudent student of human nature and a highly trained law enforcement officer, Ranger Whiteman exercised good judgment, radioed for backup, and followed the stolen vehicle at a discreet distance until additional help from county officers and other rangers arrived.

Once he was no longer the lone ranger, Bob selected a suitable spot to make a stop and turned on the blue lights and siren. That left the driver of the reported stolen car one of two choices, which gave him a fifty-fifty chance of making the right decision. Unfortunately, he made the wrong one and elected not to stop.

The good news is that the chase wasn't at high speeds—the driver simply refused to stop. It just wasn't the bad guy's day, however, and he obviously wasn't very familiar with the area. After apparently flipping a mental coin at a couple of intersections (another shot at a fifty-fifty chance), he definitely chose "heads" when he should have taken "tails" and found himself on a road to nowhere. The route in question ended at the security gate to a Coast Guard base, but wait—just before the gate, there was a narrow street to the left. Hmmm, wonder where that goes?

Well, the answer to that question is that it soon comes to a dead end, but our man didn't make it quite that far. It proved to be a good thing that our determined driver wasn't going *too* fast, but what constitutes a safe speed can be a very relative thing. As the event was reported in the local newspaper the next day, at one point the road made a sharp turn to the left, but the car continued straight ahead.

As is almost always the case in such driving errors, the car didn't go very far, because that curve in the road borders a patch of *very* thick brush and woods. Any attempt to drive a car through such terrain always has the same outcome, and the vehicle soon came to a final halt in a veritable jungle. At least the vegetation helped cushion the impact, so the driver wasn't injured and even the car was relatively undamaged.

Once again it was decision time, and once again, our guy didn't choose wisely. Rather than finally admitting that the game was up, he decided to continue his excursion on foot. After crashing and thrashing his way through the woods and down a very steep slope, the desperado found himself on the bank of the York River. Most of you haven't been there, so I'll simply explain that this is a *big* river, deep enough for oceangoing vessels, and hundreds of feet wide at that point.

Back in October 1781, the British general Cornwallis found himself in a similar predicament. George Washington's troops and their French allies had the English army surrounded in Yorktown, with their backs to the York River. Cornwallis ordered a last-ditch attempt to escape across the river at night, using a fleet of small boats. A fierce storm ended that plan, the once mighty redcoat army surrendered, and the rest, as they say, is history.

Despite the bad weather, Cornwallis had one advantage over our fleeing felon—at least the general had some boats. A reasonable person might think the saga of the stolen car was finally about to wind down, but wait—our desperado had one more brainstorm: Why don't I just swim to the other side of the York River?

The answer is: *bad idea*, but that didn't deter our outlaw. Perhaps the John Doe Delusion came into play, and he was trying to gain sudden anonymity by getting rid of *any* identification he was carrying. Another possibility is that somewhere in the dim recesses of his memory, the man recalled hearing that if you're going for a swim, you should get rid of extra clothing that will weigh you down when it gets wet.

Whatever the reason, before he waded out into the water and started swimming, the man left *all* of his clothes on the bank of the river. If he figured the "authorities" wouldn't try to swim after him, he at least was right about one thing that day. The Coast Guard base right down the road responded to the call for assistance with a boat, and before long the erstwhile swimmer was safely plucked from the water and given a ride to a nice, safe location where he didn't have to make so many decisions. He obviously needed some help in that area, since he definitely didn't "know when to fold 'em," and I'm not talking about the clothes he left on the riverbank.

My final tale in this chapter comes from former park ranger Oakley Blair. Oakley (or "Oak" as he was known in the ranger ranks) and his wife Barb were our next-door neighbors when we both worked at Glacier National Park, but his first job with the NPS was at Shenandoah National Park, in the beautiful Blue Ridge Mountains of Virginia. During autumn of his initial years on the job, one of Oak's assignments was to patrol the Skyline Drive in the park during the wee hours of the morning, looking for deer poachers.

Around 2:30 in the morning he was parked in his government pickup truck when he spied a vehicle moving slowly along the drive, shining a spotlight into the meadow alongside the road. This is a common poacher technique known locally as "jack-lighting for deer." Oak pulled onto the road, turned on the red light on his truck, and pulled over the driver. The alleged offender, as he would probably be called today, was alone in the truck, but there was a shotgun lying in plain view on the seat of the pickup.

Oak reports that this was his first encounter with a suspected poacher, and he was understandably a little nervous. He asked the driver to hand him the shotgun butt end first, and fortunately the driver complied. The ranger checked the shotgun and found that it was loaded with 12-gauge slugs.

For benefit of readers who are not hunters, a slug is a shotgun version of a single, *very* big bullet that is used for hunting large prey such as deer. If a slug were used to shoot a small animal, there wouldn't be anything left worth adding to the stew pot. By contrast, buckshot shells fire a number of much smaller pellets, which come in a variety of sizes to fit the intended prey and are commonly used when hunting birds or small game with a shotgun.

Oak informed the driver that it was illegal to have a loaded weapon in the park and asked him why he had a loaded shotgun sitting on the seat of his truck. The man responded in a slow southern country drawl, "I was hunt'n rabbits on my daddy's farm and forgot to take the gun out of the truck."

The incredulous ranger said, "You were hunting *rabbits* with 12-gauge slugs?"

The presumed would-be poacher responded in a matter-of-fact tone, "They was *big* rabbits!"

I doubt that the hunter was familiar with the writings of William Camden, a noted seventeenth-century British historian and author, but apparently he did agree with Camden's observation, "Better a bad excuse, than none at all." This excuse, however, was so lame that I'd rate it a notch below "bad," and Oak issued him the appropriate citation and collected the shotgun and shells as evidence. Court was held the next week, and the violator told the same story to the local judge about "hunt'n rabbits on daddy's farm." Everyone in the courtroom burst into laughter. The judge found the man guilty of possessing a loaded firearm in the park, assessed an appropriate fine, and the shotgun and shells that had been collected as evidence were then returned to their owner.

I trust the erstwhile hunter's future expeditions in search of humongous hares or other game were limited to daddy's farm and similar legal locales. He may have gone home from his ill-conceived hunting trip empty-handed on at least one night, but perhaps he would be gratified to know that I am hereby declaring him the Triple-A Grand Prize winner of my Anemic Alibi Award.

Sadder but Wiser?

"Hey—there's a moose, or an elk, or a bear, or a skunk!" A skunk? For many people, a highlight of a trip to the Great Outdoors is the chance to see wild birds and animals in their native habitat, and some folks even find skunks to be cute. Since most national and state parks are closed to hunting, creatures in those areas can lose much of their natural fear of humans, making it possible to approach them much more closely than would normally be the case.

This can be a mixed blessing for both man and beast, however, since even small animals can inflict a nasty bite (or a dose of air defreshener) and larger ones can be very dangerous, despite their sometimes deceptively "tame" appearances. Always check on safety information and regulations concerning wildlife when you arrive in a park or similar site. The majority of Beastly Melancholy Situations occur when people get too close to animals in search of a photo or can't resist the temptation to feed them.

Most wild animals don't have any better judgment than humans do about healthy eating. To the best of my knowledge, neither the FDA nor any other organization has developed guidelines for the Recommended Daily Allowances of fat and/or sugar for birds and animals, but suffice it to say that "people food" is definitely not good for the wildlife. Yeah, I know they're cute, but try to resist temptation and "just say no" when any creatures great or small come begging, so you won't find yourself in a situation similar to those in the following stories.

Mrs. Deb Anderson from Robbinsdale, Minnesota, shared the following good example of what can go wrong when people ignore warnings about feeding wildlife in parks. This incident occurred at

Custer State Park, which is located near Mount Rushmore in South Dakota.

> We were driving through the park enjoying the abundant wildlife that can be seen from the car. Our son Scott was four at the time so this was a perfect activity for our family. The wild burros in Custer were especially interesting, and we had our car windows cracked just enough to get in on the fun sounds and even a little donkey snot.
>
> We moved on down the road to another group of burros. Another car was already parked near the herd that was standing on the road. We pulled up behind the first vehicle and watched an older lady get out of the car with a big bag of potato chips. Her husband remained in the car while this lady walked up to a burro and began feeding it potato chips.
>
> It was great fun to watch her for about one minute, then things began to get ugly as the burros jostled and competed for the chips. The woman began to become alarmed and tried to move away, but the burros were intent on having that whole bag of chips! We continued to watch this scenario unfold as this woman's husband remained in their car, video camera fixed on his wife, with the window down just enough for the camera lens to stick out through the opening.
>
> Finally we became alarmed as the woman really began to panic and the burros continued to muscle her for more chips. By now the goodies were gone and the scene was just plain ugly. My husband Mark took matters into his own hands and maneuvered our car close to the woman. This resulted in the burros backing off slightly and our car provided a buffer for the woman to run around and escape.
>
> She ran to her car, jumped in and they literally peeled rubber into the sunset, never to be seen again. Scott, now age eleven, was inspired by your many clever and funny acronyms from your first book and has since invented an acronym that could be used with this story. He says the woman suffered from S.A.D. (**S**tupid **A**dult **D**isorder).

Scott was right on target, and I'll add my opinion that while the old expression about someone being "sadder but wiser" can be credited to the writer Samuel Coleridge in *The Rime of the Ancient Mariner*, its roots can actually be ascribed to S.A.D., which was known to occur in humanity as early as Adam and the event with that infamous apple.

The Andersons' story also confirms that those advertising geniuses on Madison Avenue sometimes do get it right, although I'm not sure they were thinking about wild burros at the time they coined one of their memorable slogans. When it comes to most snacks, it's hard to eat just one—whether you're a human *or* a wild animal.

Sadder but Wiser?   89

Traffic jam, Yellowstone style. These bighorn sheep aren't in a rush, so if you find your-self in one of these situations, just stay in your vehicle, enjoy the view—and please don't feed the animals. (National Park Service)

As further proof that denizens of the wild just can't resist even our leftovers, I offer a story from the Great Smoky Mountains National Park, located along the Tennessee–North Carolina border. A 150-pound black bear was enticed by the aromas emanating from a trash dumpster in the Cades Cove section of the park and managed to climb inside the container in search of a snack. This tale also proves that sometimes it's the animal rather than the human who is sadder and hopefully wiser for the experience.

In a classic case of bad timing, the bear was still inside when the garbage truck arrived, picked up the bin with its mechanized arms, and dumped the contents into the back of the truck.

The vehicle finished its rounds and made its way to the Sevier County solid waste facility, where it deposited its load—fortunately into a composter rather than a compacter.

The bear climbed up brackets along the composter's wall and took refuge in the highest corner of the structure until its presence was noted. A wildlife officer was notified and tranquilized the bear. In an unusual example of reverse recycling, the animal was then returned to the park and released, fortunately neither composted nor compacted, and I trust it was both sadder *and* wiser for the experience. An employee of the solid waste facility said that they'd previously collected

Hey Ranger 2

skunks, possums, and raccoons, but this was their first encounter with a bear.

Life isn't always easy for a bear, even if it tries to do the right thing, stays away from people and their garbage, and sticks to the diet nature intended. In June 2002, a young black bear in the Great Smoky Mountains National Park was mugged by a tourist. No, the bear hadn't threatened the man or anyone else—it had simply been doing what bears are naturally programmed to do.

With apologies to readers who feel sympathy for any wild creature that becomes a meal for another (usually larger) animal, that's part of the great scheme of things in nature. This system of predators and prey helps keep the earth from being overrun with mice, rabbits, and other animals that can otherwise become a serious problem when their population outgrows their own food supply.

In this case, the young bear had managed to capture a smaller mammal. Its only mistake was that it did so within sight of several people, one of whom attacked the bear. The bruin, undoubtedly shocked by this unexpected human behavior, dropped its potential meal and fled.

Unfortunately, the young bear's tribulations weren't over, and several days later what rangers believe was the same bruin caught another animal. This time Smokey Junior was besieged by a whole crowd of visitors, and once again retreated to the safety of the woods. One can only hope the bear eventually succeeded in getting a meal as nature intended, out of sight of those crazy humans, before it was forced to turn to dumpster diving or a life of crime, stealing picnic baskets in order to survive.

Many species of wildlife are proving to be very adaptable as we humans continue to expand our development into formerly "wild" terrain, and reports of a wide variety of animals in suburbs and even major cities continue to crop up in park reports and the media. In some cases development has spread to the boundaries of parks and in others, the parks themselves are located within cities and towns. This has created a whole new set of challenges for wildlife managers, as people react in a variety of ways to citified birds and animals that may live in a park but venture into adjacent housing areas for enhanced dining experiences.

Once again, the root of the problem is often food: Wild animals are either attracted to the contents of garbage cans, food set out intentionally for wildlife, pet food left in bowls outside a house, or unfortunately sometimes even the pets themselves. Bird feeders in someone's yard are certainly acceptable in my opinion, but it gets more complicated when people insist on feeding animals such as deer, coyotes, and even bears in their backyards. Those large animals can become serious nuisances as well as safety hazards for people and their pets.

Sooner or later, conflicts will develop between such animals and their well-intentioned benefactors' nearby neighbors. At my last park assignment at Colonial National Historical Park in Virginia, I received occasional phone calls from nearby residents who were definitely unhappy that Bambi and his relatives were snacking on their rose bushes and other ornamental plants. Those calls often included a demand to "come get *your* deer out of my yard!"

As a chief ranger, I had quite a lengthy list of items of government property for which I was responsible, and which had to be verified by a hands-on inventory every year. Thankfully that list never included any deer or other living animals, which are notoriously unenthused about wearing labels with serial numbers. See, you just thought *your* life was complicated if you've ever been a parent, and you received a phone call from a teacher or another adult concerning some misdeed committed by one of your offspring. At least in the eyes of some of the public, you aren't personally responsible for the conduct of countless deer, raccoons, squirrels, bears, skunks, and other creatures that are notably uncooperative with the order to "go to your room and don't come out until I tell you to."

Roderick Eime, editor of the travel website www.traveloscopy.com, provides the following great story as proof that challenges with seemingly "tame" wildlife aren't limited to the U.S. His tale is from Australia; in case you aren't familiar with the terms, *joey* refers to a young kangaroo, and an *eskie* is a Down Under term for a picnic cooler or ice chest.

> On a recent family holiday to a beachside caravan park we discovered one of the very real dangers of interacting with the local wildlife.
>
> We pulled up in the parking bay outside our beachside cabin. There was a gentle breeze, bright sunshine, plenty of shade and the therapeutic sound of waves lapping on the pristine white sandy beach. What could possibly go wrong?
>
> The children unloaded themselves and quickly ran to the cabin in excited anticipation, leaving us to lug the bags, balls and eskies. Their delighted yelps alerted us to an unexpected bonus as there, on the carefully manicured lawn, was a small mob of kangaroos lounging unperturbed in front of our accommodation.

Clearly these animals were more than comfortable with humans as they barely lifted their heads on our approach, despite us having to literally step over them with our armloads of luggage.

The kids were transfixed by this minor spectacle and on my next load I saw both of them carefully stroking a young joey lying outstretched next to its mother who seemed barely interested in their activities.

The next morning the tribe were back, about a dozen of varying sizes, all in perfectly relaxed positions around the lawn—or so we thought.

The kids were dying to feed them, so I let them take out some apple cores, banana peels and sundry scraps. It was a perfect sight as the little ones eagerly hopped up for a polite nibble from their outstretched hands. Suddenly there was a loud crash in the nearby scrub and a much larger buck hopped out onto the lawn, scattering the mob. Startled, the kids yelped and ran back inside the cabin leaving the buck to gorge himself on all that was left—a process that took all of about fifteen seconds.

Clearly unsatisfied and insulted by this paltry offering the buck, standing almost five feet tall I reckon, hopped very purposefully onto the verandah toward the last whiffs of breakfast. Doing the brave fatherly thing, I confronted the interloper and tried to scare him off with some loud hisses and barks. Forget it! In one menacing hop he was in the doorway, standing at full height, grunting and growling. The message: "Get out of my way, I'm coming in!"

I wanted to push him away, but fearful of a further escalation in hostilities, went to pull the sliding door shut. It jammed. Sensing a diminishing opportunity, the buck made one last (successful) lunge through the doorway into the kitchen and promptly slipped over on the shiny lino.

The wife and kids were now in a total panic, standing on tables and chairs screaming their lungs out. "Stop screaming!" I screamed. Equally panicked, the buck briefly righted himself, attempted a full frontal attack and, fortunately for me, fell over again in a flurry of huge paws and tail swipes. Furniture, crockery, the microwave and our unpacked luggage were quickly turning into jumble as I tried to force the frantic animal into a corner with a chair so the hostages could flee.

"Get out, get out!" I yelled.

"He can't get out, you idiot, you're waving a chair at him!" snapped the missus.

"No, YOU get out!" I retorted rather impolitely, but the hostages were scared stiff and now cowering pathetically behind the divan.

Keen to end this disastrous melee, I took one concerted prod at the beast then bolted out the narrow gap in the jammed doorway. It worked. The enraged attacker came after me, slamming himself heavily against the narrow opening—just as I had done.

To my great relief, "Skippy the mutant kangaroo" broke off his offensive and took to the bush, leaving me puffing and wheezing heavily, my traumatised family whimpering in their corner and our entire cabin "trashed."

We checked out early.

All creatures, whether great or small, have the potential to create difficulties for people, and you don't even have to *feed* them to get into trouble. A good example is a story about a man who wanted to take a picture of a ground squirrel in Glacier National Park in Montana. The animal would poke its head in and out of its den in the rocks but never fully emerge for a good shot.

Perhaps this gentleman was a fisherman, which would help explain what happened next. In what probably seemed like a good idea at the time, the photographer decided to dangle his car keys in front of the den's opening, hoping to draw the squirrel out into the open. If a lure works for fish, why not this animal?

Waving something bright and jangling in front of the family cat— or a one-year-old baby—may be a great way to get a cute photo at home, but this story took an unexpected turn out in the wild. The keys did achieve the desired result of getting the squirrel's attention, but the man didn't expect it to literally "take the bait," so he didn't have a good grip on his lure. The animal bolted from its den, snatched the keys, and just as quickly darted back underground, prize firmly in tow! All subsequent attempts to retrieve the keys were unsuccessful.

An extra set of keys for the man's vehicle was not on hand, which qualified this as an Extraordinarily Inconvenient Melancholy Situation. I can vouch from my years of working at Glacier that it is many a mile from anyplace in that park to the nearest locksmith, so the cost of having a replacement set of keys made was undoubtedly an expensive lesson. Juliet may have told Romeo that "parting is such sweet sorrow," but I'm confident there was nothing sweet about the departing of this man's keys.

Here's a free investment tip for you: If you're looking for a good business opportunity, check and see if there is a locksmith in the vicinity of any large park or other recreation area. There are countless ways that people manage to lose their car keys in the Great Outdoors, but

Ground squirrels, chipmunks, and other small animals can be cute subjects for a photo. Just don't underestimate them, as the man in this story learned the hard way! (National Park Service)

having them heisted by a ground squirrel is probably the most unusual one that I've heard recently.

Once all was said and done, I trust this unfortunate park visitor was not only sadder but also wiser for his experience. Although I wouldn't recommend his approach, the best advice I could give this man in hindsight about using his car keys as a lure would be to "get a grip!"

Assumption Junction

L ots of folks get into trouble in the outdoors by making assumptions. My trusty *Roget's Super Thesaurus* tells me that term is closely related to words like *speculate, bogus, make-believe,* and *imagine.* When you're faced with a choice that could determine whether your day turns out to be fun or frantic, none of those sound like a very good basis for a decision!

A classic example occurred during the first week of a recent April in eastern Utah. A man I'll call Mo and his wife Flo were on a four-day canoe trip on the Green River in Canyonlands National Park. The couple were in their midforties, were not amateurs on the water, and knew that the river always flows downstream. Mo was a canoe instructor and an experienced outdoorsman and had made this same trip before, so we might be tempted to assume that he'd be capable of making good decisions. If we did, we'd be guilty of some of that "bogus speculation," as you'll soon see.

It will help you appreciate this story to have just a little background about the terrain. This area of colorful rocks and sweeping vistas is remote and rugged, with limited road access to the rivers in these desert canyons. The Green and Colorado Rivers both flow in a generally southerly direction across eastern Utah until they join forces in the heart of Canyonlands National Park. For you geographers in the bunch, the technical term for the intersection of those two famous rivers is known as the Confluence.

As described on the park's website, "Both rivers are calm upstream of the Confluence, ideal for canoes, kayaks and other shallow water craft. Below the Confluence, the combined flow of both rivers spills down Cataract Canyon with remarkable speed and power, creating a world-class stretch of white water. . . . Cataract Canyon contains fourteen miles of rapids ranging in difficulty up to Class V. It is a particularly hazardous and isolated section of the Colorado River and is subject to extreme water level fluctuations."

For the benefit of you non-white-water folks, there is a rating system for rapids ranging from Class I (easy even for novices) to the extremes of Class VI (don't even think about running it). The Class V rapids in Cataract Canyon are very challenging indeed, and are described as "Expert. Extremely long, obstructed, or very violent rapids which expose a paddler to above average endangerment."

Given the above information, a prudent person would not need to make any assumptions about a trip through Cataract Canyon. This is a stretch of river for experienced boaters only, and it is certainly *not* a great choice for anyone in an open aluminum canoe. As a result, those who are not prepared to run that "world-class stretch of white water" simply end their trip down either river at the Confluence. There is no road access to that point, but, proving that the free-enterprise system is alive and well, several private companies offer a shuttle service via jetboat back up the Colorado River to the town of Moab.

Now, back to our story. Mo and Flo had prudently planned to end their trip at the Confluence and use that shuttle service after covering fifty-two miles of the Green River over four days. So far so good, but unfortunately these best-laid plans went seriously awry.

The pair arrived at the Confluence, their intended termination point for their trip, but somehow mistook that joining of two major rivers for the junction of the Green River with the abandoned channel of that same waterway at a spot named Anderson Bottom. That's a serious oops in the navigational department, since Anderson Bottom is thirty-one miles *up*stream from their actual location at the Confluence. Based on that assumption they continued downstream.

As a good example of your tax dollars at work, the National Park Service has done its part to try to ensure that boaters avoid an unplanned adventure—or an untimely end—in Cataract Canyon. A large sign has been placed in this area to warn visitors about the dangerous rapids 2½

Here's your sign. Prudent boaters will heed the information on this sign, located near the Confluence of the Green and Colorado Rivers in Canyonlands National Park. (Canyonlands National Park)

miles ahead in the canyon. This advice to reconsider and turn back before it's too late would be the government's more prosaic version of the line from Dante's *Inferno,* in which a sign at the entrance to Hell reads, "Abandon hope, all ye who enter here."

You might be tempted to think that most people would read that sign and consider carefully before proceeding further downstream. Our duo apparently did stop and consult their map, but since they had already misidentified the Confluence of the Green and Colorado Rivers, they were still convinced they were over thirty miles back upstream from their actual location.

Alas, they were already on the slippery slope of Assumption-land, where it becomes increasingly easy to allow imagination or wishful thinking to overwhelm logic.

Since there were certainly no major rapids only 2½ miles downstream from their *assumed* location, how might they reconcile that fact with the contradictory information on the sign? Apparently the answer seemed pretty easy at the time. They speculated that the sign was supposed to warn about dangerous rapids 32½ miles ahead, and that vandals had removed the initial number "3," thus changing "32½" miles into "2½." Once the inconvenient matter of a missing thirty miles was

An unusual aerial view of the Confluence of the Colorado and Green Rivers in Canyonlands National Park. You'd think this meeting of two major rivers in the middle of the desert would be an obvious landmark for boaters, but the stories in this chapter prove that's not always the case. (Anders and Barbara Lock)

resolved, our intrepid pair was ready to resume paddling their canoe merrily, merrily down the stream.

The official report does not record any of the conversation between the couple, so the following dialogue is simply speculation on my part (not to be confused in this case with *assumption*). Shortly after resuming their float downriver, they heard what must have been an unexpected and unsettling sound. Perhaps Mo asked Flo something like, "Do you hear that noise?" Mayhaps Flo replied, "You mean that loud roaring sound?"

"Yeah," said Mo, "the one that reminds me of Niagara Falls."

What they heard was "Brown Betty," the first of the major rapids referred to on the supposedly "vandalized" sign not too far behind them.

They were unable to get their canoe to shore, so thankfully the couple made one vital, life-saving decision. They quickly donned their life jackets, which in my considered opinion they should have been wearing anyway, because the water temperature was only about 54°.

Once they entered this major rapid it didn't take long for the canoe to capsize and dump both occupants into the cold water. They managed to survive the float through "Brown Betty" and two additional rapids before they were able to swim to shore on *opposite* sides of the river. The canoe with their food, water, and most of their equipment, an investment of about $2,100, continued drifting downstream, presumably to be eventually scavenged by those same vandals who lurked in the canyon and removed numbers from warning signs.

The following information is being revealed to the general public for the first time, right on these pages. Now that the truth is known, you can probably expect to see full details any day now in those tabloid papers conveniently available in the grocery store checkout line. The story will begin something like this: "Secret government report uncovered! Bandits hiding in remote river canyons are brazenly changing the information on government warning signs to lure boaters to their doom and scavenge their equipment, which is later sold on eBay."

Fortunately, Mo and Flo were uninjured and able to hike three and a half miles back upstream, where they encountered a motorboat being operated by a river tour company and were rescued. The moral to this story is to watch out for those assumptions—they can definitely get you into trouble, with or without river pirates.

Another group of boaters along this same stretch of river had an adventure that required neither assumptions nor bandits. They didn't need any outside help, since they were their own worst enemies.

On a Memorial Day weekend over twenty years ago, two men and a woman decided to participate in an annual event (water levels permitting) called the Friendship Cruise. The cruise begins in Green River, Utah, runs down the Green River to the confluence with the Colorado River, and then back up the Colorado to the town of Moab, Utah. The total trip covers about 180 miles and usually takes two or three days to complete in motorized boats.

In fairness to those who plan the event, it has evolved over several decades into what is now a highly organized, family-oriented activity, complete with rescue boats, shuttles to and from the put-in and take-out points, and ham radio operators to provide emergency communications. The event has become a tradition for many of its participants, some of whom come from distant parts of the country to participate.

At the time this story occurred, there was much less structure to the cruise, and even the best-run events can't exercise absolute control over every participant. The trio in this saga seemed determined to illustrate that point. Their first error was in failing to recognize their intended first night's destination at Mineral Canyon, about 68 miles downriver from their starting point. Like the couple in the previous story, their navigation was seriously out of sync with reality, and 52 miles later they reached the confluence of the Green and Colorado Rivers.

By that time they had navigated about 120 miles of the Green River, almost twice their planned run for the day—but hey, time flies when you're having fun. I'll reinforce the fact that the scene of this tale is serious desert and canyon country, and there are very few spots along these rivers where major waterways intersect. Even for those who failed Basic Outdoor Navigation 101, the meeting of the Green and Colorado Rivers could reasonably be expected to attract some notice.

Alas, that was not the case, and in a scenario that might be sounding increasingly familiar, our happy trio failed to recognize this key landmark. Missing the required turn back upstream on the Colorado, they instead decided to continue downstream past the Confluence and into the fearsome depths of Cataract Canyon.

But wait, there's still hope—that sign warning of dangerous rapids ahead. *Surely* they'd turn back once they read that dire admonition—but of course they didn't, or I wouldn't have a story to tell. Unlike the

No place for a canoe—or a standard power boat! The rapids in Cataract Canyon in Canyonlands National Park are among the most challenging in the country. (Canyonlands National Park)

hapless canoeists whose misadventures opened this chapter, this group's fiberglass powerboat actually made it through Brown Betty, the first significant rapid in Cataract Canyon, with the passengers still safely on board. Their boat did, however, take on some water in this encounter, and the trio finally realized things were not quite as they should be.

They made their first good decision of the trip and decided it was time to don their life jackets. A wise call, followed by an unwise choice to run the second rapid they encountered. Someone in the group then suggested that upon further review it might be a good idea to try to return upstream, where the waters had been decidedly more congenial. After all, this was supposed to be a *Friendship* Cruise.

Sooner or later in every situation, one reaches and then passes the point of no return, and that proved to be the case for our hapless cruisers. Unsuccessful in their attempt to retrace their route against the rapids, they once again decided to go with the flow and continue downstream. This final leg of their journey was thankfully short, because Mickey's little hand on the wristwatch was pointing at ten on the P.M. scale, and daylight must have been a very scarce commodity in the depths of the canyon.

Thomas Hughes, who wrote in the late 1800s, voiced the opinion that "Heaven, they say, protects children, sailors and drunken men." This group fortunately didn't include any children, and applying the term *sailors* to this trio would be an affront to anyone who has earned that title, but these characters did qualify on Mr. Hughes's third point. Divine Providence did intervene, and the little band spotted a group camped along the riverbank.

Making their best decision of the entire day, they headed for shore to spend the night near the other party of legitimate river runners—at a location a full 60 miles beyond their own intended camping spot. A subsequent interview by rangers with this second group confirmed that the trio from the powerboat was intoxicated when they arrived in camp, a fact that sheds considerable light on the day's series of miscues. Thus ended Day One of our story.

The summary of the official report that I read was silent on the following details, but I infer (notice I did not assume) that the following morning (Day Two) the experienced river runners explained the facts of life in Cataract Canyon to the trio in the powerboat. In brief, the veteran boaters' advice probably included something like, "If you expect to live to see another sunset, don't try to take that craft of yours through any more rapids in *this* canyon." Their boat was not designed for rowing, any further travel downstream would be neither gentle nor merry, and life would certainly not be a dream.

According to the park's report, at 6:30 P.M. on Day Two a hiker reached a location where a report of the situation could be made to the Proper Authorities. At 10:15 the next morning (Day Three of this ill-fated trip) a Park Service search party reached the location of the stranded boaters. On Day Four a park boat hauled the men, woman, and their equipment (including numerous empty beer cans) to safety at Hite, on the upper end of Lake Powell.

The park report also provides an excellent analysis of this saga: "If you drink don't drive. In this instance it led to not knowing or caring about location, and the inability to perceive a dangerous predicament. That nobody was injured is miraculous."

You may recall a famous poem by Robert Frost about a traveler who came to a fork in the road and decided to take the way less traveled. In that case, the poet says his decision made all the difference, presumably for the good. In the Great Outdoors the way less traveled may not always be the best choice, so whether you're on a river, a trail, or a road, when you come to a junction, think at least twice before you make any assumptions about whether to proceed on one route or the other. Above all, if you spot any signs warning of dire conditions ahead, don't engage in any wishful thinking about what you *want* it to read, unless you're prepared to "abandon all hope."

You've Got Mail

During the course of my park service career our family had the opportunity to live in several places with interesting names. We rarely had a "normal" street address, and in many cases our mail simply came to a rather mundane post office box number. However, the name of the town where that box was located often added a little extra interest—and occasionally led to some interesting conversations when we were ordering items by phone or transacting other business.

Early in my career, for example, we moved from a suburb of Washington, D.C., to a small town in northwestern Arizona. You may have heard this spot mentioned occasionally in the weather reports due to some fairly hot summer days, and I thought it was a name that had some definite character. As a result, I was unprepared for the reaction I received when I went into our big-city bank in Maryland to give them a forwarding address for our account.

The teller had probably filled out a ton of those forms and was handling my request in a rather ho-hum fashion until she asked for the name of our new "city and state." When I replied "Bullhead City, Arizona," she paused for a split second, looked up at me with an incredulous expression, and then burst out laughing. "You're kidding!" she finally exclaimed. When I assured her I was serious, she looked around, called a coworker over, and asked, "Do you think this is a *real* place?"

For the record, it is a very real place, and I thought it was a great name for a town in the West. Bullhead City has grown quite a bit since we lived there briefly in the early 1970s. The name is taken from a large rock formation near town that resembles a bull's head. Well, okay, it obviously looked that way to some early settler of the area. Based on the names given to a *lot* of natural features by explorers and pioneers, I've concluded that people had much better imaginations back in those days, a quality that has probably suffered in our era of television and video games.

Over the years we also lived in places named Lincoln City, Indiana; Yellville, Arkansas; Echo Bay, Nevada; and East Glacier, Montana. (Yes, there is also a West Glacier, Montana, but not a North or a South, at least as applied to the name of a town.) Some of the real fun came when we lived at spots that were so small they didn't even exist, at least as far as the postmaster general was concerned. In those cases we had to use an address in the nearest settlement that had a post office.

One of those "nonexistent" locations was Willow Beach, Arizona, a part of Lake Mead National Recreation Area. To reach Willow Beach, you drive south from Las Vegas or north from Kingman, Arizona, on U.S. Highway 93. About fourteen miles south of Hoover Dam you turn west onto four miles of two-lane paved road that twists and turns steadily downhill across the desert before entering a narrow canyon. Here steep, bare rocky walls close in on both sides of the road, and if you hadn't been promised by a reliable source that there really is water and other human life somewhere ahead, you'd be more inclined to think you had taken a wrong turn and ended up somewhere on the surface of the moon.

Willow Beach, in Lake Mead National Recreation Area, has some beautiful views, but you sure couldn't get mail delivered if you lived there in the 1970s. (Jim Burnett)

It's always a pleasant surprise for first-time visitors to the area to round yet another bend in the road and suddenly break out of the mouth of the canyon to a lovely view of the upper portion of Lake Mohave. The road bends northward and parallels the water for a short distance to a boat ramp and small resort that operates under a permit from the park service.

The area is a popular destination for boaters and fishermen, but back in 1973 Willow Beach was about as close as you would come to *any* sign of human habitation over those seventy miles of desert highway between Kingman and Hoover Dam. It was also the last outpost of civilization in Arizona as you headed north along U.S. 93. This created a few interesting challenges.

Since we actually lived in Arizona, we had driver's licenses and vehicle tags from that state. Our telephone number had an Arizona area code, although if you checked we weren't in the phone book, and you couldn't even find us listed by name if you called Directory Assistance. That's because Willow Beach was literally the end of the phone line stretching northward from Kingman, and there were only a limited number of connections available. As a result, the phones in the two ranger residences there were simply an extension of the phone for the ranger station. While that pretty well eliminated calls from telemarketers, it also meant we had to be sure we notified friends and family of "our" phone number.

Even though we were officially residents of Arizona, the closest town was Boulder City, Nevada, a distance of about twenty-five miles. Our mailing address was a post office box in Boulder City, which was shared by the park families and the staff of the commercial resort at Willow Beach. "Delivery" occurred whenever someone from the park or the resort happened to be making a trip into Boulder City and could stop at the official post office to drop off or pick up mail. The resort office served as a de facto post office for the residents of Willow Beach.

As a matter of convenience, the majority of our shopping was also done in either Boulder City or Las Vegas. Knowing what you probably do about Las Vegas, you can readily understand that business people there have good reason to be cautious about accepting out-of-town checks, and back in the 1970s, merchants didn't have the easy access they do today to "instant" account verification by computer. With that in mind, we often experienced the following scenario.

We would walk up to the cashier at a store in Las Vegas, a reputable institution such as Sears or J. C. Penney's, and make out a check to pay for our purchases. The check would be from a bank in Boulder City,

Nevada, and have a Boulder City post office box as our mailing address. So far not too bad, since most people from Boulder City shopped in Vegas from time to time. However, since it's a little hard to locate anyone at a post office box in case the check bounces, the first question would logically be, "What's your street address?" Now the fun began!

"Well, we don't actually *have* a street address; we get our mail at the post office box. We live at the Willow Beach Ranger Station out at Lake Mead."

"Where's that?"

"It's about thirty miles south of Boulder City."

"No address, huh? This your home phone number on the check?"

"Yes." (That was an honest answer, since that was the number of the phone in our house.)

"You got a work phone number and address?"

"The work phone is the same as our home number. Like I said, we don't actually have a street address at work or home, which is why we have the post office box."

Admittedly, not too many people even then lived at their place of employment, so the clerk's eyebrows went up another notch. "You don't have your own telephone?" (This was a polite way of asking why we couldn't *afford* to have our own phone. After all, anybody who had a checking account ought to have a phone, shouldn't they?)

"No, we just have an extension of our office phone. We're out in a pretty remote spot, and there aren't enough phone lines for us to have our own separate number."

The clerk peers again at the information printed on our check. "Hey, wait a minute, you have a *Nevada* mailing address, but this is an *Arizona* phone number."

"That's right, we live in Arizona, but the closest place to get our mail is in Boulder City, Nevada."

"This your own post office box?"

"No, we share it with the other people who live out at Willow Beach. The box actually belongs to the Willow Beach Resort."

"You work at the Willow Beach Resort?"

"No, I work for the National Park Service. The resort is just down the road from us." (That's the same road that didn't even have a name, much less any street numbers.)

The clerk ponders this piece of news with increasing skepticism. Not only can these people not afford their own *phone*, they can't even rent their own post office box!

"You got any I.D.?"

Now it's time to whip out my *Arizona* driver's license that shows my address is a post office box in *Nevada*. At least the address on the license agrees with the one printed on my check! We had quite an interesting adventure down at the DMV office in Kingman, getting an Arizona driver's license with a Nevada address, but I won't go into that.

Just about this point in the process we became accustomed to hearing something from the cashier like, "Excuse me, I'll be back in a minute." In due time, we had the chance to get acquainted with a number of supervisors, assistant managers, or owners of establishments, depending upon who had the authority to approve suspicious checks in that particular place of business.

Fortunately, not long after we arrived, banks in the area began issuing "check guarantee cards" to their regular customers. Those cards guaranteed that the bank would cover a check written on their account, so presenting one of those cards greatly simplified check cashing in that area. Otherwise, I'd probably still be waiting at a checkout counter for somebody in Las Vegas to decide if they wanted to take the risk of approving our check!

In recent years, this situation has changed, and at least partly due to the advent of 911 emergency response systems, almost every place in the U.S. now has a physical street address—even Willow Beach. In another chapter in this book I describe some of our experiences living in Greenbelt Park, Maryland, a suburb of Washington, D.C. Surprisingly enough, back in the 1970s even that location had some challenges related to our address.

Our Greenbelt Park assignment was early in my NPS career, and after about five years of living in various apartment complexes during my stint in the army and then graduate school, Velma and I were looking forward to having a place of our own for a few months—even if it was a government-owned trailer in the middle of a campground. Shortly after our arrival, we embarked on the process of getting established: You know, the usual stuff—open a bank account, get a newspaper started, call the phone company to get connected, and so forth. We quickly learned one fact of life in the Big City as opposed to rural areas: Getting *anything* delivered properly depends on your precise street address.

There was only one problem. We didn't have one.

As soon as we moved in, we learned that our *mailing* address would be the same one as the park headquarters, about three-quarters of a mile away from our humble, government-owned trailer. That building also served as a substation for the U.S. Park Police, a separate arm of the National Park Service that provides law enforcement services to NPS sites in the D.C. area. We received our mail at the park head-quarters because there were no street names or numbers for the inter-nal road system in the park, so there was no street address at our mobile home in the campground.

This system worked okay for getting our mail, but it proved to be a challenge when it came time to start a newspaper subscription. The conversation with the folks at the *Washington Post* went something like this:

"Hi, we'd like to start a subscription."

"Yes sir, what is your address?"

"Well, we don't actually have one, but I can give you directi . . ."

"Excuse me, sir. *Everybody* has an address! You get mail, don't you?"

"Well, yes, but . . . "

"Okay, now we're getting somewhere. What is your mailing address?"

"I can give you our mailing address, but that's not where we want to get the paper."

"You don't live at your mailing address? *Now* I understand, you must get your mail at a post office box. If you want a mail subscription, I can set that up, but you'll get your paper a day late. If you want home delivery, you'll have to give me the address where you want the paper delivered."

I decided to try a different tack. "O.K., please have it delivered to the Greenbelt Park Campground in Greenbelt, Maryland."

"Sure, what's that street address?"

Well, you get the picture. I was eventually passed off to a supervi-sor, who dutifully took down detailed directions to the place where the paper was to be delivered. The agreement was that our newspaper bill would be sent to our mailing address (which was not where we lived . . .) and the paper would be delivered to our trailer. I was assured that the newspaper service would start the next day.

A couple of days later, I repeated this same general conversation with the Subscription Department. Since more than one operator was undoubtedly standing by to take my order, I'm sure I talked to a dif-ferent employee and then a different supervisor. No problem. They had it straight this time, and the paper delivery would start the next morning.

A week later and still paperless, I happened to drop in at the Park Police substation in the park headquarters building early one morning. After greeting the sergeant on duty, I noticed that a copy of the *Washington Post* was lying on the table in the break room. I asked the sergeant if I could take a look at the paper, since we hadn't started getting ours yet.

"Sure, help yourself. I don't know why one started coming here a few days ago, but the guys sure enjoy having it delivered right here to the station."

A few days after we canceled our subscription, the Park Police staff finally stopped asking about what happened to the "free" paper. Sorry, guys—I think they started delivering it to someplace called Willow Beach.

Let Sleeping Bears Lie

Encounters between people and wild animals have been part of the experience of visiting parks from the earliest days of those areas, and such situations aren't limited to visitors. Anyone who lives or works long enough in bear country will accumulate their own stock of bear tales.

"Don't feed the bears" signs have long been the subject of cartoons as well as actual regulations, but sometimes these rules can take a rather bizarre turn. Many areas in Alaska offer great opportunities to observe wildlife, not only in parks but also on other public lands and private property. Because wildlife is so common in Alaska, some interesting laws are rumored to have been adopted over the years by the state or various local jurisdictions.

Although it's legal to hunt bears with a license at designated locations and seasons in Alaska, information is widely circulated on the Internet that it's against the law in that state to awaken a sleeping bear for purposes of taking its photograph. I've been unable to verify the accuracy of those claims, but there is considerable wisdom in this rule whether it's an actual regulation, a humorous cyberspace legend, or just common sense. After all, how many of your friends and relatives would be happy to be rudely roused from a nice nap with the admonition to "smile and look at the camera"? Dealing with a grumpy human is bad enough, but facing a surly bruin is definitely not a good situation.

The chance to see a grizzly family in the wild is a rare and wonderful experience, but keep your distance—and never get between the mother and her cubs. (National Park Service)

While we're on the subject of unusual laws, there are also unverified claims on the Internet that in at least one Alaskan city it's a violation to feed alcoholic beverages to a moose. I'm not quite sure why anyone would want to do that in the first place, unless the moose has just been awakened from a nap for purposes of taking a photograph, and the theory is that offering the animal a nip or two might improve its disposition.

Just for the record, a moose is a very large, often ill-tempered, and potentially dangerous animal. Approaching one too closely for *any* reason, including taking a photo or giving it a drink of any variety, is definitely a bad idea. Winters can get rather long in places like Alaska, a situation that often inspires the search for new forms of entertainment. Perhaps this regulation really was promulgated in response to people putting out moose drinking stations instead of bird feeders, and filling them with something that freezes a little more slowly than plain ol' water.

Meanwhile, back to the bruins. A friend of mine was willing to share a couple of tales from his days as a ranger in Glacier National Park, a place that is blessed with incredibly beautiful mountain scenery along with its fair share of bears.

Oakley Blair (or "Oak" for short), his wife Barb, and their two small children were assigned for part of each year to a ranger station in a very remote area of the park named Goat Haunt. Lest the name cause anyone to avoid a trip to this magnificent spot, the "goats" are of the mountain variety, and *haunt* refers to the "hangout" use of the term, not the spooky one.

Located just below the U.S.-Canadian border at the southern end of Waterton Lake, Goat Haunt can be visited during the summer months via a tour boat that makes several trips a day from Waterton, a small town where you'll find visitor services for Canada's Waterton Lakes National Park. The only other access to Goat Haunt is by horseback or a serious hike, and in these northern latitudes all of those options are limited to the warmer months of the year. During the long winter season about the only thing "haunting" this neck of the woods on a regular basis might be the Abominable Snowman.

As hard as it is for most people to imagine today, during the Blair family's time there, Goat Haunt was a place where there were not only no roads, but also no telephones or television. Their limited electricity was provided by a generator, which for the sake of conserving precious fuel, as well as peace and quiet, did not run around the clock. It's a good reminder about how quickly the world has changed to realize that as recently as thirty years ago there were no cell phones or even satellite TV as we know it today, and certainly no Internet connections.

The Blairs' primary contact with the outside world was with hikers or boaters as they passed through or via the park radio system. The park radio was handy for emergency messages and Official Government Business, but it was pretty slim on entertainment value or the daily news headlines. This limited two-way radio communication *can* be an advantage at times, such as occasions when the boss wants some paperwork completed or has a brainstorm for a less-than-desirable project. ("Sorry, your transmission is breaking up—we weren't able to copy that message. We'll try again tomorrow. . . .")

One summer, Oak's in-laws were visiting from Chicago; it was their first visit to the park and their introduction to hiking in bear country. Being prudent individuals, they asked what they should do in the event of an encounter with a bear. Their expert ranger son-in-law gave them some tips, and told them that the one thing they should *never* do is run from a bear, but make a little noise and back up slowly. He even loaned them some bear bells to wear during their short hikes.

For those of you who haven't spent any time in bear country, I should explain the difference between "bear bells" and "cow bells." Cow bells are actually sometimes worn around the neck of a cow and serve a legitimate purpose in the agricultural world, such as making it easy for Heidi's grandfather and other farmers to locate cows that may have wandered to a remote corner of an alpine meadow. The bells are also popular as noisemakers with fans at a variety of sporting events, especially in Europe, a market that probably is far more lucrative today than the one for bovine necklaces.

Bear bells, while very similar to many cow bells in appearance, are not intended to be worn by bears, and to the best of my knowledge, have never been used for that purpose. Although it would be helpful for hikers in bear country if that were the case, it's simply not in a bruin's natural disposition to be cooperative if a human were to attempt to attach a bell to a bear. I can't tell you whether or not it's against the law in Alaska or anywhere else to hang a bell on a *sleeping* bear, but legal aspects notwithstanding, I'd strongly advise against anyone trying to do so.

That being the case, the term *bear bell* refers to an accessory commonly used by people who are hiking in areas inhabited by bruins. One of the greatest potential risks to people from bears in the wild is a surprise encounter with one or more of those animals, so conventional wisdom is to make noise while hiking or biking in areas where bears occur. When it comes to meeting a bear, the best surprise is definitely no surprise.

Talking or singing loudly and traveling in a group of three or more people is believed by some experts to be the most effective deterrent to an unexpected encounter with a bruin. Many hikers prefer, however, to wear a bell on their pack, walking stick, or ankle to help serve notice to any bears in the vicinity. After hearing some people sing, I can understand why anyone hiking with them would vote for a bell rather than vocalizing.

The effectiveness of wearing bear bells is currently the subject of some debate among the experts who get paid to study such things, but until that issue is settled, the bells remain a popular item. A recent Internet search found 2,630,000 hits on the term *bear bells,* and numerous vendors offer them in a variety of decorator colors and sizes. Since the color of the bell should have negligible effect on the sound produced, I presume this is one more example of the power of advertising and human vanity. One major outdoor equipment supplier even reported that bear bells are among the most popular items in its inventory.

Now that you are fully informed about bear bells, we'll rejoin Oak and his family in the park. One evening after supper Oak, his wife, and their two preschoolers went for a short hike with her parents. They had not walked a hundred feet when they turned a bend in the path and spotted a black bear right in the middle of the trail.

Oak and his wife were leading the group and saw the bear first. They screamed "bear" and immediately turned around and ran back down the trail, carrying their small children with them! Oak reported that he saw the look on his poor in-laws' faces—an expression of bewilderment and terror as they ran past the older couple. They, too, turned and ran down the trail after the rest of the family. They never saw the poor bear again. When everyone finally stopped—and before anyone else could say anything—Oak took the initiative and remarked, "Remember, do as I *say*, not as I do!"

Oak's second bear encounter was a one-on-one adventure. In the fall of the year the seasonal staff at Goat Haunt had departed, and Barb and the two children had also moved back to a year-round ranger station on the edge of the park where they spent the fall, winter, and spring months. Oak stayed at his remote post until the end of fishing season on October 31. For about six weeks he was alone at the station to patrol the trails and lakes and check the fishermen as they came and went through his area.

One evening during the last week in October Oak had finished dinner and was washing the pots and pans. As he did, he heard the horses in the nearby corral making a lot of noise. Oak looked out the window toward the corral and saw a large black bear with its nose and paws pressed against the other side of the glass, looking directly at him.

This was a time for a little more direct action than simply ringing a bell, so Oak grabbed two pots and started banging them together and shouting at the same time. The bear looked confused and started to amble toward the screen door of the house as if he wanted to come inside. That was definitely not a desirable option, so Oak ran toward the door making as much noise as possible. This achieved the desired effect, and the bear, obviously wanting no part of this crazy person, ran off the porch and down the steps and turned the corner at the bottom of the stairs.

Wanting to make sure his unwanted Peeping Tom completely left the area, Oak ran out the door and after the bear, continuing to bang the pots together. While still on the porch he saw the bear make the turn at the bottom of the stairs, and Oak turned in the same direction as the bruin. In his enthusiasm to complete the job, our defender of hearth and home underestimated his speed, hit the porch railing, and flipped over the rail, landing on his derriere right in front of the startled bear. This all happened so quickly he reported than he was still banging the pots as he hit the ground.

The befuddled bear came to an abrupt stop, whirled around, and ran up the hillside, never to be seen again. It took a while after the escapade had ended for Oak's adrenaline level to return to normal, at which point he noticed the pots had several large dents in them. His account to me did not include whether or not future users of those cooking utensils received an explanation about the condition of those items. This story also confirms a comment many of us have made at one time or another: "If I'd just had someone filming this with a video camera, I'd have a sure winner for *America's Funniest Home Videos*."

This final story about bears is one from my own experience at Glacier National Park. Among my varied duties was maintaining several air quality monitoring stations in the eastern half of the park. This merely required changing a couple of filters each month, which were then sent off to a lab for analysis. One of these devices was located near Logan Pass, the point where the park's spectacular Going-to-the-Sun Road crosses the Continental Divide about 6,600 feet above sea level.

The Going-to-the-Sun Road is one of the scenic treasures of our country, and if you ever have a chance to make the drive, do so. Check ahead, though—the combination of high elevation and Glacier's northern latitude means that the road is only open from about mid-June until late October, although the exact dates vary each year depending on the amount and timing of snowfall. For several years beginning in 2007, the road will be undergoing some long overdue major repairs, so expect some possible traffic delays during that time. Updated information is available on the park's website (www.nps.gov/glac).

There was no road work or any other human activity in the vicinity on a late autumn day when I made what was probably the last motorized trip of that year to the pass. I wanted to leave the air quality station at that location in operation as late into fall as feasible so we could collect as much data as possible. The road had already been closed to the public in late October after a couple of storms, but it was still passable once most of the snow from those fronts melted. The next time snow was forecast, I decided it would be prudent to retrieve the equipment before the area became inaccessible for the winter.

It was an interesting experience driving up into the heart of the park with absolutely no other vehicles on the road. It became even more interesting as I got closer to the top, and I was reminded that weather forecasting in the mountains is often more art than science. The official forecast was for flurries during the day and heavier snow that night. By the time I parked my truck at Logan Pass, large flakes were already falling quickly. It tends to be windy there on the top of the Continental Divide almost any day of the year, so the combination of snow and a brisk breeze made visibility less than ideal.

Being a prudent ranger I had made sure some of my coworkers knew where I was going and when I expected to return, and I carried plenty of emergency supplies in my vehicle. In view of the weather and the fact that I might well have been the only human within many square miles of rugged mountain terrain, I called the dispatcher at headquarters by radio to let her know I was leaving my pickup at Logan Pass and told her how long I expected to be out on foot.

Proving that Murphy's Law was alive and well, the dispatcher acknowledged my call and passed on the information that they were going to have to shut down the radio "repeater" for an hour or so for repairs. The repeater is the equipment that makes it possible to talk long distances by two-way radio in these mountains, so I was effectively without any communication with the rest of the world for that period of time. Not a big problem, and as was my usual practice when hiking I grabbed my day pack with basic survival items and hit the trail.

I only had about a half-mile walk from the parking lot to the location of the air quality monitoring station, the route followed the faint remains of an old unpaved road, and I'd made the trip plenty of times before. At that elevation, some snow remained from the previous week's storm, and the new flakes were accumulating fast. I made haste to finish my chore, picked up the breadbox-sized equipment, and headed back toward my truck.

It wasn't difficult to retrace my route even if I hadn't been familiar with the area. All I had to do was follow my footprints in the fresh snow, although they were already getting a little fuzzy as the white stuff continued to come down. About halfway back to my truck I realized that the day had the potential to include a Totally Unexpected Melancholy Situation, which is one defined as encouraging the use of a popular over-the-counter remedy for heartburn.

This development occurred when I suddenly noticed that my prints weren't the only ones in the snow. Trailing right alongside my boot

Seeing bear tracks in the snow can add a lot of interest to a backcountry trip—and raise a very important question: "Where's the bear right *now?*" (National Park Service)

prints were fresh, unmistakable bear tracks. He or she had followed my inbound steps for several hundred feet before veering off the path, and given the time it had taken me to return to that point, Mr. or Mrs. Bruin couldn't have been gone very long. I made a hurried scan of the area, but visibility in the blowing snow was pretty limited. Actually, it was almost nonexistent.

As discussed above in this chapter, one of the cardinal rules in bear country is to make plenty of noise on the trail so you don't surprise a bruin. I was bereft of any bear bells, which under the current conditions would likely have been of minimal value anyway. Announcing my presence in a stiff wind and falling snow was a bit of a challenge, and I may not have been very melodious, but Julie Andrews isn't the only one who has made the hills ring with the sound of music!

Since the rest of my trip back to my truck was uneventful, perhaps the bear had decided to ignore my foray into its domain and just go take a nap. Even though I wasn't in Alaska, if I'd had any thought that the bear was headed off to dreamland I certainly would not have awakened it, especially for the purpose of taking a photograph!

Six Feet High and Rising

One situation where hindsight can get a good workout is the choice of a campsite. I realize that not all of my readers are campers, and if your idea of "roughing it" on a trip means indoor accommodations that garner at least a three-star rating in a reputable guidebook, that's just fine. You can enjoy the following camping tips secure in the knowledge that *you're* going to have a good night's sleep—although it's not a promising sign if several school buses pull into the parking lot of your hotel just before sundown, or if your room turns out to be directly above the club that advertises "live entertainment." Oh well, nothing's perfect. That's why travel is often called an adventure.

For those of you who want to get a little closer to nature, there are several factors to consider in selecting a campsite. If you're a veteran camper, you already have your own mental checklist of features that separate a great spot from a "sure glad we only paid for one night" ordeal. For everyone else, here are several observations from both my personal and professional experience to help make your outing a more positive experience.

Finding the right site or even the right campground is a lot like buying or selling real estate: It's mainly about location, location, and location. Some factors are pretty obvious if you have good information, although if you're reduced to picking out a spot based solely on a listing in a free campground directory or because you spotted one of those little tent symbols on a highway map, be aware that those decisions can be fraught with peril. Examples are sites that turn out to have an unobstructed view of a six-lane interstate highway or that lie just beyond the end of the runway of a major airport. You'd certainly have reason to be concerned if dark, ominous clouds accompanied by thunder and lightning are moving in and you noticed a large sign at the campground entrance that reads, "Warning! Flash Flood Zone. If siren sounds, evacuate immediately!" I've known of areas that meet those criteria, so just be forewarned.

Sometimes even your best efforts at finding a nice, peaceful spot will take a nasty and totally unexpected turn. Early in our camping days, my wife and I spotted a listing in a campground directory that sounded promising. It was at least a mile off a two-lane state highway and quite a distance from town. We dutifully followed a gravel road that wound through a lovely area of hills and forests and eventually reached our destination. Except for a couple of cabins tucked away in the trees we hadn't seen any signs of civilization since leaving the highway. Things were looking good.

The small campground was well maintained and we had a choice of several attractive sites. In fact, we could select from most of the sites in the area, which I will note with benefit of further experience can sometimes be an important clue that additional inquiry may be prudent before paying your fee, especially if it's a busy weekend or peak travel season. This is analogous to pulling up in front of a large restaurant at 6 P.M. on a Saturday evening and noticing that there are only two cars in the parking lot.

In our case, it was late in the day and many miles to the next campground, so we optimistically chose a spot on the back side of the area, nestled nicely into a grove of trees. All seemed well until just before dark, when the gentle rustle of wind in the pines was interrupted by a disconcerting sound. Surely that wasn't the whistle and rumble of an approaching train?

Don't get me wrong. I love trains, and some of our most enjoyable trips have been by rail. However, unlike fences, railroads don't make good neighbors if you find yourself camped too near the tracks. We soon discovered that just out of sight beyond that nice, thick forest was a major component of the transportation infrastructure of North America. In this location the answer to the question, "Can you hear that lonesome whistle blow?" was a qualified "yes," because the interval between freight trains during the night was short enough that those whistles shouldn't have been very lonely. Hey, you win some and you lose some in the game of campground roulette, but I still wonder why that rail line wasn't shown on our Official State Highway Map.

If your chosen campground passes the highway, airport, and railroad tests, there's another major factor to consider. Depending upon whether your tent or RV is equipped to handle your middle-of-the-night personal needs, you may wish to be closer to or farther away from the "comfort station," the official campground term for the structure housing the necessary facilities. The first time you have the opportunity to use a campsite adjacent to those amenities you'll understand that there is a trade-off for convenient access, and it's a slightly different twist to the expression about things that go bump in the night.

Based upon my informal survey, the national average for the number of times a comfort station door bangs shut between midnight and 6 A.M. is fourteen, which is a bit more than twice per hour during prime sleeping hours. In some locations there is the bonus of a loud squeak every time the door is opened. That probably explains why campers often tend to prop those doors open with a large rock or any other available object. The doorstop technique solves the slamming and squeaking door problem but can come at an unexpected price.

An open door in an outdoor setting allows unhindered access to the interior not only by campers but also by any and all inhabitants of the natural world, including those that fly, walk, crawl, creep, or slither. Even a room full of mosquitoes can make a visit to that facility unpleasant, and small insects are really the least of your worries. I'll leave further analysis of those possibilities to your fertile imagination, but perhaps that will motivate you to be a good citizen and remove those unauthorized bathroom doorstops.

This potential for dark-of-night encounters between humans and other life forms is why the campground management prefers doors that slam shut with vigor. When the doors stay open at night, the staff quickly tires of those midnight phone calls imploring the ranger to come with all due haste to investigate those "hysterical screams coming from the comfort station."

If you're staying in an upscale campground with flush facilities, a bathroom door left propped open also allows occupants of nearby sites to enjoy an additional auditory experience. Nearby campers will quickly confirm that comfort station designers have a strong affinity to fixtures that make the loudest possible "whoosh" when the flushing mechanism is activated. I presume this robust flush cuts down on cleaning time for those bowls, but in the nighttime silence of most campgrounds the background noise of city living is eliminated, and it's absolutely amazing how far such manmade sounds will carry.

No matter whether you're near or far from the potential sounds of banging and squeaking doors and whooshing or silent fixtures, a major factor in site selection is your fellow campers. The majority of campers make fine neighbors, but just to be on the safe side, it pays to discreetly check out the other occupants before setting up camp. Once you've moved in, it's a good idea to keep an eye on any new arrivals. Since you have no control over who may show up next door, my advice is to always pay for a site one night at a time. Refunds are notoriously hard if not impossible to obtain, especially at government sites, so if the neighborhood suddenly takes an undesirable turn, you at least don't have a big financial stake if you want to relocate.

The value of that advice is confirmed by an astute observation by a veteran outdoorsman: "When the campsite next to yours is occupied by a group that brings a drum set, you know it's *never* going to be good!"

If you really want to avoid sharing your outdoor vacation with railroads, rock bands, and the racket of comfort stations, there is another option, but it's not for the faint of heart. You might consider really roughing it and going for a campout in Real Nature, where there are no facilities and picking a spot is up to the individual or group. Whether or not this is allowed depends upon local regulations, since overuse and damage to the natural scene have prompted some areas to limit even backcountry camping to designated areas, so inquiry is in order.

In many situations along remote rivers, beaches, and lakeshores, there is often a lot more latitude in choosing a campsite, and there are definitely several factors to consider, some more obvious than others. I refer you back to my comment early in this chapter that it's mainly about location, location, and location, but a closely related factor is the weather. Here are several good examples.

It had been drizzling for two nights in early August at Canyonlands National Park in Utah. A commercial river guide and his two passengers set up camp at the mouth of a side canyon at the head of Mile Long Rapid, on the Colorado River in Cataract Canyon. The heavy clouds should have suggested the possibility of rain to this experienced boatman, but for whatever reason he ignored those signs. I'll dub their selection of a campsite Uh-oh Number One, which might lead alert readers to suspect that additional dubious choices are soon to be revealed.

Shortly after midnight, the group's camp was inundated by a flash flood emanating from the side canyon. These sudden desert floods can be extremely dangerous, but fortunately this one was on the lower end of the Noah scale. Minor flood or not, the sudden arrival of a couple of feet of water rushing through your campsite is not a welcome development, nor is that what campground guidebooks intend if they mention a site has "running water."

The boatman was knocked down by knee-deep water, and after recovering his footing, attempted without success to alert his French-speaking companions. (The first time I read this comment in the park's report, I wondered how they had been communicating during the *rest* of the trip!)

Some situations transcend mere language barriers, however, and the linguistic problem was resolved when the flood waters hit the tent of the other two campers. Fortunately, the water was still not deep enough to cause serious harm, and everyone survived Mother Nature's rather rude wake-up call.

When the excitement began to subside, the three were able to salvage a tent and sleeping bags. *Salvage* is probably the operative term, since it's a safe bet those items were seriously soggy and of rather marginal utility for the immediate future. That was, unfortunately, the extent of the good news.

The group had been traveling in an eighteen-foot raft they had secured by one rope, tied to a stake driven into the sand on the beach. Unfortunately, this stake was also located within the flood zone. This mooring method proved to be Uh-oh Number Two, and the boat, much of their camping gear, and some personal property were all washed by the flash flood off the beach and into the Colorado River.

As the raft drifted away, the boatman considered swimming after it, but fortunately made a wiser choice and remained ashore. Two other commercial river groups found the trio the following morning, left them food and water, established communications with the Proper Authorities via satellite phone, and promised to look for the lost boat and equipment. Later that afternoon another boat from the company of the stranded group picked up the party for the continuation of its journey, and the lost boat was eventually retrieved further downstream.

Despite their mishap, this group was very lucky. Camping in flash flood zones at the mouths of side canyons is never advisable, and during the time of year when thunderstorms are common, it is extremely dangerous. I hope the guide practiced better security for his boat on any future trips, keeping in mind that while a single mooring line is usually considered adequate for boats directly under the watchful eye of a responsible individual, at least two lines are recommended for overnight parking when everyone is sound asleep in camp. Some campers are uneasy about things that go bump in the night, but many experienced boaters actually sleep on top of one of the lines securing their craft to the shore, so that any unexpected movement can alert them to an impending problem.

The expression "a rising tide lifts all ships" has been applied to a multitude of situations, including the business and educational worlds. A corollary is that a rising river lifts all boats, canoes, kayaks, rafts, and similar means of aquatic conveyance. As a result, even boaters who avoid camping in obviously risky spots such as the mouths of side canyons can have some unexpected adventures.

One of my assignments was at the Buffalo National River in Arkansas, a beautiful, free-flowing river that winds its way through rocky bluffs and pastoral valleys for about 150 miles in the Ozarks. Numerous gravel bars and sand beaches along the river provide plenty of places to camp, but what makes a great site sometimes involves more than meets the eye. The steep terrain in that area can create impressive changes in river levels after a heavy rain, and anyone camping along the Buffalo or any other river needs to take that into account.

As an example of how quickly conditions can change, here's a summary from a 2004 park report:

> During the three day period from April 22nd to April 24th, about ten inches of rain fell on northern Arkansas. . . . These heavy rains caused the Buffalo River to reach its highest flood level since the record floods of 1982. In the Upper Buffalo District at Pruitt, the river surged from 3.7 feet to 32 feet. . . . In the Lower Buffalo District near Buffalo Point, the river rose more steadily beginning at five feet and peaking at almost 50 feet.

Proactive and sometimes heroic measures by the park staff to evacuate campers and close the river to boating kept the number of rescues to a minimum and prevented loss of life. Such efforts can be a challenge at times, because a few folks always seem determined to test the limits of Mother Nature.

Several years before the flood described above, two young men came into the ranger station at Buffalo Point and stated their intention to camp along the Buffalo River downstream from that location. We discussed some options but discouraged their plans in view of the forecast for heavy thunderstorms overnight. In such situations rangers can only try to give good advice and then hope for the best. To our relief, it sounded like the pair had decided to use the developed campground in lieu of a more remote trip on the river.

The night brought the expected storms and heavy rain, and the river responded with an impressive but not catastrophic rise. As is standard practice in such situations, rangers began checking the area for any potential problems and before long discovered an unattended vehicle in a secluded area. We recognized the truck as the one belonging to the pair of erstwhile river campers we had talked with the day before, and the location where it was parked strongly suggested that they had decided to venture out on the river.

People often comment to rangers about their great job—that it's just spending the day cruising the river or lake or driving around looking at the scenery. For a few brief moments in a typical year that may be the case, but more often than not the job involves time on the water or in the woods under less than ideal conditions. It's those days (or nights) when it's about 33 degrees and a strong wind is blowing the almost-freezing rain horizontally that the job looks a lot less appealing to the general public!

Conditions weren't *quite* that bad this morning on the Buffalo, but boating on a rising river at flood stage isn't most people's idea of a good time. That crystal-clear water from the day before had turned an ugly, gritty brown that looked more like cheap coffee in a bad café that's been left out on the counter overnight and gone stone cold. Any boaters out in that mess would be playing dodge ball with large limbs and sometimes whole trees that were racing downstream in the strong current. The result was that the river bottom resembled a giant pinball machine as all that floating debris careened back and forth from one side of the river to the other.

Even so, duty called, and Charlie Rogers and I launched a flat-bottomed johnboat powered by an outboard motor and set out in search of our presumably missing campers. Charlie was a superb boater, and I wisely took the observer's position near the front of the boat and left the driving to the expert.

This proved to be a lucky day for Good Samaritans and for hapless campers, and we had only gone a short distance downriver when we encountered a classic "Hey Ranger!" scene. Our quarry on this little hunting expedition were both perched on the highest point of what had been an immense gravel bar about the size of a football field when they went to bed the night before.

Gravel bars along rivers can make great campsites in locations where such camping is allowed. Just keep in mind that rivers can rise quickly—sometimes while you're sleeping—when you select a site. (Buffalo National River)

By the time we arrived, their remaining dry land was now a tiny island, closer to the size of a checkerboard than a football field, and our approach was met with much vigorous arm waving and loud shouts of "Hey Ranger, over here!" At least all of us in this situation spoke English, although their body language would probably have communicated their message effectively no matter what dialect was in use.

Their antics would have been adequate to catch the attention of a New York cabbie even at quitting time on a rainy Friday afternoon in midtown Manhattan, and it would be safe to say that they were highly motivated to accept our offer of a ride. Like the boaters at Canyonlands in the story above, they had been awakened before daylight by the rather rude entry of water into their tent, and by that time their canoe had long since taken a solo trip downriver for points unknown. Well before our arrival, as the ground above the rising water continued to shrink, much of their remaining gear had drifted away in search of the canoe on its eastward trek.

In view of the prevailing conditions and the fact that our boat was already fully loaded with four occupants, everyone agreed that a search for their canoe and gear wasn't a high priority at that moment, and we made a prudent return to higher ground.

Boats that go AWOL while their owners are sleeping are not unusual, and this can happen even if things are nice and calm in camp and the weather seems absolutely perfect. A heavy rain miles upstream can cause the water level to rise during the hours of darkness and then fall again before anyone wakes up to an unpleasant surprise.

Such a scenario occurred in Canyonlands National Park, where a couple camped for the night near the mouth of Water Canyon. As stated in a wonderfully creative report from the park, while the pair slept the river rose and subsided, and "during the interim the River Gods furtively escaped with floating booty" in the form of their rented canoe. The duo awoke to find that their craft had abandoned them in favor of the Green River. The former boaters, now reduced to hikers, decided to leave most of their gear at their campsite and trek toward the Confluence of the Green and Colorado Rivers, a distance of about four and a half miles.

Their fortune improved, and about halfway to their destination, they came upon their undamaged canoe, which thankfully still contained their all-important paddles. They were then able to continue to their scheduled meeting spot with a commercial boat operator and subsequently reported their situation to park rangers.

Two days later the park river patrol located their remaining gear, and in due time it was returned to its owners. The report did not mention whether the River Gods gave up their booty willingly, but if history holds true, those mythical deities will have plenty of opportunities for further mischief with boaters. I hope my readers, armed with the information from this chapter, will avoid being numbered among their future victims!

Camping is a wonderful way to enjoy the Great Outdoors, but in selecting a site you might consider the words of the writer John Milton: "The world was all before them, where to choose their place of rest." You do have a choice about where to camp (or not), and rather ironically in the context of this chapter, that quote is from Milton's work *Paradise Lost*. When you pick out your little piece of paradise for your next camping trip, just try to be certain your choice doesn't turn out to be a loser.

15

"A River of Gasoline"

An acquaintance of mine who was an air force fighter pilot once described his job as "long periods of routine and monotony punctuated by occasional moments of sheer terror." Occasionally, that statement could also apply to the jobs of some park rangers.

Sure, there's plenty of routine and sometimes monotony for rangers. (After all, we *are* talking about government jobs here, so there's no escaping paperwork and meetings.) Whether their day is routine or exciting, rangers are almost always busy, and in many parks there are more than enough crises to avoid any risk of boredom. Moments of anything approaching sheer terror are, however, thankfully rare.

The following story probably had the potential to provide one of those moments for me, but at the time the need for quick action didn't allow much opportunity to ponder the possibilities. Like the other stories in this book, even a Truly Melancholy Situation had its lighter moments—at least when viewed years later from the comfort of my own living room.

As is usually the case, on the afternoon in question there was no reason to suspect that the day would be out of the ordinary. That all changed when a man burst through the front door of the ranger station at Buffalo Point, at the Buffalo National River in northern Arkansas, obviously *very* excited about something.

"Hey ranger! You'd better come quick! There's been a truck wreck just across the bridge!"

That information in itself was not especially unusual. Arkansas Highway 14 crossed the Buffalo River about three miles from my office at Buffalo Point. The two-lane road made a steep, winding descent into the gorge carved by the river, with one switchback and hairpin turn after another. Quite a few large trucks had come to grief on that stretch of highway when their brakes overheated, resulting in a runaway rig. Thankfully, the drivers always seemed to make a miraculous escape, and while cleanup was a hassle, it was rarely dangerous.

The current situation, however, had a new wrinkle for our list of truck wreck sagas, and the wide-eyed man in my office definitely had some ominous news.

"There's a big fuel tanker truck on its side just up from the bridge, the tank is busted open, and there's a *river* of gasoline running downhill!"

On a list of statements that will bless your day, that one definitely has to rank pretty far down the line.

At least some of you reading these words have probably felt a little touch of envy at the great jobs we have as rangers, and perhaps you've even aspired to one of those positions yourself. Okay, just for fun, put on your imaginary flat-brimmed Stetson hat, switch places with me, and take charge of this little scenario. I'll set the stage for you and then we'll get to a truly bizarre element in this situation.

The good news is that the district of the park where you work *does* have a fire truck and a trained fire brigade, which includes a grand total of the four rangers in the district and two of the maintenance employees. The bad news is that it's late in the afternoon, which means that all of the maintenance staff has already gone home for the day. Since the rangers work different shifts to maintain coverage for as many hours of the week as possible, the total number of rangers currently on duty within an hour's drive of your location is: one. (Oh, by the way, that would be *you*.)

Two small rural volunteer fire departments have stations within five miles. The nearest towns in each direction are about twenty miles away over winding mountain roads and also have small volunteer fire departments. The closest towns with full-time fire departments (and therefore additional equipment and expertise) are well over an hour's drive away, and you're way outside their response area anyway.

Meanwhile, back at the scene, the reported "river of gasoline" would be flowing downhill toward one of the premier recreational rivers

The Buffalo National River in Arkansas includes spectacular bluffs and 135 miles of free-flowing river but
thankfully no gasoline. Protecting those natural resources
is a big job for the park staff. (National Park Service)

in the lower 48 states, renowned for its cool, clean water, excellent fishing, fine canoeing, and pristine scenery. Adding even a small quantity of
gasoline to that clear, sparkling water in the Buffalo River would be a
less than desirable situation.

Finally, it's a rather warm afternoon, and you might keep in mind
that gasoline has a very low "flash point." I'm sure you were very atten-
tive through every one of those science classes back in school, but just
in case you happened to miss that lecture, this term means that any one
of a variety of potential sources of heat, spark, or flame could ignite
those gasoline fumes. The result would be a lot more than just a "flash"
and could create a Significantly Seriously Melancholy Situation. Okay,
Mr. or Ms. Ranger, are you having fun yet?

Maybe you'd like a little bit of good news, so here's some: Thankfully this isn't the "good ol' days," so you *do* have a way to spread the word that something is amiss short of waiting for someone many miles away to say, "Hey, that's a *really* impressive pillar of smoke. Maybe we ought to go see what's up!"

A couple of calls on your two-way radio sound the alarm and get some additional help started in your direction. Among the reinforcements will eventually be someone from the Arkansas State Police, which according to state law is ultimately responsible for management of hazardous materials incidents on state highways. You'll still have to make sure park resources are protected, but once that unfortunate state trooper arrives on the scene, you can pass this trophy buck to somebody else.

In the meantime, you're the Lone Ranger, and Tonto has the day off, so get back to work and see what you can do to keep this situation from getting completely out of hand.

There's a good basic rule for emergency services personnel in a crisis that you can also apply to any calamity you may face: "Don't become part of the problem." Loosely translated, this means don't rush headlong into an incident and turn a mishap into a catastrophe.

With that goal in mind, I first drafted some local help to shut down the road at a safe distance from the reported accident site, to make sure *nobody* drove up that hill until I sized up the situation. I had also requested that the Proper Local Authorities be notified to stop traffic coming downhill on the opposite side of the river, but I had no way of knowing how soon this would actually occur. I was also hoping that the initial report exaggerated the problem, but until I knew otherwise, I sure didn't want any vehicles with hot catalytic converters or cigarette-puffing drivers passing through rivers, streams, rivulets, or even puddles of gasoline.

In addition to the extent of the spill, the other key unknown factor was the status of the truck driver, so I grabbed some basic medical gear and headed out on foot to investigate. (I refer you back to the aforementioned basic rule, "Don't become part of the problem," and I certainly had no interest in driving a vehicle through any gasoline.) After crossing the bridge, the route was also seriously uphill, and the smell of fuel became increasingly strong.

As an aside for any of you trained emergency personnel reading this little saga, I realize that approaching a leaking gasoline tanker from downhill is not considered good form. However, due to the very rugged terrain and lack of any other roads crossing the river for many a mile, the only other options were either a helicopter, which wasn't available anywhere in the area, or a wait of an unknown period of time for the first trained personnel to arrive from the opposite side of the river. Since the fate of the truck driver, or any other motorists who may have happened upon the scene, was still undetermined, it was time to take a hike. At least the good news was that I hadn't seen or heard a flash, boom, or smoke.

Before long, I did in fact find an 18-wheeler in a clearly undesirable situation. Both the tractor and trailer were lying on their sides, not quite upside down, along the edge of the road. It came as some surprise to me when I became an adult and began to travel to other parts of the country to find that an expression from my Texas childhood apparently isn't universal to the entire world. However, this term would have aptly described the current status of the truck: it had definitely *tumped over*.

Confirming that this is not yet an Official Word, at least according to Microsoft, the spell-checker on my computer immediately responded by putting one of those red squiggly lines under *tumped* as soon as I typed it. I promptly corrected that oversight by clicking on "add to dictionary." You are welcome to do the same for your mental word list if you wish, in the event you ever find yourself in places where the term is in use.

This stretch of highway was literally carved out of the side of a very steep rocky bluff, and there was almost no road shoulder. When the big rig tumped over, it slid on its side for some distance along the face of the jagged cliff and the rocky ground alongside the road until friction won the battle with momentum, and the vehicle finally came to a halt.

This impolite treatment had a detrimental effect on the nice, shiny skin on the gasoline tanker—as it would on any similar object. If you saw the movie *Titanic*, think back to that scene of the iceberg ripping open the hull of the ship. If you missed the film, I trust you still get the picture, and it was not a pretty sight. At this point, we had a smorgasbord of news, including good, mixed, bad, and very bad.

The good news was that there was no river of gasoline running down the road, although there was a serious puddle under the tanker, and as best I could tell, only one of its compartments had been torn open. Good news was in short supply, however, so this paragraph is accordingly rather brief.

The mixed news was that there was no sign of the truck driver. This confirmed that he had managed to escape from his truck, hopefully more or less unscathed, but it left open the question of his status. We'd have to conduct a search to be sure he wasn't lying injured somewhere in the vicinity.

Now to the bad news.

This particular tanker had the capacity to carry about eight thousand gallons of gasoline, divided among several compartments. In the absence of the driver, some rather important information was not available: Had the truck been full, partly full, or mostly empty at the time it came to an untimely end? This was certainly a case where the devil is in the details, and the details mattered a lot.

Since at least one compartment of the tanker had been seriously abused by those jagged rocks, there was the possibility that we had as much as two thousand gallons of gasoline unaccounted for. The flow from the ruptured tank had diminished to a dribble, and there was very little liquid visible on the surface of the rocky ground, although the fumes were still very strong. So, if the tank had been full, where had the gasoline gone? That leads to the *very* bad news.

If you've ever visited the Arkansas Ozarks, you may recall that a good word to describe the area is "rocky." As a very short refresher from your Earth Science class, this is a classic example of a *karst*, a term that describes "landscapes characterized by caves, sinkholes, and underground drainage. In this kind of terrain, streams disappear into the ground and reappear elsewhere as large springs." Any liquid falling on the surface (usually rain or melted snow rather than gasoline) soon makes it way down into the depths through countless cracks in the porous and fractured rock.

The result was that whatever gasoline had escaped from the tank and not evaporated was now somewhere underground, either trapped in crevices or perhaps even a cave. In the worst case, the fuel was making its way at an unknown rate via underground water courses or other passages to springs or even down to the river itself. Not a happy scenario!

During the next couple of hours we learned that the driver had survived with minor injuries and flagged down the first vehicle that came upon the accident. He convinced *that* driver to turn around and give the trucker a ride to a nearby phone to report the mishap to his boss. The problem of the missing driver was at least solved, and we also confirmed that the truck had been fully loaded at the time of its mishap.

Reinforcements arrived in due time from area volunteer fire departments, rangers called back to duty, state police, the state department of transportation, various environmental protection agencies, and a variety of experts, either real or self-appointed, from the aforementioned and several other entities.

Now, as promised, we're almost ready for the comic relief in an otherwise undesirable situation. All the great minds assembled at the scene agreed that there were two main goals to be accomplished: (1) safely remove the truck and all remaining gasoline from the scene; (2) minimize harm to the environment, which primarily meant keeping the fuel from reaching that pristine water in the Buffalo River. As is often the case, figuring out how to actually *accomplish* those goals was a bit more complicated.

One man, however, had a simple solution for goal number one. (Well, *he* said it was simple.) This gentleman, the owner of the trucking company, arrived in a pickup truck followed by another gasoline tanker. This one was empty and would be used to haul away the off-loaded cargo once it was removed from the wrecked tanker. There was only one small difficulty.

Due to the risk of an explosion or fire, the consensus of the various experts was that no one wanted to try to get the damaged truck and trailer back on their wheels until the fuel had been removed. One little spark during that maneuver would have rather undesirable results, and righting the trailer might spill additional fuel from the hole in the side of the tank. However, the position of the tanker made the fittings normally used to empty the cargo inaccessible, and it appeared they had also been damaged in the accident. So, how to get the gasoline from the wrecked tanker to the other one?

No problem, said the owner. He reached into the back of his truck, grabbed an axe, and began to clamber up the side of the overturned tanker.

By now, it was well past nightfall, so the lighting at the scene was a little limited. As a result, it took a few seconds for the rather surreal scene that was starting to unfold before our eyes to sink in. About the time the trucker, armed with his trusty axe, reached a position with more or less secure footing, and began to heft his tool, someone from the assembled crowd called out, "Hey! What do you think you're *doing?*"

The reply from the man atop the wrecked tanker was very matter-of-fact. "I'm going to chop a hole in the top of this tank so we can drop in a hose and pump out the gas. Then I'll do the same thing on the other compartments."

I know the expression "stunned disbelief" is probably a little overused, but it certainly applied to the assembled bystanders in this situation.

The state trooper who was the Incident Commander (IC) was probably the person who spoke first, and although his exact words have faded from my memory with the passage of a couple of decades, they were something like, "Hold on just a minute there, Leroy!"

An interesting debate ensued, while Leroy (or whatever his name really was) delivered a rather persuasive discourse on the merits of his plan. He assured one and all that he had done this "several times before," which caused me to silently wonder about the track record of his drivers. He went on to explain that the axe was made from a particular type of alloy that would absolutely, positively, definitely not cause *any* sparks in the process of chopping a hole in the metal surface of the gasoline tanker.

Perhaps most telling was his challenge, "anybody here got a better idea?" Another rather timeworn expression is to "put your money where your mouth is," but it certainly applies here, and I will readily concede that Leroy was clearly willing to do just that—and more—since he was going to be the one wielding the axe.

In the process of writing this chapter, I called several experts associated with the petroleum and trucking industry to inquire if Leroy's approach was in fact unusual. There are accepted procedures for solving this problem, but both the equipment and knowledge were lacking at that moment in rural Arkansas. Thus far I've not found anyone who would either endorse or has even heard of Leroy's approach, suggesting that there *are* times when it may be better to be lucky than smart.

I'll have to admit in retrospect that there were probably more people hanging around the general vicinity of this accident than were absolutely necessary—or prudent. However, upon Leroy's pronouncement of his planned course of action, a very interesting phenomenon occurred. Just about everyone within earshot suddenly realized that their services were no longer needed, and furthermore, they recalled that they had pressing business elsewhere, probably in the next county or points beyond. I cheerfully admit that I included myself in that number, although duty required that I merely withdraw a safe distance until Leroy had completed his work.

We may not have been able to cite the exact source of the expression that "discretion is the better part of valor," but we certainly understood the principle. Among other things, I was personally responsible for that fire truck parked nearby, which was property of the United States government, and I certainly didn't want to put that investment by the taxpayers at unnecessary risk.

Before long an agreement was reached: Any personnel who elected to remain in the vicinity and their vehicles would be withdrawn a prudent distance, and everyone else was free to leave. Leroy would then be allowed to prove his point about his magic axe, which to his credit he did with efficiency. In due time, the damaged tanker was emptied, returned safely to its upright and locked position, and along with the salvaged fuel, hauled away.

That brought the now considerably smaller crowd of assembled experts to goal number 2, which you may recall was solving the Case of the Disappearing Gasoline.

As ideas about how to handle the underground fuel were bounced back and forth, someone in the group came up with a real show-stopper. In fairness to the true experts present, I believe this suggestion came from a local resident who had managed to talk his way past the checkpoint, perhaps claiming to be a local volunteer fireman or using a similar ploy. Some folks just can't resist getting in on the action, whether real or imagined, and this situation was probably the most exciting event in the neighborhood for some time.

Irrespective of who he was, in view of his suggestion I'll refer to him as Boomer. His plan went something like this: "Hey, I've got one of them flare guns back at the house. We could all pull back a ways, and I could lob a flare down here where the gas smell seems to be strongest. That should catch it on fire, and it would all just burn up, and then we wouldn't have to worry about it messing up the river."

I *will* give Boomer credit for being concerned about the environment and at least thinking outside the box. There was, of course, at least one fairly serious flaw in this plan.

In the process of researching my facts for this book, I was reminded that information obtained from the Internet can't always be taken at face value. As a case in point, I recalled hearing on several occasions over the years that a gallon of gasoline has the explosive power of a certain number of sticks of dynamite.

I thought it would be interesting to include that information to illustrate this story, so I ventured into cyberspace in quick search of the definitive answer. I soon found several seemingly reliable sources whose figures for the explosive equivalent ranged everywhere from six to thirty-three sticks of dynamite per gallon of gasoline.

The variation may be explained in part because it depends upon whether you're talking about gasoline in liquid or vapor form and lots of other factors, possibly including the size of the stick of dynamite. I cheerfully admit that I have no idea if those sticks come in more than one size, since my personal experience with dynamite is thankfully virtually nil.

Either way, the bottom line is that if one gallon packs a big wallop, a couple of thousand of gallons of gas trapped underground in a space of unknown size and shape was a force not to be taken lightly. Furthermore, the explosive power of gasoline is much greater if the fuel is in a vapor rather than a liquid state.

This fact was not lost on the local representative of the state highway department who was part of the remaining brain trust at the scene. Being an engineer, I suppose he had more experience with dynamite/gasoline ratios that I did, but he summed up his concerns pretty succinctly. They went something like this, and all things considered, I thought he exercised impressive tact and diplomacy in putting Boomer's idea to rest.

"Well, that's an interesting suggestion, but it's been a pretty warm day, and I'll bet a lot of that gas has turned into vapor somewhere underground. That means if we touch off those fumes with a flare or anything else, we'd probably blow at least half a mile of this highway right off the side of the mountain. I don't think my boss, the governor, or the taxpayers would be too pleased with that outcome, and besides, a lot of that rock and dirt would end up down in the river." Hey, this guy was thinking about the *big* picture. I was mainly concerned a little earlier about the value of a fire truck, and he was pondering the cost of rebuilding an expensive stretch of mountain highway.

Suffice it to say that Boomer's plan was not accepted. By this time a professional hazardous materials cleanup crew had arrived, and among their assignments was to scout the area downhill from the wreck for any places where liquid gas was returning to the surface—not an easy job in the rugged terrain. If any such places were found, their job was to keep the fuel from reaching the river and then remove it from the area. There were lots of other details, which I won't inflict upon you, but I'm pleased to report that the river remained pristine, life eventually returned to normal, and Boomer went back to his think tank to refine his skills in contingency planning.

So, the next time you drag yourself through the front door at home and your spouse asks, "How was your day at work, dear?" perhaps you can take some comfort in the fact that occasionally it really could have been worse! You may recall a movie named *A River Runs Through It.* At least in *that* case, it didn't contain any gasoline!

Doing the Wave

Fishing is an activity enjoyed by about one out of six Americans, at locations ranging from remote mountain streams to ocean beaches, vast lakes to tiny ponds, the open sea to lazy winding rivers, and almost anyplace else with enough water to justify dropping in a lure or baited hook. According to the U.S. Fish and Wildlife Service, Americans take about 437 million fishing trips a year, providing more than ample opportunity to confirm Eugene Field's observation, "I never lost a little fish. . . . It always was the biggest fish I caught that got away." Occasionally, however, even the one that *didn't* get away can provide a fun and unusual tale.

Willow Beach is located in the Arizona portion of Lake Mead National Recreation Area, and fishing is one of the primary attractions of that area. When I worked there in the 1970s the management of a resort operating under a permit from the government had astutely parlayed angling into a good combination of positive customer relations and effective advertising.

Their program was based on a simple invitation: If you caught a fish in the area that tipped the scales at five pounds or more and brought it to the resort, they would take a photo of you and the fish and hang the picture on the wall. Almost all of the lunkers in those days were rainbow trout, and the walls of the restaurant, store, and other public areas in the building were pretty well covered with those photos. In addition to minimizing interior decorating decisions for the resort staff, it also provided a popular and informal form of competition among the anglers.

Fishing is a popular activity in many parks. This angler made a nice catch at Curecanti National Recreation Area in Colorado. (National Park Service)

The area is still a prime fishing destination, although I'm told that striped bass have replaced most of the big trout, and the current resort keeps some photos in a scrapbook rather than on the wall. That was probably a good call, since by now they would have long since run out of any space to hang additional "Kodak moments."

One day during my years in the area I was on the lake with my boss and fellow ranger John Chew. We were aboard a boat manufactured by a company called "Boston Whaler" and headed back to the marina at Willow Beach. The weather was nice and we were making good time when there was a sudden, loud *thunk* from the underside of the boat.

John was an expert boater, I had been keeping an eye on the water ahead, and both of us were very familiar with the area, so we exchanged surprised glances at this development. Neither of us had seen anything on the surface of the lake, but it was obvious that the boat had hit something, so John immediately throttled back the engine and began a U-turn to see if we could solve this mystery.

We soon had our answer, and it was quite a surprise. Floating there on top of the water was a really nice trout that had apparently been right below the surface or had made an unusual leap from the water directly into our path. John eased the boat to a stop and we leaned over the side for a closer look. We hoped the fish had just been stunned and would gather its wits and swim away, but it was soon apparent that this was a definite TKO (Trout Knock-Out) and this guy was down for the final count.

It was much too nice a fish to waste by leaving it behind for the scavengers, and since John had a valid fishing license, we talked it over and decided he should just take it home. Inadvertent or not, he had "bagged" the fish, and we certainly didn't want to be guilty of "wanton waste" of a prime specimen. We were only a few minutes from the marina, and John could ice it down as soon as we arrived.

It was a slow weekday morning, and we were the only boaters in the area, so it was almost inevitable that the marina manager would see us arrive and come over to say hello. He immediately spotted the fish and congratulated us on our "catch." Before we could give any further explanation, the manager insisted that John bring the fish in to be weighed, since he was almost certain it was well over the five-pound limit for the photo wall of fame.

Sure enough, John had a winner, and almost before he could say "cheese," the bemused "fisherman's" picture had been taken to immortalize his achievement as part of the collection on the resort wall. This unique if impromptu method of fishing couldn't be allowed simply to fade into oblivion, and some time later I conspired to help some friends recognize John at a special occasion. He was transferring to a job at another park, and I talked the resort manager out of the photo. At a send-off party prior to his move, John was presented with the infamous picture, with an added inscription declaring him to be the "Colorado River Record Holder for the Largest Trout Bagged with a Boston Whaler."

Even a more conventional approach to fishing can still include a surprise, as illustrated in a story shared by Eric Blehm. He's the author of *The Last Season* (www.lastseason.com), a wonderfully written book in which he eloquently details the life and mysterious disappearance of a veteran backcountry ranger in Sequoia and Kings Canyon National Park in 1996. Blehm is a veteran outdoorsman who has great respect for the wilderness and for park values. He has spent many a day and night in the remote High Sierras of California, including numerous trips during eight years of meticulous research for his book.

One of those expeditions found him on an unexpected solo hike on the John Muir Trail, after two companions who planned to make the trip backed out on short notice. Following a grueling climb in the rain over a 12,000-foot pass, Blehm slipped and slogged his way downhill toward a campsite, wet, hungry, and ready for a good night's rest. It had been two days since he'd seen another human being, so it was an unexpected but pleasant surprise when a backcountry ranger suddenly appeared alongside the trail.

Even more welcome was the invitation for Blehm to take a break and dry out in the ranger's cabin before he continued on to his nearby campsite. The term *cabin* was perhaps a bit of a stretch for a ten-by-ten-foot tent with wood sides, but it was warm and cozy, and Blehm's appreciative sniffs of something tasty simmering on a Coleman stove brought an invitation to share a hot dinner.

True to good backcountry etiquette, Blehm offered to repay the hospitality by seeing if he could bring the ranger "something from the lake for breakfast the next morning." Blehm was up with the sun, put the fishing gear from his pack to good use, and soon arrived back at the cabin with a stringer of freshly cleaned trout.

The ranger eyed his guest's catch and commented, "So, you caught a few of those last night, eh?"

"Nope, caught 'em all this morning," Blehm replied with a touch of pride. "One right after the next. Every cast a fish . . . ."

"Hmmm," the ranger interrupted. "That would leave me in a bit of a pickle. You sure you caught *all* of those this morning?" He held up his hand before Blehm could continue. "Because . . . you're three over the limit for a day's catch, and so I just figured you must have caught some of them last night, and kept them on your stringer in the lake."

Suddenly finding yourself in a self-inflicted Melancholy Situation can bring a unique sinking feeling to the pit of the stomach.

"Oh man," Blehm thought to himself. Actually he thought something a bit stronger, realizing he had just delivered himself right into the hands of The Man. In sharing this story, he commented, "Thankfully this ranger knew the difference between malice and stupidity, and I definitely qualified for the latter. He let me slide, and for more reasons than one, those were the best trout and potatoes I've ever had, then or since."

"I also keep special track of limit regulations. Religiously."

Like Blehm, most anglers are honest, even if they occasionally lose track of local rules that change from time to time. A few others, however, just can't resist seeing how much they can get away with. At any park where fishing is among the available activities, one of the rangers' many duties is checking to ensure that anglers have the necessary fishing license and are otherwise abiding by the rules.

Most parks have been shorthanded for decades, and there's always more to be done than time and staffing allow. As a result, rangers have become adept at finding often ingenious ways to make the most of those limited hours. A good example can be found in a technique for discouraging fishing without a license—I'll call it "The Wave."

Like the first story in this chapter, this one takes place at Lake Mead National Recreation Area, and there are good reasons why this park is a favorite with fishermen. At least two Colorado River record catches in the "hook and line" category are on the books from the Willow Beach area, including a 21-pound rainbow trout and a 67-pound striped bass that measured a very respectable 47.5 inches in length. We'd consider that to be a bit beyond "pan-sized" even in Texas, but I noted when I checked the official state fishing records that a category for "bagged with a Boston Whaler" was conspicuously absent from the list.

If you bring your own boat to Willow Beach or rent one at the marina, you have access to more miles of river and lake than you can effectively fish in a weekend, a long vacation, or probably a lifetime. Those who prefer to fish from the bank can just continue for about 150 yards past the resort, find a place to park, and climb down a short slope to the shoreline. This popular fishing beach runs for about a quarter mile before it and the road dead-end at a federal fish hatchery that helps keep the surrounding waters well-stocked with future catches.

I spent a little over two years at Willow Beach, and when other duties permitted the other ranger assigned to that area or I would take a few minutes to check fishing licenses and limits. During busier days there were far too many fishermen on the shoreline for us to contact them all and still tend to other essential matters.

As a result, one of our primary goals was simply to weed out in the shortest possible time those who didn't have the necessary license. This was not an uncommon occurrence, since Willow Beach is located on

Aerial view of Willow Beach, Lake Mead National Recreation Area. The fishing beach described in this story is along the road on the left side of the water. (National Park Service)

the Arizona side of the river, but most of our visitors came from nearby Nevada or Southern California. Our license/no license culling process was actually pretty simple—and very time-efficient.

In those years the ranger vehicles were a distinctive light green color and were conspicuously marked with reflective "Park Ranger" decals on the front fenders and tailgate, a National Park Service arrowhead logo on the doors, and the usual red lights on the roof. In short, there was no undercover skullduggery involved—when the ranger arrived via the one road in the area, anyone with at least 20/100 vision saw him coming from a considerable distance.

If only one ranger was available for this job, he'd drive his vehicle to one end of the road that ran parallel to the fishing beach, park, and stroll down to the edge of the water. He'd engage the nearest fisherperson in pleasant conversation, and sooner rather than later the topic turned to, "May I see your fishing license, please?"

The first person the ranger contacted was a captive audience, so there was no sense in trying to dodge the "license or no license" question, although plenty of alibis were offered if the required paperwork wasn't on hand. It was while the ranger was discussing the state of the world with the first one or two anglers that the real fun was getting underway nearby.

If you've ever attended or seen a sporting event where the crowd does "the wave," you can easily picture the scene on our little fishing beach. In the sports stadium version, a group of fans will all start to cheer and wave their arms above their heads at the same time. Fans standing next to them pick up that process, which is repeated and passed quickly from person to person until the cheering and arm-waving ripples through the crowd in a motion resembling a wave moving across a body of water.

As soon as it became obvious to the assembled fishermen that the rangers were out and about checking licenses, a similar situation developed. There wasn't any cheering or waving of arms, but there was plenty of activity. Up and down the length of the beach, a few of those anglers suddenly realized that they were overdue for very important engagements elsewhere. Seized by a real sense of urgency that they not delay their departure even a minute longer, they hastily packed their fishing tackle, folded up their lawn chairs, grabbed their coolers and other necessary accoutrements, and scrambled up the bank to their vehicles.

The amount of paraphernalia required to pursue the wily trout in relative comfort varied considerably from one person to another. Some of these folks had enough stuff that it took two or three trips from their vehicle to haul all their equipment down to their chosen fishing spot. However, when duty elsewhere suddenly called, it apparently did so "loud and clear," and time was obviously of the essence. It was sometimes almost comical to see the juggling act that was required for those individuals to haul all of their gear back up the bank in a single trip.

It's too bad we couldn't have borrowed the Goodyear blimp for a few minutes during one of these exercises. If this process could be viewed from above, it would bear a definite resemblance to that "wave" in the sports stadium, beginning with the fishermen nearest the ranger and moving steadily down the entire length of the beach. A slightly different effect occurred on those rare occasions when both rangers who worked in the area teamed up for license checks. One of us would start at one end of the fishing area, while the other would drive to the opposite end and begin there. In this case, a unique double wave occurred, starting at each end of the beach and meeting in the middle.

I rarely made a serious effort to intercept any of these departing brethren, but I'd be willing to bet that a significant percentage of those beating a hasty retreat were angling without benefit of license. An interesting spin-off would occur if the fish were really biting at the time one of these waves occurred, because few serious fishermen could bear the thought of heading for home before they had caught their limit.

Under those circumstances the nearby resort, which sold fishing licenses, would experience a sudden rush of sales of those magic pieces of paper. The resort staff remarked several times they always knew when a ranger was doing his duty on the nearby beach, simply by noting that a line of license seekers had suddenly formed at the counter in their store. I believe I even heard the term *Oklahoma Land Rush* applied to a couple of these license feeding frenzies.

It usually took only a few minutes of this little game to flush out all those who needed a license, and the rangers could then go on to more pressing duties. Here's my tip of the week for all of you anglers out there: If your plans for an outing include a little fishing, just ask about the local regulations, and make sure your license is up to date. If that's the case, you can enjoy your trip with a clear conscience, and the only wave you'll need to use is one that goes along with a friendly greeting if the Proper Authorities decide to drop in for a visit. Your day will be a lot more fun if you don't find yourself saying, "Hey Ranger! I sure didn't expect to see *you* here!"

Skip These Tips

You may have heard it said that babies don't come home from the hospital with instructions for new parents pinned to their diaper. A lot of outdoor equipment (and the out-of-doors itself) is the same way. For example, a canoe doesn't usually have a label indicating "this end first," and most rivers lack signs reading, "Downstream is this way →." However, in an era when there may be more lawyers seeking clients than people looking for an empty site at your favorite campground on Memorial Day weekend, makers and sellers of recreational gear are probably adding more warning tags and information than in years past.

In the case of canoes, an appropriate label would note that those watercraft are easily tipped over while afloat—and those are "tips" the occupants usually prefer to avoid. Perhaps manufacturers and companies that rent canoes to novices could borrow a page from the airline industry and permanently emboss the following in large letters in a highly visible spot inside the craft: "Warning—please remain on your seat until this vessel has come to a full and complete stop at the shore."

Notice that I said "on" rather than "in" your seat, since most canoes don't really have seats per se, although many models have a little platform of sorts on a cross brace, and it is possible to buy backrests that loosely resemble chairs. One key to successful canoeing is to keep everything on board as low and as close to the center of the boat as possible, and that especially applies to the occupants.

Printed instructions or advice from experienced boaters notwithstanding, most beginners still have to learn that concept by experience. Unless it's a warm day and you really want to take a swim, here's one tip you *do* want to observe: Don't stand up in a canoe once it's in the water. Just keep in mind that when a canoe capsizes, *every*body and everything on board gets wet, so it's a good idea to have consensus in advance about whether a dunking is part of the plan for the day. If you'd like to test the validity of my suggestion, just go to any popular canoeing spot on a nice summer weekend and position yourself where you can observe people embarking on their voyages. You are likely to see at least one or more rookie boaters attempt feats that defy logic, the laws of gravity, and/or the information on those suggested labels.

For "Exhibit A," I offer the following story submitted by a Candid Contributor about his first canoe trip:

> My wife and I took the canoe ride down the Buffalo River in Arkansas. We decided our first trip should be the shortest one (three miles). After being bused to our drop-off point we put our cooler, lawn chairs, cell phone, and the rest of our stuff in the canoe and

"I told you not to stand up!" Canoeing is a fun activity, but always wear your life jacket—and be prepared to get wet, just in case the unexpected happens. (Buffalo National River)

started down the river. Well, then I had a brilliant idea. I thought, why not put the lawn chairs across the seats of the canoe and view the river that way?

Rule number 1: Never sit in a lawn chair in a canoe. It was all right until my wife said, "Oh, look at the deer," and I turned quickly to look. SPLASH! Into the river we went. It wasn't that deep and we had a big laugh and after retrieving all of our items out of the river we started again.

Rule number 2: Remember that the water may not be deep, and the rocks may be small, but when you see a rock with paint scrapes on it in the middle of the river, stay away from that part of the river! We didn't.

Yep. Second time in the river. Anyway, we stayed wet the whole time and had a wonderful trip and will go back again next spring. It is a beautiful ride down the river.

You can glean some good tips from the above account, but for those of you who have limited experience with canoes, here are a few more tidbits of Rangerly Wisdom:

1. *Use it and you might lose it.* Don't take anything in a canoe you can't afford to lose, or at least don't want to get wet. If you feel compelled to carry along that expensive video or digital camera to capture some special memories of your aquatic adventure, at least purchase a good waterproof container for it and make sure that container is securely tethered to your canoe. I know a photo taken from your boat while you're running a major rapid would be a nice one, but I'd suggest that's a prime time to stash your camera in that waterproof bag or box. (Besides, you're *supposed* to be paddling to help steer around those rocks in the rapids!) Don't let the "one that got away" refer to your great camera.

   It's also a good idea to enclose your name, address, and phone number on a waterproof card inside that container with your valuables. If your stuff gets separated from you and your canoe and ends up drifting merrily, merrily down the stream, maybe you'll get lucky and your gear will be found by someone who will contact you and return your property. (Yes, I plead guilty to believing in Santa and the Tooth Fairy until late in childhood, but there *are* still some honest folks out there.)

2. *Face the facts—not each other.* All occupants of the canoe should sit or kneel in the canoe facing the same direction, which incidentally corresponds to the front of the canoe and to the direction you intend to travel. The idea is to move the canoe *forward* by having everyone paddle in the *same* direction. It still amazes me how many first-timers get into a canoe and sit down facing each other. (That's a great way to go nowhere fast, unless your goal is simply to travel around and around in a circle.) Perhaps some people picked up that idea from watching an old movie where the guy is *rowing* a boat (not paddling a canoe) while his lovely lady companion sits gracefully facing him, gazing romantically at the noble boatman as the craft glides smoothly across the water.

3. *Pick the right trip.* Making a canoe travel in a straight line isn't quite as easy as it might seem, even if all the paddlers *are* facing the same direction. Practice makes perfect, but for better or worse, most people just pick a river, rent a canoe, and head downstream (well, hopefully downstream!) with little or no instruction. If you're in that category, I trust you'll at least avoid choosing a river with any challenging whitewater until you have the basics well in hand. Serious tip: *Everyone* should *always* wear a life jacket when they're on the water. Even experts take unexpected spills, and a knock on the noggin against a rock cancels out the skills of the best of swimmers.

4. *Team but don't scream.* The person in the back of the canoe does most of the steering, but the individual in front must also be able to lend a competent hand (and paddle) in controlling the boat. Teamwork and communication are especially important when sudden changes of direction are needed to avoid obstructions, such as that rock with all those paint scrapes from close encounters with previous boats. In addition to paddling, the person in the *front* of the canoe is supposed to be the primary lookout for such obstructions, sound the alarm when they appear, and at least suggest a change in direction.

You may have noticed from the above discussion that canoeing can teach you a lot about interpersonal relationships: How much advice, for example, does the steerer in the back take from the observer in the front? If you add another paint scrape to that rock, whose fault *was* it, anyway? In canoeing as in the rest of life, there is need for balance between "give and take" and "get it done." It is possible to be *too* polite, and navigating a rapid or dodging a giant boulder in the river is not the time for the following civil discourse:

Front paddler: "Big rock ahead! Want to go left or right?"

Back paddler: "Gosh, it doesn't really matter to me. What would you prefer?"

Front paddler: "No, I decided about the last boulder. It's your turn."

Back paddler: "Are you sure? I want to do what you'd really enjoy . . ."

Both paddlers: Splash!

If you're a sociologist looking for a great research topic, I'd suggest you consider examining a possible correlation between the incidence of divorce and how much time the two people spent together in a canoe within the previous year. If you're thinking about getting married, perhaps it would be a good idea to take a half-day canoe trip with your potential mate *before* you set the wedding date! You'll probably gain some new insights into his or her character, and I bet they'll be different than those that come up during the standard premarital counseling session.

Author Kevin Callan has written extensively about canoeing and other outdoor activities, and he includes confirmation of my theory with the following insightful comment from his article on www.paddling.net/, "Bow Paddlers Are People Too." He notes, "One of the negative aspects of canoe tripping is that you're forced to spend time in cramped quarters with another person all day; and even worse, you have to communicate with them if you want to get anywhere. I've even heard some people compare canoeing to that of riding a two-seater bicycle. Maybe that's why kayaking is on the rise (kayakers are just canoeists who never got along with their canoe partner)."

The insights into relationships provided by canoeing also extend to children. Bob Marley and Susan Groth are veteran river runners who have an interesting and useful website "for self-reliant outdoors enthusiasts" (www.kwagunt.net). One of the newsletters on that site describes a five-day float trip on the Green River in Utah, during which they provided expertise and logistical support for a group of friends including five kids under ten, one teenager, and nine adults. Their narrative includes a wonderful observation about the differences between adults and children that can become evident during a lengthy river trip.

"We had never traveled with a group that included this many children before, so getting used to their eating habits took some time. Children don't seem to eat on the same schedule as adults do and they have some differences of opinion as to what is good to eat (e.g., 'I don't eat anything that's green.') This made for massive ingestion of white bread with peanut butter and jelly, at weird times during the day."

Hey kids, don't feel too bad. After several days on some river trips, I didn't want to eat anything that's green either, but probably for different reasons. As most parents know, you don't have to be on a canoe trip to find that the operative word for many kids presented with vegetables at mealtime is *balking* (**B**ig **A**nd **L**ittle **K**ids **I**ngest **N**othing **G**reen.)

Finally, a canoe trip can provide some interesting life lessons for the workplace. While I was working at the Buffalo National River in Arkansas, a government agency came up with an idea for a unique training program for about two dozen new managers—a three-day canoe and camping trip on the river. The plan was to paddle for a while, then come ashore at a convenient sandbar for a couple of hours of seminars or discussion groups, then paddle a few miles further.

A local canoe outfitter was hired to provide the equipment and help with logistics. Other locals shuttled guest speakers who didn't want to make the whole trip to scheduled stops for their presentation and then took the speakers back to the nearest road to return to civilization. A key part of the whole event was the anticipated team building from the combination of canoeing and camping together.

I had a chance to observe some of this strategy in action when the group came ashore for a lunch break. The water was quite chilly, and the air temperature was also a bit cool, but due to a recent dry spell the river level was a little low in places. As a result, there were some stretches where it was necessary to get out of the canoes and drag them through the shallow spots, then climb aboard and resume paddling.

With both occupants of the canoe helping, this was not especially difficult. All of the group seemed to be taking this in stride as they hauled their canoes the last hundred feet to the shore for the lunch stop, and it looked like team building was right on track until I spotted the last boat in the flotilla.

One of the new managers had been paired up for the day with a top executive of the organization, an opportunity that probably produced a little envy in his peers. After all, what a great chance for some serious bonding with the top dog! This attitude proved to be short-lived once the trip got underway. As the rest of the group all pulled their canoes onto the gravel bar (a stretch of beach covered with smooth river stones instead of sand) I noticed that there was something a little different about the last boat in line.

It was being tugged along, slowly but surely, by a determined but rather exasperated looking young manager. He was thoroughly wet from the knees down and based upon the sweat stains on his shirt had obviously completed quite a workout during the past couple of hours, dragging the canoe through the shallow spots. Sitting comfortably in the back of the boat, his crisp khakis still nice and dry, was the executive!

Yep, a canoe trip can definitely tell you a lot about relationships. Just don't count on finding that subject covered on any instruction tags, although an important clue can be found on a bumper sticker that is something of a folk legend in canoeing circles. The sticker reads, "Love many, trust few, and always paddle your own canoe." Perhaps someone needs to write a book along these lines to expand on an earlier popular volume, and I'll even suggest a title: "Everything I need to know about life I learned in a canoe."

This Ambulance Was Hot Stuff

Last year Lake Mead National Recreation Area, on the Arizona-Nevada border south of Las Vegas, received over 7.6 million visits, making it one of the busiest areas in the National Park System. Early in my career I worked at a location in that park called Willow Beach, where two rangers were assigned to assist the general citizenry in their efforts to enjoy life, liberty, and the pursuit of fun on the water.

To aid in that effort, the government motor pool had assigned two vehicles for our use, a Dodge pickup truck and a 1968 Chevy Carryall, the basic version of the current Chevy Suburban. This was before sport utility vehicles became fashionable, and a Carryall from that era was strictly a heavy-duty workhorse. In short, this Bubba rig was long on "utility" but seriously short on "sport."

When I arrived at Willow Beach my supervisor was a top-notch ranger named John Chew. Later in his career, John served as the first Emergency Medical Services (EMS) director for the entire National Park System. He went to work for the National Highway Traffic Safety Administration, and in both jobs played a key role in developing the modern EMS system that we now take for granted across the country.

Thanks to lots of hard work by John and many others over the years, EMS has come a long way in most national parks during the past three decades. Numerous lives have been saved through the work of rangers who do extra duty as emergency medical technicians or even more highly trained park medics. Many of these men and women have invested countless hours of off-duty time to develop the skills needed to provide those services to park visitors.

Our Chevy Carryall converted to an ambulance may not have been the fastest or "coolest" rig on the road, but it filled a need at Willow Beach in the early 1970s. (Velma Burnett)

In the early 1970s, however, EMS as we know it today was still in its infancy. John and I were both interested in that field, and although we provided the only available emergency services in a sizeable chunk of territory, we didn't have much to work with. As a result, John decided to adapt our Carryall to serve as both a patrol vehicle and an ambulance.

John did some skillful politicking and probably a little diplomatic begging and rounded up an ambulance cot, a jump seat for an attendant, and a pretty good selection of EMS gear. We removed the back seat from the vehicle, installed all that equipment, and *voilà*—we were in the ambulance business. We were, in fact, the *only* ambulance available at that time in this remote corner of northwestern Arizona.

Don't forget my earlier statement that these were the pioneer days of modern EMS, and our "ambulance" was still pretty basic. If things were *really* serious, the fire department from Boulder City, Nevada, would occasionally send their factory model ambulance out to meet us about halfway to the hospital. Otherwise, we were on our own.

Our trusty Chevy was equipped with a not-so-mighty six-cylinder engine, and I often wondered what some drivers along U.S. 93 must have thought when we were making an emergency run on that major highway. If we were on a downgrade we could get up a good head of steam, and people were pulling over on the shoulder to let us roar by, lights flashing and siren wailing. A mile of so down the road, when we came to a long, steep uphill stretch, we'd gradually start losing momentum, and before long those same vehicles (including big 18-wheelers and ancient station wagons towing oversized travel trailers) were passing *us* as we crept our way up to the crest.

Once we made it to the top and started back down, the same process was repeated all over again. We certainly got our share of puzzled looks from more than one driver during these games of highway leapfrog. At least out there in the literal middle of nowhere we couldn't be accused of simply being in a hurry to get to the donut shop.

Our trusty Chevy had one other interesting shortcoming. It had originally been assigned to Death Valley, up the road in Southern California, but that park's staff finally convinced the government motor pool in Las Vegas that the truck just wasn't suitable for their location. Their reasoning? The vehicle was only equipped with the infamous Model 4-60 air conditioning, which means that any interior cooling was limited to having all four windows down while driving at sixty miles per hour.

I'd be the first to agree with the staff at Death Valley that this was more than an inconvenience, and I was amazed that even the cost-conscious purchasing agents for the federal government would ever consider buying a vehicle without air conditioning for use in serious desert country. In hindsight, perhaps there was some method to their apparent madness. If the load of an air conditioner had been added to that six-cylinder engine, the vehicle might have crawled to a complete stop on a steep hill!

Faced with the dilemma of what to do with the orphan truck, someone at the government motor pool was seized with a stroke of genius: Just reassign the vehicle to Willow Beach, where the average temperatures throughout the year are somewhere in the range of five degrees *cooler* than Death Valley. I occasionally thought about volunteering to drive the rig to a motor pool in an area with a climate better suited for its equipment package, such as northern Minnesota, but I concluded that was a lost cause.

This inability to maintain great forward speed on upgrades resulted in a major drop in efficiency for that Model 4-60 a/c, so there was no avoiding the fact that a midsummer ride in this baby, even at midnight, was not something to revere. Once it was purchased by the government, however, regulations required that the vehicle be kept in service until it acquired a sufficient number of years or miles to be eligible for retirement.

Despite those limitations, the vehicle did prove to be very handy on a number of occasions when there was an urgent need to safely transport someone to town for medical care. During cooler weather, which occurred for about five months out of the year, a ride in our ambulance was actually pretty comfortable. In retrospect, the lack of air conditioning was sometimes even an advantage. Functioning as a somewhat primitive form of triage, it helped us separate the urgent from the optional when it came time to determine just how serious an emergency *really* was, and whether it was necessary for the rangers to provide a ride to the hospital.

The setting for some of these events coincided with the Arab oil embargo in the 1970s. During that time, fuel prices skyrocketed, and long lines sometimes formed at the pumps when gasoline was hard to find. As a result, visitors to Willow Beach with an injury or medical condition that *might* require transportation to the hospital about thirty miles away in Boulder City were quick to call the rangers and request the use of our ambulance. "Hey, we pay taxes," the theory went, "so let's just use Uncle Sam's gasoline for this trip to town instead of ours."

In cases where the emergency was actually pretty marginal, there was an additional factor involved. If they could talk the rangers into taking the victim to the emergency room, the rest of the group could get in at least two or three more hours of fishing before they had to drive to town to retrieve their unfortunate companion. Most people apparently figured that their time was much better spent sitting in a boat on the lake rather than in a hospital waiting room, and I'll admit that it's hard to challenge that philosophy.

These scenarios occasionally resulted in a little gamesmanship on the part of the ranger, the victim, and his comrades. The patient or friends sometimes tended to exaggerate the extent of the problem to improve their chances of a free ride. For our part, the rangers had to evaluate whether the person *really* needed our help in reaching medical care as quickly as possible, and whether our presence during the trip was necessary in case the victim took a turn for the worse. We'd always err on the side of caution, but there were valid reasons to avoid unnecessary drives other than the cost of gasoline.

With only two rangers assigned to cover a sizeable area of a *very* large park, committing one or both of us to a trip to town meant that the hundreds or sometimes thousands of other visitors in the area were left to their own devices in the event of a more serious emergency. We had good reason, therefore, to make sure an ambulance ride was really necessary, and that's where our "no air conditioning triage" came into play. Here's an example of how that worked.

It was a hot summer day, I was literally the lone ranger on duty at Willow Beach, and ironically I was en route back to the area from a trip to the hospital. I was about twenty minutes away from the ranger station when my wife called on the two-way radio to ask about my estimated time of arrival (ETA). In remote locations such as Willow Beach, the spouses of rangers were often the only people available to receive reports of emergencies by phone or from visitors who showed up at our front door.

I realized, therefore, that her inquiry about my timetable was not so she'd know when to have lunch on the table. I replied and waited to see what tidbit she had to share that would undoubtedly make my day a lot more interesting.

"The resort just called with a report that a visitor is being brought in by boat. He's an adult male with severe abdominal pain, and they think it's appendicitis. They're asking you to meet them at the boat ramp and transport him to the hospital. Their ETA at the marina is about fifteen minutes."

I replied that I was on the way. My spouse had her secret ranger message decoder ring and therefore understood not to expect me for lunch. The good news was that from my current location, it was downhill almost all the way back to Willow Beach, so I could expect maximum cooling effect by operating the a/c at its top 4-65 setting.

As predicted, I arrived at the marina about five minutes after my potential passenger. By then his friends had wisely moved the patient to the much cooler interior of the adjacent resort. I'm very familiar with the comment about desert weather, "But it's a *dry* heat." That may be true, but when the temperature in the shade is flirting with the 120-degree mark on the Official United States Government Thermometer, it's just downright hot—wet or dry.

I parked the Chevy, headed inside, and went through the standard initial assessment of the man's condition and medical history. His vital signs weren't unusual, and except for a somewhat tender tummy he seemed to be doing pretty well. I also learned that his group had driven down from Las Vegas for a day of fishing and had been enjoying considerable success in the angling department until interrupted by this untimely medical situation.

This was one of those marginal calls about whether an ambulance ride versus a trip in a private car would be suitable, so I asked his three companions whether they had a vehicle that could be used to take the patient to town. Their boat was docked year-round at the Willow Beach Marina, so they wouldn't have to waste any time loading their boat on a trailer. Unspoken was my knowledge that the man would reach the hospital in much greater comfort if they had suitable (i.e., air-conditioned) transportation for his journey.

This inquiry was met with immediate and vigorous protest that the poor man would be *much* more comfortable lying down on that nice cot in the back of our ambulance, and besides, what would happen if he suddenly took a drastic turn for the worse? None of them had any medical training, and so on. Although they were genuinely concerned for their friend, I had a strong suspicion that their primary interest was really in getting back to fishing. I was willing to make the trip if it was absolutely necessary, so I decided this was a good time to gamble on the "no a/c triage." My ace in the hole would be to point out that since I'd have to drive the ambulance, one of them would need to ride in back and keep an eagle eye on the patient, just in case that dreaded "turn for the worse" occurred while we were en route to town.

I asked one of the man's friends to go with me and help bring in the ambulance cot. He readily agreed and we headed for the door. We had all been inside the building long enough to cool off nicely, and the effect of walking out the door from that comfortable building into the summer air was about two notches below opening the door of a blast furnace. Even with all of the windows open, my trusty Carryall had been efficiently capturing plenty of solar radiation.

When you live and work in a place with serious summer heat, you quickly adopt certain coping techniques. One is the ability to open a vehicle door with minimal contact time between your bare hand and the hot metal handle. I quickly swung the two big rear doors of the truck wide open and reached inside for the lever that would free the ambulance cot from the locking mechanism that held it securely in place.

I turned my head and spoke to my draftee assistant as I did so. "I'm going to release the stretcher, and then you can pull it straight out toward you. Just grab that silver-colored handle on the foot of the cot."

My companion did as instructed, but as soon as his hand touched the sizzling metal, he let out a sharp yelp and jumped back. "Man, that thing is *hot*."

"Sorry," I replied. "Here, let me get it started, and you grab the side rail as it comes past you. Just be ready, it'll be pretty warm, too."

My volunteer was now a little less anxious to help but stood obediently to one side, ready to do his duty. We got the cot safely on the ground without scorching any fingers by using a little tap dance with our hands on the toasty metal, and I leaned down to tow the cot up the sidewalk toward the building.

"Hey, wait a minute," my assistant called. "It's *really* hot inside that ambulance! Don't you think you ought to go ahead and crank it up and turn on the air conditioning, so it will be cooler inside when we bring my buddy back out?"

Ah, the moment of truth had come. "Nah," I replied as I started toward the building with the stretcher trailing along behind. "Unfortunately, this vehicle doesn't *have* any air conditioning."

This news was met with speechless disbelief, which lasted almost long enough for me to get back to the entrance to the building. "How about holding this door open so it doesn't hit the cot when I pull it inside?" I asked.

My companion rejoined me and found his voice at about the same time. *"No air conditioning?"*

"Yeah, sorry about that. Tight budgets and all that stuff, you know."

We returned to the small group clustered around the potential patient, and my new assistant spoke up. I was gratified to see there was reason to hope that friendship would trump fishing.

"Guys, you won't *believe* this, but that ambulance doesn't have any air conditioning. It's like an *oven* inside!" To confirm this stunning news, he pointed to the cot. "Here, feel the sheets and metal on this thing."

The other two members of the group dutifully followed his instructions, which were quickly followed with suitable exclamations of amazement. The patient was taking all of this in with a clearly skeptical expression, and an earnest discussion immediately broke out among the group. The victim himself apparently had some fairly strong opinions about the plans for *his* immediate future, and I withdrew a tactful distance to allow a free and open exchange of ideas.

I realize that the application of heat is an appropriate treatment for certain medical conditions—but a possible case of appendicitis is not one of them. I had also previously discovered that the mere suggestion of a summertime ride in the back of a non–air conditioned SUV could sometimes produce a near-miraculous improvement in the medical condition of some individuals.

In short order, the designated spokesman for the group approached me. "Hey, we really appreciate your offer to drive our buddy to town, but he seems to be feeling a *lot* better, and we think it will be safe to just take him in ourselves. We've got a big car, and three of us can ride in the front while he lies down in the backseat."

I confirmed that the man did in fact seem much improved, and after ensuring that they were all satisfied with this plan, I watched them head off into the midday sun. At least the windows of *their* vehicle were all rolled up, confirming the presence of a much more modern—and efficient—air conditioning system.

On other occasions our ambulance came in handy for reasons in addition to strictly medical emergencies. One such event occurred on a spring evening shortly after dark, when I answered the phone at home to receive some disconcerting news. According to the nearly hysterical caller, there had been an explosion in a mobile home occupied by an employee of the nearby resort, and I was implored to "come quick!"

Based on this sobering information I did exactly as requested and was relieved upon my arrival to see that the trailer was at least still intact and there were no visible smoke or flames. Those facts provided hope that this potential crisis had been a bit overstated. This was very good news indeed, because my fellow ranger at Willow Beach was away on vacation, and I was the total extent of emergency forces available within many a mile.

I was met at the door of the trailer by the woman who had phoned, and she was still considerably agitated. She motioned for me to come in and excitedly pointed toward her husband, who was sitting on the kitchen floor in front of the oven. His expression was a curious combination of slightly dazed and clearly unhappy, and there was a distinct and not especially pleasant odor that I couldn't immediately identify, hanging in the air.

To avoid any misunderstanding, let me note at this point that the current resort at Willow Beach is under entirely different ownership than existed at the time of this story, and even that management was cooperative and congenial. Neither of those adjectives applied to the subject of this tale, who was quickly coming back to his senses—and he was *not* happy with the state of his world.

Here's a brief summary of the events as I later reconstructed them: Our leading man, whom I'll name Flash for purposes of this saga, had come home from work intent on trying a new recipe for supper. A key component in his experiment was a sauce containing rum, and the would-be chef had apparently felt the need to sample a significant quantity of that product in its original form, prior to using it for culinary purposes. After all, any cook worth his salt wants to ensure that all essential ingredients meet his exacting standards.

These quality control measures had apparently followed the consumption of a hefty dose of another beverage that cannot be sold legally to minors, a situation that greatly amplified the effect of the rum. It's been said that too many cooks spoil the broth, but I'd also suggest that too much broth can foil the cook—especially if the "broth" consists of the aforementioned ingredient.

Once primed and ready to embark on his kitchen adventure, our chef dutifully followed step one in the instructions: preheat the oven. His wife had almost immediately detected the smell of propane and suggested that the "pilot light on the oven is out again." This is a situation where it *always* pays to follow instructions, and a failure to do so can result in an Instantaneously Melancholy Situation.

You may have thought such events occur only in cartoons and old slapstick movies, but Flash was the exception to the rule in several categories. He failed to immediately turn off the gas for the main burner, didn't allow any time for the fumes to dissipate, and yes, he really did strike a match and then open the oven door to try to relight the pilot light. The resulting minor explosion was predictable, but Flash (along with his spouse and the mobile home) was very fortunate on several counts.

First, he had turned the oven on to a very low setting, so only a limited amount of gas had accumulated inside the stove before he opened the door and ignited the fumes. Second, he was a man large in stature, both vertically and horizontally, and therefore moved rather deliberately. As a result, there had not been time for him to lean very far over the open oven door when the appliance behaved in this unseemly manner. Finally, he was wearing eyeglasses, which probably prevented potentially serious injury to his eyes.

Even so, he had not escaped totally unscathed, and as I approached him to offer assistance, at least part of the source of that unusual odor became apparent. Flash now sported a new, and shorter, hairdo, especially in the front, but it at least matched his singed eyebrows. The previously abundant hair on the back of his hands and forearms was in a similar condition, but amazingly he seemed to have only minor burns.

Now that the initial shock was wearing off, the effects of Flash's recently consumed sauce ingredients were moving the situation in an undesirable direction. He began to direct his ire at his spouse, who responded in a predictable manner. Flash outweighed me by at least a hundred pounds, and as the lone ranger in the territory I had no desire to allow this problem to deteriorate into a classic domestic disturbance. At that point, the availability of our trusty ambulance came to the rescue.

Employing my best bedside manner, I was fortunately able to redirect the focus of Flash's attention to his potential injuries, and I'll readily confess I played it to the hilt. Even though the thick eyeglasses had fortunately protected his eyes from any obvious injury, I suggested that a trip to the hospital would be wise, because in such situations it was possible to suffer damage to one's vision from the sudden flash of the explosion.

Upon questioning, Flash admitted that his vision was in fact "a little blurry." No big surprise there, given his recent liquid intake, but that provided just the opening I needed. I suggested that to prevent any chance of further eye damage, he should remove his glasses, close his eyes, and let me cover them with a loose sterile dressing until he had been examined by a doctor.

Fortunately, my Official United States Government First Aid Kit even included several oval-shaped eye patches, which I was quick to point out were provided "just for situations like this one." Once these patches were applied and held in place by copious amounts of wide gauze bandages wrapped around his head, Flash was effectively blindfolded—and now relatively harmless. Just for good measure I also swathed both hands with additional wraps of gauze, which had the added benefit of immobilizing his fingers and thumbs. I'll have to say that the overall "mummy" effect was rather impressive, but most important, Flash was now a much more cooperative patient.

A friend volunteered to ride in the back of our ambulance with Flash, and his wife agreed to drive to town and retrieve him once the hospital said he was free to go. By the time the emergency room evaluation and paperwork were all completed, the effects of his pre-dinner libations had worn off, and a considerably subdued Flash returned home, fortunately none the worse for wear—at least on a long-term basis.

Sometimes, a little detail like the lack of air conditioning isn't such a big deal after all, and on this occasion our hot ambulance provided a pretty cool solution to a potentially volatile situation.

When in Doubt . . . Don't

O ne of the concerns (okay, let's be honest, fears) that quite a few people have when they venture into the Great Outdoors is having a close encounter of the worst kind with a snake. Contrary to popular opinion, the vast majority of snakes are not by nature aggressive, and if you use good judgment your odds of being bitten, mugged, or otherwise accosted by a snake or any other reptile are very slim.

Just to help you avoid ending up in a future version of this book, here's a bit of free Rangerly Advice—good judgment about snakes mainly comes down to two key rules: First, when you're out of doors don't step, sit, or put your hands or any other portions of your anatomy anywhere without looking first to see if that spot might already be occupied by some other life form. Examples include stepping over a log lying across a trail or reaching above your head for a handhold on a ledge while scaling a cliff. In rare cases you may not be able to avoid those actions, but they can put you in a Painfully Melancholy Situation involving more than just snakes, so if you choose to do so, please don't say I didn't warn you.

Second, if you happen to see a snake, simply stand still, or if there's adequate distance between the two of you, back off slowly and leave it alone. I apologize if that seems too obvious, but you'd likely be amazed at how many people just can't resist doing otherwise, such as jabbing it with a stick or even picking it up. You'll read shortly about a couple of folks who, upon further review, wished they had let snakes, sleeping or otherwise, lie.

I realize that some of you are skeptics, convinced that these reptiles are lurking out there, just waiting for a chance to brazenly leap from their hiding places and mug a likely-looking innocent victim who outweighs them by a factor of at least twenty to one. Should you happen to encounter one of these rare kamikaze serpents, by all means feel free to defend yourself.

I'll mention that while I don't have any unusual fear of them, I'm also not a big fan of snakes when it comes to getting up close and personal. I appreciate their useful role in the great scheme of things, but I've never had any desire, for example, to have one as a pet. Since I chose a career that allowed me to spend quite a bit of time in places that snakes call home, I came to a kind of vague understanding with reptiles in general—I'd do my best to just leave them alone if they would return the favor.

I admit that this agreement was rather nebulous, since I never had any formal discussions with an official representative of any reptilian organizations. However, word apparently got out, or my guardian angel worked overtime, since I encountered plenty of their brethren during thirty years of rangering without any untoward events.

Occasionally it is necessary for rangers to capture and relocate snakes from places frequented by park visitors, especially if the reptiles are of the poisonous variety. Such actions are taken to reduce the chance that someone might have an unfortunate experience with the creature, which always results in the need to complete a bunch of Official United States Government Reports. These events qualify as an exception to the "just leave them alone" rule, but for those of you who think you'd like to be a ranger, be aware that reptilian relocation is often part of the package.

One such event occurred at Willow Beach, in the Lake Mead National Recreation Area. Late one afternoon I received a phone call from the manager of the resort to "come as soon as you can." He wasn't very specific but did mention that the problem had something to do with a rattlesnake, so it seemed prudent to deal with this promptly. It was quite a drive to the hospital from our little oasis out in the desert, and I didn't have any desire to put my emergency medical—or report writing—skills to use.

An unlikely place for a snake. The marina at Willow Beach, Arizona, as it looked during the author's years there. The same facility today is much smaller. (Jim Burnett)

I met the manager and one of his employees, who told me that a visitor had rented one of the dozen or so small boats available from the marina. The man reported that as he started to load his gear into the vessel, he spotted a rattlesnake in the bottom of the craft. The tourist suddenly found that he was not nearly as interested in fishing as he thought and promptly returned to the office to request a refund of his boat rental fee.

The manager of the resort explained the situation and then demonstrated his executive skills by delegating the task of solving this problem. The delegates were one of his employees, who was responsible for the boat rentals, and yours truly, who as the Official On-Site Representative of the United States Government was presumably responsible for the snake. The manager then departed to resume managing.

The park staff did keep a couple of useful tools on hand for such occasions. These implements had handles long enough to allow corralling the target while presumably keeping the operator at a reasonably safe distance from the snake. I went to my truck to retrieve those items and sent my partner in this assignment, whom I'll call Charlie, out to the pier. His instructions were to keep a close eye on the boat in case the snake decided to relocate or reveal its present location.

I returned promptly to find Charlie standing on the dock, peering cautiously into the boat.

"See anything?" I asked.

"Nah. He probably crawled off before we got back out here," Charlie replied hopefully.

I tend to be optimistic by nature, but in this case I had to be the chairman of the cold water committee.

"Could be. Unfortunately, if that's the case, we'll have to look through *all* these rental boats, just to be on the safe side, so hopefully we can just locate the rascal and get him out of here."

Charlie somewhat woefully agreed that was the case, so we decided to get to work. He even had a plan.

"How 'bout if I bang on the inside of the boat with a paddle? Maybe he crawled under one of the seats, and the noise will flush him out into the open. Then you can jump in and grab him with that contraption of yours."

I had to give Charlie bonus points for a preemptive strike with his strategy, which allowed him to remain in relative safety on the pier while I headed into close quarters with our quarry, if it decided to show itself.

So that you can fully understand what happened next, I'll have to take a brief time-out to give you a little technical background. As usual, I was carrying a portable, two-way radio that allowed me to stay in contact with park headquarters and my fellow rangers scattered around the nearly 1.5 million acres included in this huge park. This particular radio didn't have a case to allow it to be worn on my belt, so in order to have both hands free for whatever adventures might lie ahead, I had stuffed the radio into the back pocket of my trousers. Such radios in those days had several small knobs on top, including a channel selector, a volume control, and an identical knob for the "squelch" setting, which controlled the sensitivity of the reception. Too much sensitivity produced a steady rush of static; too little might cause you to miss a radio call. The trick was to carefully adjust the squelch by turning the knob slowly until it was set just a tiny fraction back from the point where the static kicked in.

Now, back to the task at hand. Charlie took up his position on the dock next to the boat, grabbed a long, wooden paddle, and glanced over his shoulder at me.

"Ready?"

I checked my grip on my snake catcher. "Go ahead."

Charlie gave the inside of the aluminum boat several vigorous thumps while we both peered over the bow. In the midst of Charlie's whacking on the hull, I thought I heard a call on my portable radio but wasn't sure due to the noise he was making. Charlie suddenly stopped thumping and leaned over a little further to try to get a better look inside the boat. At that same moment, I reached rather awkwardly around to the radio in my back pants pocket to be sure the volume on my radio was turned up.

I don't think Charlie ever fully believed me afterward, but it really *was* an honest mistake on my part. I was keeping both eyes on the boat—and any possible action that might develop—and as I felt for the volume control on the radio, I accidentally bumped the squelch knob. The volume had in fact already been set close to the maximum, so when I moved the squelch knob, the afternoon's silence was suddenly shattered by a *very* loud burst of static from my radio.

That unexpected rush of noise really didn't sound much like the rattle of a snake, but under the somewhat tense circumstances, as the old expression goes, it was close enough for government work. Both of us gave a startled jump, but in his position leaning over the boat with the paddle, Charlie was already poised at a critical and awkward angle.

I'm sure under the circumstances he fully intended to leap further back onto the dock, but gravity overcame good intentions, and with a startled yelp, Charlie tumbled right into the front of the boat!

In a very impressive series of moves that ought to be considered for future Olympic gymnastics events, Charlie made a remarkable recovery whose agility was eclipsed only by its lightning speed. In less time than it takes to recount, he was back on his feet, out of the boat, and standing next to me on the dock. Thankfully for a lot of reasons, including Charlie's well-being and the fact that I wouldn't have to complete more Official United States Government Reports, the only thing injured was his dignity.

"What was *that*?" he demanded.

"Charlie, I'm really sorry! It was just the radio in my back pocket."

For the sake of your time and to preserve the family-friendly tone of this book, I'll skip over the rest of our conversation and simply report that our search of that and other nearby boats failed to turn up any occupants, reptilian or otherwise. Perhaps our quarry really had decided to depart before we arrived on the scene, or maybe the visitor making the report changed his mind about renting a boat and just wanted a good excuse for a refund.

Regardless of the background for this little adventure, for Charlie it was always a classic example of a close encounter of the GERD kind, otherwise known as a gut-wrenching experience. (If you don't recognize the medical term GERD, watch for one of those ads for the "purple pill," or just translate this as a case of serious heartburn.)

Another example of "sure wish I hadn't done that" occurred on the afternoon of June 21 in a recent year at the Little River Canyon National Preserve in Alabama. That date normally happens to be the summer solstice and is therefore the longest day of the year. Under the following circumstances it probably seemed like the longest day of this young person's life.

The chief character of this little drama was a 15-year-old boy from Georgia, who was visiting the area with his family. The group had been to a popular swimming area and was returning to their vehicle when they encountered a copperhead on the trail. In case some of my readers aren't the outdoors type, I'll clarify that a "copperhead" is not a penny with Lincoln's head face-side up, but one of the varieties of poisonous snakes found in the U.S.

Just for the record, I refer back to my Sage Solutions for Serpent Situations cited near the beginning of this chapter. More specifically, I remind you about my Rule Number 2: If you encounter a snake—just leave it alone.

Our hero had obviously not been instructed in the above guidelines, and when he attempted to move the snake off the trail with his foot, the snake responded in a fairly predictable manner, and the boy was bitten on his right foot. I might cut this young man just a little slack due to his age and therefore potential lack of experience in such matters, but he loses that potential leniency by virtue of the rest of the story. His error in using his foot to try to nudge a snake off the trail was compounded by the fact that he was barefooted at the time! Let's see now, I wonder how *easy* I could make it for this snake to bite me?

Ben Franklin mentions the value of shoes in a slightly different context in *Poor Richard's Almanac*: "A little neglect may breed mischief: for want of a nail the shoe was lost, for want of a shoe the horse was lost . . ." and so on. In this case, for want of both a shoe and a little discretion, a perfectly nice day at the park was lost. Fortunately, the boy was treated by trained park employees and then transported to an area hospital, where he recovered after spending a night in ICU.

Our next lesson in how *not* to do it involves a 26-year-old man, whom I'll simply refer to as C. L. Without casting any aspersions on this individual, you are free to note or disregard the fact that those initials bear a close relationship to the term *clueless*. C. L. was one of sixty-five participants in a program offered by the Appalachian Mountain Club called Wilderness Awareness School. This is an excellent activity by a highly respected group, and at least C. L. was attempting to learn something about the outdoors. Unfortunately, he either wasn't paying close attention in class, or they hadn't yet gotten to the session on reptiles.

This particular course was being taught in July at a facility called Camp Mohican, which is located within the Delaware Water Gap National Recreation Area. According to the park's report, C. L. spotted a four-foot-long rattlesnake in a brushy area near one of the camp's cabins. The camp's director warned him that the snake could strike, and others in the area warned C. L. that he was getting too close to the reptile.

Despite the aforementioned sound advice, the report states that while camp staff and group leaders were away from the area, C. L. continued to "be involved" with the snake for about 45 minutes. I'm not sure exactly what activities with poisonous reptiles fall under the heading of "involvement," but I once again refer you back to my advice at the beginning of this chapter: The only good involvement with a snake is *no* involvement.

As with many other activities forbidden by parents, teachers, laws, or plain old common sense, one small misdeed often leads to another, and once you start down that slippery slope of foolishness, the situation eventually gets away from you. Such was the case for C. L., whose involvement with the snake eventually emboldened him to the point where he decided to pick it up with his bare hands.

Witnesses reported that the snake was initially calm but became agitated as time passed. Fortunately, there was only one eventual victim in this story, even though C. L. was not content to handle the creature himself but reportedly "allowed those around him to touch the snake." Eventually tiring of this game, C. L. put the snake down and attempted to release it. By then, the reptile's patience had clearly worn thin, and once it was free to move at will, it responded by biting our erstwhile naturalist.

The man was taken to an area hospital, where he learned that there was good news and bad news. The good was that the hospital did have the necessary antivenin on hand to treat his bite. The bad was that C. L. was allergic to the medication. Fortunately, at the time of the report he was recovering, but more slowly than would have been possible had he been able to receive the antivenin.

Not very far from the site of this mishap, on another day in July two years earlier, a group of scouts was hiking on the Appalachian Trail at a point where that popular hiking route passes through the Delaware Water Gap National Recreation Area. The reasons for his actions weren't included in the report, but a 42-year-old leader of the group, Mr. B., apparently attempted to handle a snake. In the absence of good information, I'll give him the benefit of the doubt and trust that he had good intentions of simply removing the reptile from the trail.

Once again, I refer you back to my cardinal rule about snakes. According to a succinct summary of the incident in the report, the soon-to-be victim "lost control of the smart end" of the snake and was bitten on the left hand. Fortunately the group was able to establish cell phone contact to call for help, and the leader was evacuated by a litter to a waiting ambulance and admitted to the same hospital that would treat C. L. two summers later. I trust that my readers will benefit from these experiences and avoid giving the good folks at any hospital further practice in dealing with snakebites.

Encounters with snakes *can* have a peaceful resolution for all concerned. As proof, I end this chapter with the award of my "Cool Hand Under Fire, Reptiles Category" to Susan Conrad Ream, a former seasonal park ranger at Golden Spike National Historic Site in Utah. Mrs. Ream was giving an interpretive talk for visitors on a patio at the park's visitor center, when, according to a written account on the park's website, "I had to interrupt the program for a moment and ask a woman and her two small children to move from the bench they were sitting on. A snake was crawling right towards their feet."

"They quickly moved and we went on with the program. After the program was over, a woman asked me if it had been a rattlesnake. She said I stayed very calm if it was! It wasn't. It was a Bull Snake, in Utah commonly called 'Blow Snake' and was about three feet in length." In all fairness, I'll also give bonus points to the woman and her two children, who apparently kept their cool and simply relocated versus bolting for the exit when they were advised of the presence of the reptile.

The French philosopher Voltaire noted, "Common sense is not so common," and several folks in the preceding stories seemed determined to prove that human nature hasn't changed much over the past several hundred years. I trust that you, like Ranger Ream in Utah, will be the exception when it comes to reptiles of any variety. If you ever have any doubts about whether you should become "involved" with a snake—don't!

Don't Believe Everything You Read

I n any discussion about a trip to the Great Outdoors, I always stress the importance of getting good information from a reliable source. More than one outing has taken a nasty turn because someone set out with the best of intentions on what they thought was an easy family hike, but which turned out to be more suitable for an Iron Man Triathlon.

Accurate information for an outdoor trip doesn't include a brief conversation with a guy at the water cooler at work, who made a similar excursion "not very many years ago," or a tip from the clerk at a convenience store near your destination, whose sister's second cousin's boyfriend "used to work at the park." In the same vein, acceptable maps for hiking or boating do not include those you sometimes find printed on paper napkins or disposable placemats at restaurants near a park or recreation area.

I'm confident that readers of this book are reasonable and responsible individuals who would never rely upon such flimsy information, so you may think the above advice is unnecessary. However, consider the following information from The Michigan Lawsuit Abuse Watch (www.mlaw.org/), which conducts an annual "Wacky Warning Label Contest." A recent prizewinner was a cocktail napkin imprinted with a map of the waterways around Hilton Head, South Carolina. The napkin included the following disclaimer: "Caution: Not to be used for navigation." Considering the type of beverage this napkin was intended to accompany, perhaps this admonition was not such a bad idea.

Conditions can change, sometimes quickly, so even though tight budgets are making it harder and harder to find a ranger in many parks, at least make an effort to get firsthand, expert advice. If nothing else, check the park's official website as close to your departure time as possible. Links to every park's site are available at www.nps.gov. If you aren't part of the computer generation, enlist a little help from a 12-year-old relative or neighbor, most of whom are more computer literate than we adults are these days anyway.

"Slim" Woodruff from Grand Canyon, Arizona, is now an accomplished hiker and outdoorswoman. She was gracious enough to share the following experience from some years ago, as proof that even the written word isn't always reliable, and it doesn't take long for guidebooks to get out of date. I'll let her tell the story in her own words:

First, let it be understood that I will go to a great deal of trouble to see an arch, a petroglyph or a fossil. So, when at the end of a summer job I found myself footloose and child-free in Yellowstone National Park, I immediately looked for any of the above items. When I heard that one could see fossil trees still in the upright position, I had my objective.

Working from a ten-year-old guide book I had purchased at a thrift store (I will also go to a great deal of trouble to save a buck) I found the description of a set of fossil trees a mere half mile from the Lamar Road. I parked my 20-year old Ford Falcon, which at that stage of my life served as conveyance, storeroom and spare bed near what I fondly hoped was the trailhead.

Since it was such a wimpy hike, I wore running shoes, shorts and tee shirt. I brought no food, but being a child of the desert, I put in a liter of water. I set off briskly. I gained the top of the hill—no fossils. I searched up and down the side of the hill—no fossils.

I looked at my guidebook again. There were more fossil trees a couple of miles along the way which "couldn't be missed." Okay, that was my new objective.

Striding along purposefully it occurred to me that I was, after all, in grizzly country. But, I told myself, I am in an open plain. *Surely* grizzlies hunt in the *forest*. Later, of course, I found out that grizzlies adapted to hunting on the plains long before Anglos were around, but I found the thought comforting at the time. I picked up a large stick and told myself I could fight off a bear if I had to, and if anyone saw me, I would pretend it was just a hiking stick.

I found the correct drainage and hiked down. Once again, no trees. I clambered up and down fruitlessly (and tree-lessly) for about a half hour. By now I was very, very hungry and a little chilly. I was about to admit defeat when I heard voices. I saw khaki green. A ranger hike! Surely they were heading for the fossil trees!

I surreptitiously joined the end of the line, and yes, they were headed for the trees, and yes, said trees were worth it to a fossil freak like me. By now I was ravenous, and I had to get back to my car before dark. I could have caved in, admitted my error, and begged a snack from someone in the party. Surely the Ranger would have a candy bar secreted about his person for just such an emergency. Someone might even give me a ride back to my car if I were piteous enough.

But along with being a fossil/arch/petroglyph freak I am proud of my hiking prowess. I didn't want anyone, particularly a scion of the Park Service, to know I had (a) gotten lost; (b) set out on a hike with no food and no extra clothes; and (c) thought I could fight off a griz-zly with a stick. I told my stomach sternly to wait its turn, and climbed back up the hill.

I covered the next few miles in record time, trying to beat the dark, the cold, the hunger, and the bears. Obviously I made it unscathed, pulled on a sweatshirt, and gulped down a peanut butter sandwich.

I mentioned my adventure to a Ranger the next day, and was told that, yes, there were fossil trees where I had first looked, but they were quite far down the ridge, difficult to get to, and almost impos-sible to find. "What idiot told you to look for them *there* when there is a perfectly good trail just down the road?" she demanded.

I mumbled something about not trusting anybody these days and wandered off to find a geyser or two. I was fairly sure I could locate those!

These days, it doesn't have to be a slightly dated guidebook to lead you astray in the Great Outdoors. Even the latest technology isn't always the final answer, as the following recent park report demon-strates.

On a day in late May three men set out on a backcountry trip in Utah's Zion National Park. Their intention was to traverse a piece of fairly challenging terrain named Behunin Canyon, a route that requires eight rappels of up to 150 feet.

For benefit of those of you who prefer to keep your feet firmly on the ground, a "rappel" is a technique using ropes and other specialized gear that allows a (hopefully) controlled descent from a higher starting point to a lower ending point. That starting point may be a ledge on a steep cliff face, a hovering helicopter, a tall building, or any other loca-tion from which a free fall would be a most undesirable experience. Rappelling is a necessary skill for those who engage in mountaineer-ing, caving, rescues, and similar adventurous activities, but it requires training and practice as well as the right equipment.

Zion National Park in Utah includes miles of magnificent canyons. Unless you know the terrain, it can sometimes be hard to tell one side of the canyon from another. If you're planning a hike in the backcountry, choosing the right one makes a big difference! (Phil Stoffer, USGS)

If you've ever spent any time in the canyons of the west, you know that to anyone unfamiliar with the area, one rocky chasm can look very much like another. In this particular adventure, the trio of hikers decided to use a high-tech device called a GPS unit to locate their starting point at the head of Behunin Canyon.

GPS (Global Positioning System) units are the current rage in outdoor navigation and even in the big city. In basic terms, these small, handheld devices use satellite technology to pinpoint your location anywhere on the face of the earth and display that information on a small screen. You can even get units for your vehicle that will not only display a map but actually give you audible directions through a small speaker: "Go one block, turn left," and so on.

GPS has been a real boon to people who work and play in the outdoors, but like any other manmade object, it is subject to malfunctions, operator error, and other potential pitfalls. Like all such technological wonders, these little electronic tools also confirm an age-old principle: You get what you pay for. In the case of GPS units, much of what you pay extra for is accuracy.

In retrospect, this group may have been better served to use a reliable standby, a detailed topographical map, to locate their starting point. (As mentioned above in this chapter, this advice does not include the use of maps printed on cocktail napkins or restaurant placemats.) Topographical maps may be considered by some to be old-fashioned and they also require a bit of experience in translating all those squiggly lines into meaningful information, but they're hard to beat for accuracy. At a minimum, such a map or even a detailed written route description could have provided confirmation of the reading on the group's GPS unit. However, if they had used a map, I probably wouldn't have this story to include in my book.

Since I provided a significant clue in the previous sentence, it should come as no surprise to you that this expedition got off to a less than promising start. An inch may be as good as a mile in some circumstances, but not on a GPS screen (or a map) if you're on a backcountry trip, and in this case the error on the ground was actually about a quarter of a mile. That's the distance between their intended jumping-off point and Heaps Canyon, which the group located with the help of their trusty GPS unit, mistook for Behunin Canyon, and entered to launch their adventure.

Some of you who are in the "seen one rocky canyon, seen 'em all" school of thought may be wondering what difference that made, so I'm glad you asked. In contrast to their intended route, a trip through Heaps Canyon is described in the park's report as "a multi-day trip that includes swims through numerous potholes with water temperatures in the 40s and many rappels, including one of 300 feet." If you start such a trip equipped for only a 150-foot rappel and suddenly find yourself faced with one twice that distance, you are definitely in a Major Melancholy Situation and will soon find yourself at the end of the literal rope.

When the men reached the first cliff, they failed to find the expected anchor points for their rappel. Here's one more hint about mountaineering: If you plan to defy gravity, lean out into thin air to descend a steep cliff, and entrust your life to a rope (preferably *two* ropes, including your belay, or safety, line), it's a really, really good idea to be sure the other end of that rope is firmly attached to a *very* secure anchor point.

Our trio discussed discontinuing their trip at this point but instead created an anchor of their own and forged ahead. This decision is an excellent example of what I call macho mania, a close relative of the

HOSS syndrome. Although it's not limited to the male of the human species, this malady does occur more often in that group.

HOSS is closely related to that other underlying cause of numerous bad decisions known as peer pressure. Put an average guy under the age of about sixty with at least one other person in a situation requiring even a hint of daring, and he will usually experience at least a fleeting desire to prove that he's a "real hoss," and therefore up to facing whatever challenge lies ahead. The photo on the cover of this book provides a good example of HOSS in action.

There is a valid physiological explanation for this behavior that explains the derivation of the term HOSS—Hormones Override Sensible Solutions. The passing of years and/or successful escapes from enough close calls eventually diminishes this syndrome in most adults, but that was clearly not the case for our group down in the depths of Heaps Canyon.

Once they realized their mistake, the men were past the point of no return and were unable to backtrack to the canyon rim. I mentioned above that further travel through Heaps Canyon requires swimming through numerous potholes filled with very cold water, another situation for which the group was not equipped. This would have been a really good time to call it a day, find a safe perch, and wait for rescue. They had at least obtained the required permit from the park for this trip, so their failure to return as scheduled would have been noted. HOSS reigned supreme, however, so instead of cutting their losses, they forged ahead.

Fast forward to the next day. The park report states that by then one of the men decided that he'd had enough of swimming through the frigid pools and he climbed to a nearby knoll to await rescue. At last a good decision; better late than never. Violating yet another basic rule of any outdoor trip, the group split up, and the remaining two members continued into the narrowest section of the canyon.

This little adventure was originally intended to be a single day trip, so on the previous evening, the group had been reported overdue. Rangers began a search of their intended route in Behunin Canyon the next morning, but by afternoon concluded that the missing trio were not in that area. A helicopter was then brought in to search a wider area, an expensive step that should gladden the hearts of taxpayers everywhere.

The aircraft did prove to be the key, and all three men were located. A landing was certainly not possible in the canyon, so necessary supplies and radios were lowered to the strandees to allow them to get through another night in relative safety and comfort. Since specialized gear such as thick wetsuits or drysuits are normally required to safely make this trip through frigid waters, rangers were surprised that the two were not victims of hypothermia.

On the following morning, additional equipment was lowered to the pair of "hosses," which enabled them to complete the trip through Heaps Canyon on their own. The one man who had wisely known when to say when and stopped earlier on higher ground was flown out safely by helicopter.

Although this saga had a happy ending, there is a definite moral to the story, ironically provided by the name of the canyon they took by mistake. Don't believe everything you read, including directions on a high-tech GPS unit. Most important, if any outdoor trip just isn't going as planned, be willing to admit that fact and call it a day, before you find yourself in Heaps of trouble.

Λ Nice Place to Visit, But . . .

Λs I mention elsewhere in this book, only a small percentage of park employees actually live on-site. Rangers and others who reside in government quarters are there either to provide round-the-clock security and emergency services, or because the park is so remote there simply aren't any other alternatives within a reasonable distance. If they work for the National Park Service and most other federal agencies, employees pay rent to Uncle Sam, at sometimes pretty expensive rates, so this isn't the great fringe benefit many people assume it to be.

Living in a park, especially one in a rural or remote area, can add a little extra dimension to daily life that may not occur in the big city or even the average suburban neighborhood. Among other things, you learn to plan *way* ahead for your shopping list, since it's often many a mile to the nearest grocery store or other shopping opportunities.

Weather as well as distance can also be a factor when it's time to pick up a loaf of bread or gallon of milk. Glacier National Park in Montana has some of the finest scenery on the planet, but it also has some serious wintertime that occasionally makes travel a challenge. As a result, people who live in that and similar parts of the world learn to stay stocked up on essentials.

Throughout my ranger career I was blessed with a spouse who is a great cook, so I was highly motivated to be sure we were always well-supplied with the raw materials for the most essential food groups: desserts and other home-baked goods. William Camden was an English writer and historian who noted in 1605, "Better halfe a loafe than no bread." While that's certainly true, as the man of the house I felt it was my duty to be certain that the ingredients for whole "loafes" were available at all times.

As part of that effort, I learned that we could buy flour right from the mill at a small town just over the border in Canada, so we'd make that drive occasionally and stock up on a hundred pounds at a time, to go along with fifty pounds of sugar and other basic commodities we kept on hand.

Stocking up does have a flip side, including the need for extra storage for all those goodies. During my assignment at Glacier, we lived in half of a duplex that was well past the age to qualify for listing on the National Register of Historic Places, and which a real estate agent would politely describe as "snug." Both living and storage space were at a premium for a family of four, so we had to be a little creative in stashing our supply of extra provisions.

Our quarters had a tiny attic of sorts, and during the cooler weather months, which in that area extended from about September until the following May, this was a great spot for storing extra groceries. We bought a couple of big, shiny galvanized trash cans with tight fitting lids and kept the extra bags of flour and sugar inside those cans as defense against any unauthorized raiders.

That proved to be a good plan, and sure enough, late one night we heard the unmistakable pitter-patter of little feet above our heads. I borrowed a live trap from a neighbor the next morning and soon found it occupied by an unharmed but otherwise rather unhappy squirrel. I knew it would be futile to simply release him right outside the house, because he had already discovered a relatively warm spot to spend his winter nights.

I drove a mile or so out of town, found a nice grove of trees that closely resembled the one around our house, and turned our unwelcome guest out to his native environment. With a million or so acres in the adjacent park, I hoped the squirrel would find a new, more suitable home.

The above steps confirm two things: I'm an optimist, and squirrels can be very persistent. Two days later, what I presume to be the same critter was back. It took a couple of nights and an upgrade to more tempting bait to lure him back into the live trap, but success was finally

You'll want to keep the snow shovel handy if you're a ranger at Glacier National Park in Montana, as this midwinter view of the author's house proves. (Jim Burnett)

achieved, and this time I made a longer drive before releasing the little rascal back to the world of nature.

In answer to a question some of you may be asking, yes, I did try to locate places around the building where an animal the size of a squirrel could gain entry into our little house in the big woods and I secured a couple of likely suspects. However, the construction of this old two-story dwelling made interior access to parts of the attic virtually impossible for any life form much larger than a squirrel. Well, no problem, you may say. Just get a ladder and have a good look all around the exterior.

That's a great concept, but it was hampered somewhat by the fact that the entire perimeter of the house at ground level was buried under about five feet of snow, which had been sliding off the metal roof for several months and packing into a miniature imitation of a glacier. That made footing for a ladder rather dicey.

To add to the fun, the ambient air temperature at the time didn't move very far above the positive side of zero during the daytime, even excluding the windchill factor. The steeply pitched roof on the two-story house also meant I would need either a Mega-Bubba extension ladder or a nonexistent aerial ladder or bucket truck to reach the highest points on the gables. I'll readily admit that under those circumstances, I was a wimp when it came to wintertime exterior home

Hey Ranger 2

improvements, and this old house needed a lot more work than plugging a few exterior holes. It had a lot of character, but it was also a good candidate for a very extreme makeover. Besides, I'd solved the problem by relocating our temporary resident to another location.

Yeah, right, but at least this time the squirrel's return trip took four days. By now he was pretty wary of that cage, so it required some of Velma's best homemade cookies and an extra night to lure the little rascal back into the live trap. In retrospect, maybe he figured the hike was worth it just to keep getting those snacks, especially since they got increasingly tasty with each succeeding visit.

For my part, this game was growing old, so I made certain it wouldn't go into extra innings. No, I didn't harm the furry raider, but I did drive far enough before releasing him that if they use voter registration cards in the world of squirrels, this critter was definitely in a different precinct, and he would also have to file a permanent change of address to continue receiving any mail.

Adventures with wildlife for park residents aren't confined to the attic or even the house. A fellow ranger spent several years in a park located in a rural area of the West. For purposes of this story and for reasons that will soon become apparent, I'll call him Peter, or just Pete for short. His car didn't get a lot of use, since he normally drove his truck instead, but one day Pete had to take the car to town to have a muffler replaced and get the annual safety inspection.

"Going to town" from that park involved a drive of about 30 miles, so this was one of those errands that required taking some time off work to get to the repair shop during normal business hours. Pete arrived just in time to get the muffler replaced before the mechanic called it a day, but as the young man was writing up the paperwork, he remarked that he was going to reject the renewal of the vehicle's safety inspection.

There turned out to be two problems: a burned out taillight bulb and windshield wipers that weren't working. It's easy to understand how any driver would have been unaware of either situation on a vehicle that isn't on the road very often. It's pretty hard from the driver's seat to know that a taillight isn't working, and I have a hunch that the windshield wipers didn't get a lot of use in this rather arid part of the country.

Pete asked if he could help make those repairs on the spot, to save another long drive to town and the need to take more time off from work. The mechanic agreed, and while he was replacing the light bulb,

Pete went to work on the wipers. The best scenario for a quick fix was a blown fuse, but that would have been way too easy, and the fuse checked out okay. It was time to move on to potentially more complex issues, and time was of the essence.

Some automakers and drivers like to brag about how many "horses" their vehicle has under the hood, but I don't think what Pete found when he popped this hood would be a big selling point with those Madison Avenue advertising executives. Huddled there in the engine compartment was a cottontail rabbit!

The furry hitchhiker had evidently crawled into the vehicle during the time the car was sitting unused out at the park and had taken up residence. It apparently made the ride in this unlikely location all the way into town and was cowering down near the wiper motor, afraid to move. If you've ever approached a rabbit in the wild, you'll know this is not unusual behavior. The animals are apparently genetically programmed to believe, "If I don't move, I'm invisible."

The mechanic was afraid to get near this unexpected auto accessory, referring to it as a "*#@ rodent," but some action was obviously required, so Pete tried to grab it. The rabbit decided it was time to thaw out from its defensive freeze and made a break for it. In a good imitation of the Energizer Bunny, it headed into the back of the shop with our trusty ranger in hot pursuit. The animal got under a large rack of tailpipes that clanged together and sounded like a huge wind chime as Pete and the cottontail played a brief game of tag.

The critter was finally cornered, captured, and put in the trunk of the car for safekeeping. Returning to the business at hand under the hood, Pete soon found that the animal had made a single, razor-sharp cut right through three of the wires leading to the wiper motor. Repairs were made and Peter and the rabbit were on their way, but with a detour to a meeting in another town. The cottontail didn't have much choice other than to go along for the ride, but the return trip in the trunk of the car should have been a lot more comfortable than the journey into town in the engine compartment. He was eventually set free as soon as his chauffeur returned to the park.

Pete notes, "As I released him, I couldn't help but think: 'If rabbits could talk, what a story this one would have to tell his buddies!'" I would certainly agree that this cottontail had probably traveled both farther and faster than any of his kin.

Other contacts with wildlife while living in a park can fit in the "close encounters of the worst kind" category. Early in my career at Grand

Canyon, my wife and I became acquainted with a seasonal (temporary) ranger who lived with his new wife in an ancient mobile home in an outlying area of the park. He and his spouse occasionally came to the village on the South Rim of the park, but one early winter day they seemed to be keeping their distance from acquaintances and strangers alike.

The reason for their unusually standoffish behavior soon became apparent, especially for anyone who happened to be downwind from the pair. Our friend's explanation was short and to the point: "Two skunks had a fight under our trailer last night—and *we* lost!"

The end result was that they, their clothing, and everything else they owned bore ample olfactory evidence that he was telling the truth, and despite all efforts at defumigation, the results of their unintended ringside seats for the polecat version of the WWF (Wildlife Wrestling Federation) lingered for some time. Their problem was complicated by the cold weather, which made it distinctly uncomfortable to leave the windows open to help air out their trailer. This was clearly a case of the lesser of two evils: shiver or stink, and it certainly qualified as a Persistently Melancholy Situation. Shakespeare must have had some experience with skunks because he described this unmistakable odor perfectly when he wrote about "The rankest compound of villainous smell that ever offended nostril."

The opportunity to view the wildlife—skunks excepted—and the scenery are among the pluses of living in many parks, and people who need their daily fix of electronic entertainment probably wouldn't be very happy in some of the rural or downright remote areas. The situation today has probably changed considerably in some of those areas with the advent of small satellite dishes for TV, but during most of my career that option wasn't yet available.

The result was some interesting adventures in attempting to get television or even much in the way of radio stations. Perhaps the most extreme example in my career was at a spot called Willow Beach at Lake Mead National Recreation Area in Arizona. Our only hope for television was to capture a stray signal from Las Vegas, about sixty miles to the north, but that challenge was complicated by two topographical facts of life: There was a large mountain range between us and Las Vegas, and we lived in the bottom of a deep canyon.

Our little residential compound housed two rangers and two maintenance employees and our spouses in a compact quadraplex unit that shared a common roof. Thankfully, none of us was seriously hooked on television, which was a very good thing in our situation. However, we thought it would be nice occasionally to watch a sports event or some special program, so the four families pooled their resources, and my fellow ranger and I accepted the challenge of bringing the miracle of television to our little corner of the desert.

Armed with the largest antenna we could find, some coaxial cable, and several signal amplifiers, we went to work. Placing the antenna anywhere on the four connected houses was a no-go, so we upped the ante a bit. A ledge about fifty feet up the rocky bluff above the houses looked like a promising spot, mainly because it was the only piece of semi-flat ground on the otherwise steep slope. Two of us hauled the antenna to the site, slid the metal antenna pole over a small pipe driven with considerable effort into the rocky ground, and ran the antenna cable down to the houses.

Our home was on the end of the complex nearest the antenna, so we became the reception test site. Proving once again that ranger spouses are worthy of sainthood, my wife endured seemingly endless hours of experiments for the sake of bringing a little culture, or at least *Monday Night Football*, into our home. Thomas Edison would probably have been proud of our persistence for the sake of science, which involved the following process.

Living in a park miles from town can have its pros and cons. The housing area at Willow Beach, Arizona, was a tough place to get a TV signal in the days before satellite dishes. (Jim Burnett)

Velma (The Evaluator) would stand at the open front door of the house where she could both see the television and be within earshot of The Antenna Adjuster (usually me.) The Adjuster scrambled via a circuitous route up to the ledge where the antenna was located and proceeded very slowly to rotate the antenna to various points of the compass to see if anything remotely resembling a picture magically appeared on the TV screen. This process was complicated by the fact that direct eye contact between the two parties of this experiment was not possible due to the terrain.

Something like the following dialogue, shouted vigorously back and forth, then ensued.

Adjuster: "How's that?"

Evaluator: "Nothing."

The Adjuster would then rotate the antenna about two compass points and try again.

"How about now?"

"Nope."

After seemingly endless attempts, a glimmer of hope:

Adjuster: "Got anything yet?"

"A little, but it's *really* snowy."

Hey, that's progress, so try just a little more tweaking.

Adjuster: "Any better?"

Evaluator: "Yeah, I can *almost* make out a picture."

If you've ever had your eyes examined, you've been through that process of looking through that weird device at an eye chart while the optician tries several different possible prescriptions for your lenses. "Tell me which one is better, number one or number two." After a bit, it can get hard to tell much difference. This was similar to the technique with the TV antenna, and "improvements" from one tweak of direction to another soon became speculative.

Evaluator, after the latest adjustment: "I think it was better just a minute ago. Back up to where you were last time."

In retrospect, we later learned from the park's radio technician that under certain atmospheric conditions, whatever TV signal we captured was apparently being bounced off several major electric transmission lines in the area. These lines were located at distances ranging from about three to five miles away as the electrons fly and a thousand vertical feet or so above us, so there was no apparent logic from day to day about which direction the antenna pointed to get the "best" signal.

Eventually, both parties tired of this fun, and so the Adjuster asks the Big Question.

"Do we have a Watchable Picture?"

The spell-checker on my computer didn't recognize the word *watchable,* and we quickly concluded that this is a very relative term. On some days, we actually had a choice between *two* Las Vegas channels, although changing stations usually required going back through the antenna adjustment process. As a result, we quickly settled on one as the consensus favorite most of the time.

We'd occasionally have guests from the outside world spend a night or two with us, and at the appointed hour first-timers would sometimes ask, "Is it okay if we catch the news and weather on TV?" I realize this is a ritual for many Americans, and since our company saw a television set sitting in our living room, this seemed like a reasonable request.

We would agree, but warn them as we pulled the set's "on" button that we might or might not have a Watchable Picture, depending on factors such as the weather, sunspots, the phase of the moon, or whether a recent strong wind had rearranged the direction of our antenna. That was a foreign concept to anyone used to a choice of multiple channels back home in the city, but our meaning quickly became apparent as the screen on the set slowly came to life with a nice black-and-white simulation of a blizzard. Interspersed with the static coming from the speaker there might be a sound vaguely recognizable as human speech.

"Mind if I change the channel?" our guest would ask. "I think the dial must have gotten accidentally switched to a station you don't get out here." (Yes, I know this may come as a shock to some of my readers, but this was also before the days of remote controls and digital tuners. You changed channels by turning a knob on the front of the set, which made an audible clicking sound as you moved from one number on the dial to the next. You can probably find one of those models today somewhere in the Smithsonian.)

"Actually," I'd reply, "that's a pretty Watchable Picture. It helps if you back away from the screen a bit."

I'm sure some engineer reading these words can explain it, but the further you got from the set, the less obvious the "snow" on the screen became, and the better the picture *seemed* to be. The ultimate solution was to go stand outside on the front porch with the door open and view the TV from a distance of about twenty feet through the screen door. Something about the fine mesh on the screen filtered out even more of the snow, although that advantage was offset somewhat by the fact that the size of the picture on our 15-inch set left something to be desired from long distance.

Unfortunately, this "view the screen through the screen" approach was suitable only during certain seasons, since temperatures at Willow Beach were well above 100° much of the year. Under those conditions, the front porch was not highly sought after as a place to position the easy chair and watch your favorite show.

As a joke I tried rounding up a piece of scrap screen mesh and putting it over the front of the TV screen, but the effect just wasn't the same. In retrospect, maybe we could have made up some special eyeglasses, like those you'd get at the movie theater to watch a 3-D movie, but with window screen instead of multicolored lenses.

A plus to this whole scenario is that we got pretty well weaned from television during our time at Willow Beach, and our daughter, who was born there, became an avid fan of books. Both she and our son, who was born five years later in Montana, are still good readers. Life with limited television was a major shock to some people who visited us in several remote locations where we lived, so despite the great scenery, I think some of them ended their stay with the conclusion that parks are a nice place to visit, but they sure wouldn't want to live there!

When All Else Fails, Read the Directions

Let's begin this chapter with a little survey. Nope, you don't have to raise your hand in class or answer out loud, just in case anyone else happens to be within earshot. Simply answer this single question in your mind, right in the privacy of your own home, or wherever else you happen to be while reading this book.

How many times have you acquired an item that required either some assembly or installation and concluded that there was no reason to waste your time reading the instructions? Come on, be honest now! Whether or not batteries are included with the item is not germane to this discussion, and the fact that the instructions were obviously translated from an Oriental language into something only remotely resembling American is not an acceptable alibi. (You'll notice that I didn't say translated into *English*, because there is a chance that the interpreter in Hong Kong or wherever was trained in the classical British version of the language, and perhaps those instructions actually *do* make sense in some neighborhoods of London.)

The amount of time it took you to finally get the item out of the box after managing to remove that seemingly indestructible layer of industrial-strength plastic shrink-wrap is also no defense for jumping right into assembly without benefit of instruction. I'll confess right up front that I've been guilty as charged on multiple occasions, for products including computer software ("Hey, it runs in Windows, how hard can this be?") and various household electronics.

One place where I strongly urge you to draw the line, however, is in the setup of a tent. During the course of my years in the parks, I spent many a day and night working in campgrounds, and I can testify

These campers found a great site at Dinosaur National Monument (Colorado). Such trips are a lot more fun if you know how to set up your tent—and don't leave home without all of the necessary components. (National Park Service)

from personal experience that few situations are as fraught with potential peril as trying to assemble a tent for the very first time. There are several reasons why this is the case, and most of them are closely related to various corollaries of Murphy's Law.

First, based upon a totally unscientific but extensive personal survey, I estimate that there are at least 1,576 different configurations for tents and their accompanying poles currently in use in the world today. Despite what you might think, aptitude in logical thinking or good mechanical skills is of relatively little use in guessing how those parts fit together to form a completed whole, unless you've been through that activity at some time in the recent past with this specific tent.

Second, unless you confirm by an actual test setup before you leave home that all of the necessary poles and other accoutrements are present and accounted for, the odds are strongly stacked against you that one critical piece will be missing when you try to erect your tent in the campground. This axiom holds true whether this is a brand-new tent still in the Original Factory Carton or one you borrowed from a friend or relative, although the odds of trouble are considerably higher for a previously used tent.

I can definitely verify this last statement from personal experience, based upon the number of miscellaneous tent parts I have found in vacant campsites over the years. For whatever reason, a vast assortment of tent pegs, poles, ropes, and other accessories are left behind when the owners depart. I decline to speculate about whether this phenomenon is a function of breaking camp in haste, in the dark of night, or other factors, but I will go out on a pretty stout limb and predict that many a tent that has actually been used at least once in the Great Outdoors is now missing at least one important component.

Finally, there is a direct correlation between the discovery that a key item is missing, the time of day, the weather, and the distance back to the place where the tent was borrowed or purchased. Irrespective of plans for an early daylight arrival at the campground and assurances from the meteorological experts that climatic conditions will be ideal, any campers who are making their initial attempt to erect a tent will likely find themselves trying to do so both in the dark and under assault by either rain, sleet, snow, hail, high winds, swarms of mosquitoes, or some combination of the above.

Snoopy probably got the idea for the beginning of his infamous novel from these situations, because many a camper has found it was indeed a dark and stormy night as he hastily unrolled that bundle of nylon or canvas and attempted a speedy setup. There is apparently a religious dimension to these situations, perhaps analogous to those foxhole conversions you read about in wartime, because I have heard numerous vocal imprecations for divine intervention uttered in the midst of such trials. (I have also heard some occasional comments during these experiences that fall into the blasphemy category, but this book is rated for All Audiences, so we won't go there.)

I can confirm point number two above (do a trial run before leaving home) from recent personal experience. My wife and I purchased a new tent not long ago and, taking my own advice for a change, decided to set it up in our living room before attempting to actually use it out in Real Nature. Okay, I'll admit that my wife strongly suggested this test, but I had the grace not to object. For most guys, simply agreeing to go along with such an idea from their spouse earns the same number of points as initiating the plan themselves.

We cleared a suitable area on the floor and unpacked our future outdoor home. This particular model was touted as being freestanding, with the nylon shell supported by an impressive external skeleton of sturdy metal poles. In the real world, of course, the perimeter of the tent would be firmly attached to the ground with stakes (also known as "pegs"), but that was a step we obviously omitted during this test drive in our living room. For essential information about the very important subject of tent stakes I refer you to the separate chapter in this book, "There's a Lot at Stake."

Our previous tent from many years ago had been both smaller and less complex than this new version, so I graciously consented to scan the printed instructions. This proved to be a wise move, since after considerable time trying to translate the instructions into American and then correlate the array of poles with the minuscule drawing on the single-page Owners Manual, we concluded that we were in fact missing one piece. Congratulating ourselves on our wisdom in discovering this fact in the comfort of our own living room, I concluded that we could at least run through a setup and get the general idea.

Due to the missing section of pole, the end result was a tent with a distinct list to one corner, which turned out to have an unexpected advantage. Since I am about six feet tall and at this point in life have absolutely no interest in trying to get dressed while kneeling in a low-roofed tent, I had insisted on a model with more than enough head room to allow me to stand fully upright inside. That's still a great plan, but I discovered that there is a good reason that campgrounds out in the Real Outdoors don't have ceiling fans. Fortunately, the sag resulting from the missing pole allowed us to complete our living room run-through without damage to the overhead fan blades.

There are a couple of points to this discussion. The obvious one, of course, is that I'm glad I learned my lesson from the experience of countless other campers who didn't discover that a critical part was missing until they were well into that setup in the dark and rain. Perhaps just as important is the advice that *you* should make a similar practice run as far in advance of your outing as possible. Don't wait until the night before your departure. Here's why.

Upon discovery of the missing section of pole, we located the toll-free number for the manufacturer, and my spouse volunteered to ring them up and request a replacement part. She soon learned that Customer Service was staffed only during Regular Business Hours on Weekdays. This is another lesson you might take to heart if you discover a missing part for your own tent and assume that Operators Are Standing By at all hours to take your call.

Upon resumption of Regular Business Hours the next day, my bride resumed her mission. Fortunately, we still had the Original Factory Carton and the Owners Manual, so she was able to provide the model number of the tent and the specific part number for the

AWOL pole. I'm willing to bet that in most cases involving a borrowed tent, the original box, instructions, and parts list are no longer available. Even with all of that information a fairly lengthy conversation with Customer Service was required, a pretty strong hint that obtaining the correct replacement would border on the impossible without the magic part number.

Some of you veteran campers are probably thinking, "It's *only* a tent pole. How hard can this be?" For the benefit of anyone who hasn't had firsthand experience with the current generation of tents, I should explain that our model included poles in a surprising variety of lengths, diameters, and shapes. The complexity involved was confirmed several days later, when our friendly UPS driver arrived with a box from the tent maker.

After supper that evening, I opened the package, dumped out the promised pole, and had one of those "Uh-oh" moments. I had to consult the Owners Manual once again to confirm my suspicion but soon determined that we now had an extra of one pole section but were still missing the needed replacement. A second phone call to Customer Service finally produced the needed part, but I'm sure glad we weren't sitting around a campground waiting for this item to arrive before we could set up our home in the woods.

In case any novice campers are reading this chapter, I'll give you some insider information that will make you sound like a real pro when you start to set up a modern tent. For convenient packing and transporting, most tent poles break down into short sections. It takes several such sections to form a complete pole, and to keep each set together, a heavy elastic "shock cord" often runs through the hollow innards of the pole. Each end of this cord is attached to one of the far ends of the pole. This cord has several purposes.

First, it keeps the sections of that particular pole joined together and reduces the time required to match up the correct parts from a stack of very similar poles. Otherwise, most of us would spend the entire weekend trying to sort out Pole Section AA from the almost but not quite identical Pole Section AB.

Second, once you get the technique down pat, the shock cord allows you to simply grab one end of the sections of pole, give it a little flick, and *voilà!*—the elastic shock cord causes all of the sections to spring quickly into position, forming one unified whole. I will not take the time to research the derivation of the term *shock cord* as used here, but I will note that the term is an appropriate one for anyone who has not previously experienced the above phenomenon. Should an unwary camper pick up one of those disassembled stacks of shock-corded poles and inadvertently give it a shake, the action of that stack of little short poles suddenly transforming itself into one long pole *can* be quite a shock. Furthermore, that shock is greatly magnified if another member of your group happens to be located within the impact zone of the extended pole. Jesting aside, this could be a potential safety problem, so be forewarned.

There is yet one more tip to be learned from the above information. If you're new to camping, it is a good idea to try to borrow the requisite gear from a trusted source prior to making an investment in your own stuff. If you discover that tent camping just isn't for you, it's better to reach that conclusion before you spend a bundle on equipment. Camping is a lot like broccoli—either you like it or you don't, and there's not a lot of middle ground, but you won't know until you try it.

If you do borrow equipment for camping or any other outdoor activity, just recall my earlier admonition about having the owner show you how all that stuff works before you leave home. The old expression "something borrowed, something blue" is traditionally applied to items used in a wedding ceremony. I'll amend it slightly to say that something borrowed for a camping trip can definitely *make* you blue if you find yourself miles from civilization without a clue how to use it—and even if you actually have the directions, they're notoriously hard to read in the rain by flashlight.

23

Old MacDonald Had a Farm—
But Not a Park

One of the great things about working as a ranger is that you never know what weird situation may be lurking just around the next bend in the road or trail. I learned several years into my career to avoid thinking, "Surely I've seen it all by now," because *no* one lives long enough to experience all the surprises life in the parks can hold!

An example occurred about 10 P.M. on a late September night at Willow Beach, Arizona, one of the developed areas in Lake Mead National Recreation Area. Like all good rangers I was making one more "routine patrol" through my little domain to be sure all was well with the world before calling it a night, but this trip was about to depart from whatever passes for normal in a major recreation area.

As I approached the boat ramp and marina, I had to slam on the brakes of my trusty government pickup truck to avoid driving into the back of an unlighted trailer parked squarely in the middle of the road. I turned on my emergency lights, climbed out of my truck, and was immediately greeted by the unmistakable sound and smell of a barnyard.

Lake Mead is serious desert country, and even outside the park there's not much in the way of agricultural activity, so domestic livestock were not exactly a common item in this neighborhood. I walked up to an obviously homemade trailer about the size of a double bed with wooden sides apparently constructed from salvaged lumber. The trailer was hooked to the back of an ancient station wagon, which sagged somewhat dejectedly toward the left rear tire.

There was no sign of the humans who had presumably driven the vehicle to this unlikely spot, but the dim glow from a nearby streetlight and the beam from my flashlight revealed a rather unusual cargo in the trailer: a large sow with four piglets and a crate containing two rather bedraggled chickens. Before I had time to fully conclude where this scenario might be headed, I heard the sound of a sheep bleating off to my left. Ever so briefly, I wondered if my spouse had been correct when she admonished me recently about working too many hours out in the desert heat.

I glanced in the direction of the sound and spotted the apparent driver of the car, followed by what I presumed to be his spouse and children. There were approximately four to six youngsters, but that number was only a guess, since they were obviously running off some energy after being cooped up in the vehicle. Perhaps you've heard the expression about "kicking the anthill" and the swarm of activity that quickly results in the insect world. This was a similar scene except the players consisted of small human beings rather than ants, and getting an accurate count in that melee was not a high priority for me at the moment.

The eldest of the offspring appeared to be about twelve years old, and rather than frolicking with his siblings he was leading a sheep back up the ramp toward the car and trailer. My guess was that he had been giving the animal a drink in the river at the foot of the boat ramp. Whoever said "you can lead a horse to water, but you can't make it drink" had apparently not spent much time in the desert, because horses, cows, and any other life forms usually gladly lapped up what-ever water was available in these dry climes. The evening was still warm, and I suspect the sheep had enjoyed his or her trip to the river. Thankfully the animal had been sheared and was sporting a short sum-mer haircut.

I waited for the group to make their way back to the vehicle, and a polite conversation ensued. The man said they had bought the ani-mals in Oregon and were taking them home to Georgia. While driving down U.S. Highway 93 they had seen the sign for the turnoff to Willow Beach and deduced that if there was a beach, there must also be some water. Fortunately for the sake of their animals their assumption was correct, and they had stopped at our little oasis to let the animals cool off and get a drink.

I was definitely relieved to learn that water had already been brought to the pigs and chickens, which would remain securely in the trailer. My firsthand experience with pork on the hoof was pretty limited, but I suspected that mama pig and her four little piglets would not have responded very well to an attempt at orderly herding down to the river and back to the trailer.

The idea of a piggy rodeo there on the shores of the river wasn't very appealing to me right at that moment, and the last thing I wanted was ham on the lam if any of those animals decided they'd had enough of traveling and chose to make a break for it. Under the circumstances, if they'd done so I can't say that I would have blamed them.

Upon further investigation, I learned that there weren't any functioning lights on their trailer because the wiring had all been safety-pinned together and had come apart somewhere along the way. The essential ingredient for all such projects, duct tape, had apparently been in short supply when this group assembled their rig.

There was considerable wisdom in their desire to get as far down the road as possible during the relatively cooler nighttime hours, but it was obvious that I couldn't let them continue on their way in the dark without any lights on the trailer. Kindhearted folks that we are, rangers never want to see anyone unnecessarily placed in harm's way, but I also had an ulterior motive for ensuring the safety of this little band.

In this rather isolated corner of northwest Arizona, the two rangers from Willow Beach were the first responders for any accidents along a lengthy stretch of U.S. Highway 93. We also operated the only thing that passed for an ambulance for many a mile. If this entourage was involved in a "situation" anywhere nearby, guess who would get the call? The thought of having to render emergency care in the event of an accident to the man, woman, and a bunch of kids, not to mention mama pig and four piglets, a sheep, and two chickens, was not a cheerful one. I definitely had plenty of incentive to get them back on the road in a safe and orderly manner.

A quick foray into the essential supplies in my truck came up with not only some duct tape, but also some electrical tape and wire. A few minutes' work had the trailer wiring roadworthy, if not exactly up to code, and with a sigh of relief I watched the group head up the hill and out of sight.

Some of you probably have the same question I did that night, but I was afraid to ask if there was a sudden shortage of livestock in Georgia that required that they be imported all the way from Oregon! I can only presume that the price was truly right, and it just seemed like too good a bargain to pass up.

There may not have been any other sheep or barnyard animals in the neighborhood at Lake Mead, but that's not always the case at Dinosaur National Monument on the Colorado/Utah border. One of the prime visitor activities at that park, in addition to observing dinosaur fossils, is a raft trip on the Green River. Along with some fine scenery and premier river running, one of the attractions of those trips is the chance to see wildlife, including bighorn sheep.

In the summer of 2006, rafting groups began to notice something unusual along the riverbank—a small flock of *domestic* sheep. These animals apparently had no connection to anyone named either Mary or MacDonald, nor were they en route from Oregon to Georgia, but they did present a problem. Any time domestic sheep and wild bighorn sheep share the same territory there is the possibility of transmission of disease between these distant relatives. That risk made it a matter of

The Green River in Dinosaur National Monument (Colorado and Utah) can provide a great river trip, but it's a rare day when the passengers on rafts are anything other than humans. (National Park Service)

Old MacDonald Had a Farm—But Not a Park

some urgency to conduct a sheep roundup and return the wandering woollies to their usual home on the range.

In this rugged canyon country, where access to the river by vehicle, horseback, or even foot is limited, this was a job easier said than done. The sheep had obviously found a way to reach the water, but perhaps their clandestine route was some distance from the location where they were most recently spotted. Even if their path could be determined, there was no assurance humans could use it to escort the sheep back to greener pastures. When herding animals, wild or domestic, is involved, the reverse of "what goes up must come down" isn't necessarily true.

The likely owners of the sheep were contacted and taken down the river to confirm the identity of the animals and help plan for their removal. Because the sheep were found in an area where they could not easily be herded over land, it was determined that the best solution was to evacuate them by water. Even though most sheep may be white as snow, that doesn't mean they are engineered for a swim, especially through whitewater, so some other means of getting them downstream was going to be required.

On Saturday, July 15, 2006, it is possible that history was made on the Green River, or for all I know, on any other river in a national park—a river rafting trip was completed by a small flock of sheep. Four park employees and eight ranchers made their way downriver from Rainbow Park, successfully collected and sedated six of the animals, and placed them aboard the boats.

In case you wonder about the sedation, I'd simply ask if you have ever traveled in a vehicle with a cat, dog, or any other animal that really didn't want to be there. If so, I think you can readily understand why the people who would be sharing the confined space in an inflatable raft on a river with these critters weren't interested in a floating rodeo event. Sheep have a reputation for being gentle, docile animals, but they are also easily spooked and can be quite a handful if they are determined not to participate in an activity.

I suspect that being loaded onto a raft and taken on a ride down the Green River would put the needle on the Bleat-O-Meter into the red zone, resulting in a distinct lack of cooperation on the part of the sheep. I certainly agree that sending them off to dreamland before their adventure was both a wise plan and much kinder to the animals. In answer to the obvious question, I have absolutely no idea what (if anything) sheep count when they are trying to go to sleep, but I'm confident their dreams in their induced slumber were a lot happier than the nightmare of a wide-awake boat trip. Depending upon the water level in the river on that particular day, it could have been a wild and woolly ride.

Once the animals were safely dozing and loaded, the rafts were rowed down the Green River to the nearest boat ramp at Split Mountain, where their passengers were offloaded and returned to more familiar territory. I'm sure all the humans involved hope this event made a strong enough impression on the sheep that they will avoid any future visits to the shores of the Green River.

An unwanted guest of a totally different variety provided an unusual experience for a park ranger at the Golden Gate National Recreation Area in California. Other beneficiaries of this adventure included an unknown number of commuters trying to cross the famous bridge that gives this park its name.

On a late afternoon in August 2005, Ranger Sam Eddy was in his patrol car on the bridge, stuck in northbound traffic along with other motorists due to an accident up ahead. Ranger Eddy noted that the southbound traffic had also come to a halt for an unknown reason. Since motorists who are rubbernecking and trying to get a look at an accident in the opposite lane often end up causing a mishap themselves, such tie-ups in both directions on any highway are unfortunately not uncommon.

In this case, however, Ranger Eddy soon noted the cause of the southbound gridlock. The ranger spotted a 300-pound ostrich walking toward him in the opposite lane. Eddy made a U-turn and, with the assistance of bridge patrol officers and one of their tow trucks, managed to herd the bird into a nearby maintenance yard.

Their prudence in handling this roundup was justified, since according to the American Ostrich Association, these are the world's largest living birds. Fully grown adult males are eight to nine feet in height and weigh 350–400 pounds, while females will weigh up to 300–350 pounds. It's also a good thing a chase didn't ensue, because these birds are capable of running at speeds of about 40 mph, which is probably faster than rush-hour traffic at times on this busy bridge. Fortunately the entire episode was over in about ten minutes and the AWOL bird was returned to its owner.

Investigation revealed that the escapee was one of two ostriches being transported in a northbound van when it broke out of the back of the vehicle and made a run for it. Perhaps this Big Bird had left her

The Golden Gate Bridge is a famous landmark and scenic attraction as well as an important transportation route. It's crossed by thousands of vehicles a day—but not by very many runaway Big Birds. (Phil Stoffer, USGS)

heart in San Francisco and was determined to go back and find it, or maybe she simply saw a chance to select a different destination than the van driver had in mind.

Fortunately, my own experience in ostrich herding is virtually nonexistent, and I'm happy to omit that from my life list of adventures. This is yet another unusual example of those tasks that fall under the "other duties as assigned" category in a ranger's job description. This situation confirms that a bird in the van is worth two on the lam, and as the result of his successful roundup, Ranger Eddy is awarded first place in the "What did *you* do at work today?" award. Some of you may have jobs that involve even more bizarre incidents than those faced by the people who work in parks, but if you think you've "seen it all" by now, I'd offer one piece of advice on behalf of this ol' ranger: Don't bet the farm on it.

Over the Hill and into the Woods . . .

I realize the title of this chapter is not quite the same way to get to grandmother's house as described in that famous poem and song, but a significant percentage of parks have hills and/or woods, and those can provide the setting for some unusual and unexpected detours. That was certainly the case at the Buffalo National River in the Ozarks of northern Arkansas, a very scenic part of the country and apparently a very difficult area in which to drive a large truck. I base that observation on the fact that during my five years as a ranger at that park we seemed to deal with an inordinate number of 18-wheeler accidents.

This situation was largely the result of the steep, winding roads that crossed the Buffalo River in four locations along its more than 150-mile length. Those switchbacks and sharp downgrades were simply too much for the brakes of a number of trucks in the hands of inexperienced drivers, although amazingly, injuries to the drivers themselves were almost always minor. The trucks and cargoes, however, didn't fare as well.

My fellow rangers and I had the dubious opportunity to deal with spilled loads of frozen chickens, live chickens, chicken feed, chicken fat, thousands (or maybe it was millions) of tiny fiberglass beads headed for a nearby boat factory, table legs, charcoal, gasoline, and, perhaps most bizarre of all, live catfish.

In that case, a truck carrying a load from a fish hatchery had overturned and dumped hundreds of small fish all over the roadway. We were unable to muster enough containers of water in time to rescue most of the escapees and the truck driver didn't want the fish to go to waste. The solution was to simply declare it a "no limit day" for fishing in the middle of Highway 14, no license required, and nearby residents and a few passing motorists took home the makings of quite a few fish dinners.

Okay, so these fish *were* a little on the small side, but the price was right, and it just takes a few more "catfish fingers" than filets to make a meal. This situation was also a pretty good demonstration of the power of the grapevine in a rather sparsely populated rural area, and it didn't take long for enough "fishermen" to arrive at the scene to complete the cleanup.

During my career I observed that "civic duty" cropped up frequently among the general population whenever something went amiss out on the fringes of civilization. Perhaps people everywhere were a little more willing several decades ago to get involved and help a stranger in an emergency, and that still tends to be the case in remote areas of the country. Given our limited staffing in the parks, helpful bystanders often came in handy. Sometimes, however, the best of intentions can go awry.

That was the case when I received one of those infamous middle-of-the-night phone calls at Lake Mead National Recreation Area. My duty station was at Willow Beach, a rather remote outpost in far northwestern Arizona. The information was sketchy, but the county sheriff's office had received a report of a possibly serious 18-wheeler accident on U.S. 93.

About twenty miles of that major highway ran through the part of the park that included Willow Beach, and as the closest emergency responders the two rangers stationed there were sometimes called upon to help the state and county authorities when something untoward happened on that road. The county dispatcher explained that a state trooper was en route, but since I was at least a half-hour closer, perhaps I could run up and see what I could do in the meantime?

The four-mile drive from Willow Beach to U.S. 93 was a steady, winding upgrade, and the best guess about the location of the accident was a mile or two south once I reached the main road. About halfway up the hill, I began to see an ominous glow on the horizon. One thing I didn't have was access to a fire truck, and for that matter, neither did anybody else for many a lonely desert mile. Under those circumstances, this light in an otherwise pitch-black night suggested a Potentially Very Melancholy Situation.

The color of this glow was an unusual but vaguely familiar pinkish-red, and as I reached the highway and turned south toward the scene, it continued to grow in intensity. I rounded the final curve, topped the last hill, and had my first look at the accident site. Well, not exactly, because my view of the entire highway was obscured by a weird cloud of fuchsia smoke.

Fuchsia is the term fashion designers use to describe a range of hues that's a cross between pink, red, blue, and purple and that otherwise defies classification on the color charts. It comes into vogue from time to time, and if you're a male, you'll probably recognize it from a conversation with a spouse, daughter, or other lady that went something like this.

"How do you like my new blouse (or sweater, scarf, or . . .)?" The first time this question arises you may make the mistake of asking what that color is *called*, after which time *fuchsia* is probably indelibly entered into your memory as a color you're glad isn't a guy thing. I make this unusual digression in this tale to help you picture the bizarre scene that lay before me on an otherwise dark desert night.

The air was very calm and almost damp, which in that climate meant the relative humidity was somewhere in the neighborhood of 10 percent. As a result, this glowing cloud of smoke was just hanging there on the road as it gradually grew in volume. It looked like a scene from a rock concert whose smoke machine had experienced either a bad drug trip or a nervous breakdown, or perhaps from a Hollywood action movie that had a very limited budget for special effects.

One of the basic lessons in emergency response is, "Don't become part of the problem," which translates into: Don't barge headlong into a situation until you have some idea of what you're facing. This dictum was thoroughly emphasized in a hazardous materials course I once attended, during which the instructor boiled all those complicated chemical names down into one basic rule: "Just assume it's *all* methyl-ethyl bad stuff!"

Following that advice, I pulled my vehicle to the side of the road well short of the scene to size up the circumstances. Thankfully, my dilemma was quickly solved when what to my wondering eyes should appear but a human form, walking toward me apparently unscathed out of the depths of the fiery smokescreen.

Before I could fully react to this development, he or she paused and a smaller, bright fuchsia glow suddenly appeared in his hand, then fell to the ground. At that moment, I realized why the color of the apparent "fire" looked so familiar.

You've undoubtedly driven past an accident scene or a disabled vehicle and seen a few emergency flares in use—those devices that slightly resemble a stick of dynamite and that can be ignited to emit a small, bright flame to warn others of a hazard. As they burn, they also produce a small cloud of smoke. I'm willing to bet, however, that you have never seen as many flares burning in one place at one time as I did that night. Once the number of simultaneously burning traffic flares moves into three digits, the overall effect is something almost impossible to describe.

I eased my trusty Chevy Carryall up the road, got out, and approached the King of Flares.

"Hi there, what's the situation?" I asked.

"Hey, Ranger. Got a big rig jackknifed up ahead, on its side. Most of the road's blocked, so I thought I'd better put out a few flares to warn any other traffic."

I decided to defer any discussion about "a few flares" until I had the rest of the essential information.

"Any other vehicles involved, and anybody hurt?"

"Nope. Think the driver may have started to doze off and he overcorrected on the curve, but he's okay. He's sitting up there on the side of the road."

I silently hoped the driver was upwind of the scene and knew it was now time for the obvious question.

"Where'd you *get* all these flares?" I asked.

"Off my truck," the man replied in a very matter-of-fact tone. "I drive for a big auto supply chain, and I've got at least a couple of hundred cases on this load. It was sure lucky they were right at the back of the trailer so I could get right to 'em. Didn't figure the company would mind if I used a few to help out in a real *emergency*. Good public relations, and all that, you know." My helpful citizen paused as an idea clearly had just surfaced in his mind. "Hey, maybe you could write a letter explaining how I helped out and all?"

Before we parted company, I did write a note explaining the circumstances and gave it to the driver before he resumed his journey. I hope that satisfied any questions that arose from the folks in charge of inventory control for his company, because he certainly arrived at his destination more than a few cases shy of a full load.

Several years later and back at the Buffalo National River in Arkansas, a different kind of truck accident provided some excitement for a group of park visitors. Ed Winfrey from Sibley, Missouri, shared the following story, which occurred at the Buffalo in the summer of 2001. Ed was leading a Venture Crew of boy scouts—older boys with some hiking experience—on a fifty-mile backpacking trip on the Buffalo River Trail.

The group had just completed shuttling vehicles to the end point of their hike and was enjoying a picnic lunch at the South Boxley Trailhead before starting out on their expedition. Little did they know that they were about to have a totally unexpected adventure.

As they were finishing their lunch, they could hear a big truck laboring down the hill on the highway just above their location. Suddenly there was a tremendous metallic slapping sound and a tractor trailer rig crashed through the trees and brush and slid down the steep slope, passing within forty feet of the scout group. This was a very undesirable case of down the hill and through the woods, and the truck continued out into one of the hayfields that cover most of the river bottomland in the area.

The rig was on its side as it crossed the road ditch and tore through a fence. Ed dropped his half-eaten apple and ran to the cab seconds after it came to a halt. The front wheel up in the air was spinning 'round and 'round, and the diesel engine was still running. Ed could smell the hot brakes, and there was smoke of various sorts coming from the truck.

I know that any good scout or leader is supposed to "Be Prepared," but I suspect this is a situation that isn't covered in a standard merit badge manual. I'll let Ed tell you what happened next in his own words:

I paused a second to evaluate whether it was safe to get any closer and just as I was going to climb up and look into the cab, lo and behold, a hand reached out of the open window and the driver's head appeared. He started to climb out. I hated to do it but I stopped him and asked if he could switch off the engine first. He did so and soon joined me on the ground. "Praise Jesus" was his only comment!

I was equally thankful that I didn't have to look into that cab and see a severely injured driver. The boys and the rest of our leaders joined me but the only first aid we could apply was to get the driver to sit down. He had not a mark on him. After he regained some composure he said his brakes had overheated and failed on the hill. He had been driving the truck for less than a week. Maybe he needed a little more training before tackling those steep mountain roads?

It turned out that the wrecked truck was a "reefer," a refrigerated rig that was hauling something like thirty thousand pounds of fresh chicken parts. When the trailer hit the ditch, the top tore off and there was chicken everywhere! Chicken in the road, chicken in the ditch, chicken in the field, chicken in the trees.

According to a slogan on some of the state license plates, Arkansas is the "Land of Opportunity," and although this opportunity only knocked once, it wasn't wasted. Some of the local housewives were there with dishpans to collect some fryer parts for supper even before the ambulance arrived!

We talked to a ranger a couple of days later, and he told us that they have those kinds of accidents often enough that the chicken company keeps a contractor on-call for cleanup. When we went back to South Boxley to pick up our vehicle, it was five days after the accident and the only clue that there had been a wreck was the torn up fence. It was an impressive clean up job—or maybe the "locals" had been eating a lot of chicken!

My favorite part of the story earns Ed and his group the Most Creative Title for a Truck Wreck Award. He notes that "ever since, whenever we talk about eating chicken, instead of fried chicken, we say '*slide*' chicken!"

A totally different kind of slide occurred on a winter afternoon at Olympic National Park in the northwestern corner of Washington. That park is a hands-down winner for a spot on the list of crown jewels in our National Park System, and with its wide variety of resources it has something to appeal to almost everyone.

Included among Olympic's more than 900,000 acres are magnificent mountains and glaciers, and spectacular rock formations along more than sixty miles of wild Pacific beaches. The old-growth temperate rain forests on the park's western side receive an average of 140 inches of rain per year, but less than 40 miles to the east, the town of Sequim records an average of only about 17 inches of annual precipitation. If you want variety, this park has it!

Among the favorite locations in Olympic for locals and tourists alike is Hurricane Ridge, which is reached by a 17-mile drive that winds up forested slopes to an elevation of 5,242 feet. This is a great spot for postcard-quality summer views, and it's even popular during the wintertime for hardy snow lovers. Nearby Mount Olympus receives most of its 200 inches of annual precipitation as snowfall, so the road to Hurricane Ridge is normally open only on weekends in the winter— and even on those days travel is "conditions permitting."

One couple making that trip on the afternoon of February 25, 2006, received a lot more than they bargained for, and they can thank the combination of alert fellow motorists, daring rescuers, and a hearty dose of divine intervention for the ride of a lifetime.

The park dispatch center received a report from a motorist of tire tracks in the snow along the Hurricane Ridge Road. That in itself is not unusual, but these particular tracks ran off the side of the highway and then disappeared over a steep cliff. This version of over the hill and into the woods is neither a positive nor a desirable sign under any circumstances, unless you happen to be one of those special effects daredevils from Hollywood filming an action-packed scene.

The witnesses stopped and were able to make voice contact with the occupants of the missing vehicle, but they were unable to see them due to the terrain and vegetation. These helpful citizens made an educated guess that the errant car was a considerable distance down the hillside.

Help soon arrived from the park, Olympic Mountain Rescue, the Clallam County Sheriff's Search and Rescue team, and the ski patrol from the Hurricane Ridge Ski Area. That may sound like a big response for a single-vehicle accident, but this is not your typical car-in-the-ditch scenario. Rescuers had to contend with 45- to 80-degree slopes in the snow and vegetation to descend to the final resting place of the vehicle.

I can only imagine their amazement to find that the occupants had suffered only minor cuts and bruises and had been able to extricate themselves from a 1992 Jeep Cherokee. The rescuers' surprise can't have even come close to the relief experienced by the driver and passenger of the vehicle, which had incredibly rolled approximately 450 feet down steep slopes and over two cliff faces before landing on its top, wedged between two trees!

The people who design rides for theme parks spend a sizeable sum to stay ahead of the competition and come up with the latest and greatest in the "thrills and chills" category. I suspect that there is a fertile field for opportunity if some engineer could just recapture what the pair in that Jeep must have experienced on their off-road journey!

Aided by rescuers, the duo were able to make their way back up the difficult slope to the road. This was a case where, under the circumstances, everything worked in favor of the vehicle's occupants. If you ever doubt the value of wearing seatbelts in a vehicle, this couple's situation provides one of the best testimonials that I've heard in a long, long time.

I know that kids of all ages enjoy sliding on the snow, and I've seen that activity conducted using everything from plastic sleds to trash can lids to pieces of cardboard. However, this pair's experience confirms

Over the hill—with vigor. The two occupants of this vehicle are living proof that wearing a seat belt is a great idea. Incredibly, the pair walked away from this scene after their Jeep plunged 450 feet down a mountainside in Olympic National Park. (National Park Service)

that vehicles do *not* make good substitutes for snowboards, hang gliders, bowling balls, or any combination thereof. Since their Jeep's final ride was an unplanned adventure and the result of a number of factors including a snowy, slippery highway, I can't in good conscience award them any bonus points for bravado. Even so, in contrast to the earlier story of the truck at the Buffalo River, *their* amazing ride and slide was definitely not one for chickens!

There's a Lot at Stake

For the benefit of any of you who are not tent campers, one of the essential accessories for setting up tents is the stakes. These are items that roughly resemble a very large nail that's been on steroids. Stakes are passed through loops sewn around the bottom edge of the tent and are then driven into the ground, thereby anchoring the tent in place against the effects of wind or other elements that might seek to displace it to a location that was not of your choosing.

Tent stakes, incidentally, are sometimes referred to by the alternative term *pegs*. I sometimes like to use the word *pegs* as a reminder that when you are ready to set up your tent, you're in deep tapioca if you've forgotten to bring the necessary number of pegs, which is the plural form of a word that means **P**ositively **E**ssential **G**ear.

If you prefer the term *stake* for these items, that's also perfectly appropriate, because I will stake my reputation as an expert observer of campground adventures on the following prediction: If for some reason you decide to erect and occupy one of those freestanding models of tents without using a sufficient number of tent stakes to secure the tent to the ground, natural factors seeking to relocate your tent *will* occur.

The weather may be absolutely clear and calm when you set up camp, and your site may appear to be totally sheltered by the terrain, but you can count on sufficient wind to suddenly arise out of nowhere and challenge your decision to omit those stakes. This event will create considerable inconvenience and almost always occurs at the most inopportune time—such as in the middle of the night during a driving rainstorm.

I'll concede that if your tent is small enough and the weight of the items inside the tent—including the occupant(s)—is large enough, it may be possible to win this battle. The victory, however, can be a hollow one, since it will often come at the cost of a good night's sleep, so my advice is to save yourself some grief and be sure you take and use enough stakes. Some backpackers who use small, lightweight, free-standing tent models prefer to shun stakes altogether for the sake of saving weight and time, so the choice is yours.

While we're on the subject of tent pegs/stakes, I'd suggest that when you're conducting the recommended pre-trip test setup of your tent, you make careful note of two key factors. The first is how many pegs are needed to properly anchor the tent to the ground. You can determine this by counting the number of loops sewn into the bottom edge of the tent, and then multiplying this number by at least two. I'll explain the reason for this formula in a moment.

From the looks of their nice, tight tent, these campers in this historic photo from Yellowstone had all the stakes they needed—and knew how to use them. (National Park Service)

The second item to note about the tent pegs is their size and construction. In Olden Times, when the *only* option for campground accommodations was a tent, stakes were often made of wood, with one end sharpened to facilitate driving the item into the ground. As technology advanced, pegs began to be made of other materials, including a variety of metals and plastic.

I strongly suggest that you try to make an educated guess about the nature of the ground at the place(s) where you intend to erect your tent during your upcoming outdoor adventure. If you plan to go to the beach, where you'll be driving the peg into loose sand, almost any type will work. Wood, metal, or even plastic will withstand being driven into that surface. The primary requirement in this case is that the pegs be approximately five feet long, so you can drive them deeply enough into the loose sand that there is reasonable hope that the peg will stay in place when the first strong gust of wind blows against your shelter. (Well, okay, five feet long is a bit extreme, but you get the idea.) Some veteran beach campers prefer to use sandbags placed on top of more conventional stakes to help weigh down the corner of the tent and hold the pegs in place.

Recognizing that it is possible that some of my readers have spent their entire lives within the interior portions of their mother country and have never visited an oceanfront, I think it would be prudent to share one camper's experience in the event you ever decide to go camping on a beach. Should that be the case, you may recall this discussion about the potential inadequacies of standard-issue tent stakes when driven into loose sand, and I would feel guilty if I omitted this vital information and you repeated this individual's error.

I observed this particular situation while I was visiting Padre Island National Seashore on the Texas coast in the role of a tourist rather than in my official capacity as a ranger. Since the family in this story was from Dallas, for the sake of the story, we'll just call the main character J.R.

It was early on a summer afternoon when J.R. and his group arrived at the seashore. I was just finishing the job of setting up my own, thankfully small, tent, despite a stiff on-shore breeze and the challenges of getting the tent stakes to find a firm foothold in the soft, shifting sands. My new neighbors selected a spot a little closer to my own location than I would have preferred, but that did provide the opportunity for me to observe and hear what was to follow.

The apparent leader of this band was a middle-aged man, accompanied by what I presume were a spouse and two children, about ages ten and twelve. Under his direction, the group went to work setting up their tent, a rather large model that was probably described on the Original Factory Carton as something like "Three Room Family Tent, Comfortably Sleeps Six."

The size of this temporary dwelling meant that there was sufficient square footage of tent wall to function as a very nice sail in the wind. It was therefore quickly apparent that the woefully short stakes included in the Original Factory Carton were not going to perform their intended job in the loose sand. About the time two stakes had been driven into the ground and work was begun on a third, the sea breeze began its game.

First there would be a great flapping of canvas, a shouted admonition by J.R. to his young assistants to "hold it down," and then almost instantly a parting of the ways between sand and tent stakes. All hands then scurried about to wrestle the tent to the ground before it set flight for distant points inland. This scene was repeated several times with identical results.

I will have to give J.R. credit for one thing. It was obvious that this was a losing battle, and he recognized that some other tactic was called for if they planned to experience camping on the beach. Unfortunately, his solution left something to be desired.

After directing his crew to "take a break" by sitting on the collapsed tent, J.R. strolled closer to the water and made a startling discovery. At a particular point between the dune line and the surf, the composition of the sand suddenly changed from nice, soft, loose powder to a much firmer surface. This different variety of sand was slightly darker in color and was just the tiniest bit damp. The slope of the beach toward the surf was very slight and it was still quite a distance to the edge of the water.

"Hey!" J.R. shouted. "Bring one of those tent stakes and the hammer down here." One of the children quickly complied, and J.R. performed a test drive with the peg into the sand in his new spot. The stake seemed to hold quite well in the much firmer surface, and a solution to their problem seemed to be at hand.

J.R. and his assistant returned to their original location, rolled up the tent, and the whole crew hauled it down to his newfound site. I had been watching this scene unfold with some interest, but up until then I was simply an innocent bystander. At this point, however, I was faced with a decision: mind my own business, or risk offering some (hopefully) helpful advice and try to head off an impending minor disaster.

This would obviously be a great time for a ranger to pass by and intervene, but that didn't seem to be in the cards, and we were located a considerable distance from the ranger station.

With some trepidation, I left the comfort of my lawn chair and strolled down to the group.

I decided to try the friendly greeting opening.

"Hey, how are you guys doing?"

This was met with some suspicion by J.R. and his family, which is understandable. After all, I was a stranger, just another guy camping on the beach. I received a polite but cautious response, but the tone was clearly, "Can't you see we're busy here?"

I countered with what I hoped sounded like a casual question. "Setting up your tent, huh? How long are you guys going to be here?"

Before J.R. could cut him off, the youngest member of the clan replied cheerfully, "We're going to spend the night, *right* here by the ocean. We've never been to the beach before."

This confirmed my fears of a worst-case scenario, so I decided to follow another cardinal rule of dealing with the public: Make every effort to avoid embarrassing the leader of a group, especially if that happens to be a husband, father, or other individual of the male gender.

Trying to look as harmless as possible, I glanced at J.R. and asked, "Could I talk to you over here for just a minute?"

This definitely raised his suspicions, but at least I had the appearance of a reputable citizen, so with obvious reluctance, J.R. joined me for a short stroll out of earshot of his family.

"I'm sorry if it looks like I'm butting into your business, but I thought maybe you haven't been to the beach before, and wondered if you realized you're about to set up your tent below the high tide line?"

It was clear that I was right on at least one count. J.R.'s response confirmed that he was totally clueless about the basics of oceanography or even eighth-grade earth science.

"So what?"

Okay, kind reader. If you were in my spot, how would *you* respond to that one?

Back before my park service career, I spent one year teaching general science and biology in a high school in Houston. I tried to think of an appropriate answer to J.R.'s question, but it was pretty obvious that even tenth-grade-level data were going to be a stretch for him.

"Well, right now it's just about low tide, which means the edge of the water is where you see it. Before long, the tide will start to come in, and over the next few hours, the ocean will gradually come further up on the beach. By the time it gets to high tide, where we're standing will be in the water. That's why the sand is so much firmer here. It's under water twice a day."

J.R. glanced down briefly at the damp sand, looked out at the distant surf line, and then back at me. He was clearly dubious, and in the absence of the solid basis for a rebuttal, fell back on that most basic of responses for such situations.

"Oh, yeah?" Loosely translated, this means, "What makes you think you're so smart?" and there was a mild but definite challenge in his tone, confirming that some aspects of human nature don't change much over the centuries. As Samuel Johnson noted in the 1700s, "Advice, as it always gives a temporary appearance of superiority, can never be welcome, even when it is most necessary or most judicious."

It was clear my attempt at good neighborliness was headed south in a hurry and, realizing that what lay ahead for this group was going to be more inconvenience than real danger, I decided it was time to make a tactful withdrawal. I apologized for intruding on his business, J.R. returned to the business at hand, and I retreated to my own camp.

One thing was certain: those little tent stakes *did* work a lot better in that nice, packed sand below the high tide line. Before long, their tent was set up, the kids were happily playing in the edge of the surf, and J.R. and his missus were relaxing somewhat smugly in their own chaise lounges in the shade of the tent awning.

I'm glad to report that the eventual outcome was more embarrassing than hazardous for J.R. and company. Amazing but true, as the afternoon wore on, those waves lapping gently on the sand began a slow but steady march up the beach toward the tent. On the plus side of the ledger, it became easier as time passed for J.R. to give instructions to the kids, since their position at the edge of the water was drawing ever closer to home base at the tent.

Deciding that diplomacy was in order, I moved inside my own shelter to continue relaxing with a book. That allowed me to keep an occasional but private eye on unfolding events through the mesh screen of my tent door. As a result, I was out of view when J.R. finally had to admit defeat. His group managed to break camp and get everything loaded back into their vehicle before anything actually got wet. I was just thankful that they kept on driving when they passed my location. I don't know where they finally settled for the night, but I'm willing to bet the phrase *surf's up* had a whole different meaning to them after this little informal science lesson.

Not every camping trip is to the beach, so if your future tenting expedition will take you to places where the ground may include rocks rather than soft beach sand, the length of the stake is of less importance than its strength. One corollary of Murphy's Law says that in such locations there is a 98.5 percent probability that the place you select to drive a tent peg will be directly over a rock. Not any rock, you understand, but one at least the size of a football. No problem, you say, just shift the tent a little bit, and try again.

That's all well and good until you consider how many pegs are required to properly anchor the tent. The design of the tent will determine this number, which ranges from a minimum of four to as many as a dozen or more for the Bubba Family Model. Once you've managed to secure at least two corners of the tent, your freedom to shift locations to drive the remaining stakes quickly diminishes.

I submit to you that under such circumstances, a plastic tent peg may not be the item of choice, especially since many such materials tend to become brittle as they age. In deference to the skills of chemical engineers, I'm sure that there are varieties of plastic tent pegs that were developed as spin-offs of the space program and are just as strong as tempered steel. The choice is yours, but don't say I didn't warn you.

Even if your tent is equipped with metal stakes, I'd suggest you take a good look at their construction. If you are headed out on a backpacking expedition and weight is a serious issue, then those skinny aluminum pegs that are just slightly larger in diameter than a paperclip might appeal to you. For everyone else, I'd suggest something considerably stouter. Finally, examine carefully the apparent strength of the metal itself. If you can bend the peg with your bare hands, perhaps a little more durable model might be prudent, especially if you're headed into rocky terrain.

A while back, I suggested that you determine how many pegs are needed to set up your tent, and multiply that number by at least two. There are several reasons for this safety factor. Since we've been talking about rocky ground, one reason is pretty obvious. There are few objects of lesser value than a metal tent peg that roughly resembles a corkscrew after repeated attempts to drive it through that boulder lurking just below the surface of the ground. A few spares are therefore in order.

I will also predict that sooner or later, anyone who uses a tent will find himself trying to set up camp in the dark or in adverse weather—or more likely, both. Under those circumstances, it is amazing how many tent pegs set down preparatory to driving them into the ground will suddenly disappear.

The military spent a lot of our tax dollars developing a new material for building the stealth bomber, which reportedly makes that aircraft essentially invisible to radar. I'd suggest that long before that project was conceived, the manufacturers of tent pegs had already come up with a secret metal alloy that becomes invisible to the human eye when pegs made of that substance are laid anywhere upon the surface of the earth. The color or nature of the soil, presence or absence of grass, or any other factors make no difference. Set a metal tent peg upon the ground, take your eyes off of it for just an instant, and chances are good it will suddenly vanish. Hence, a few *more* spare pegs are certainly useful. This phenomenon may go a long way toward explaining the popularity of those brightly colored plastic models.

Once you've driven a few tent pegs, you'll develop a good gauge for the nature of the soil simply by using your ears. To a person assigned that task, there are few sounds sweeter than a nice, muted, dull thud when you strike the end of the peg with your hammer. That indicates you have hit the mother lode of campsite dirt, a nice, firm texture that will securely hold the peg with a minimum of driving effort.

Conversely, a piercing, ringing sound that occurs when your hammer hits a metal peg indicates the worst-case scenario, one of those dreaded rocks. Under optimum conditions, usually about midnight when everyone else in the campground is trying to sleep, that sound of metal hammer against metal peg against rock will carry for an incredible distance. Repeated enough times in the course of trying to set up a tent on rocky ground, that noise becomes a rustic version of the infamous Chinese water torture, and it is guaranteed to earn you a special place in the memory of other campers in the vicinity. If this hammering continues long enough in the dark of night, you may even get the chance to meet some of your new neighbors and learn some interesting things about their dispositions.

If you're using a wooden or plastic stake in rocky ground, fewer of your neighbors will be disturbed, and the sound is more like a hollow *whack*. (*Whack* is definitely preferable to *crack*, the other common sound made by plastic tent pegs when you try to drive them through a rock.) No matter what variety of tent stake you choose, you will soon develop an ear for these sounds and be able to predict whether this is going to qualify as a good day or a bad one strictly on the basis of auditory evidence.

Here's one last piece of free, unsolicited advice about tent pegs or stakes. Take along a good, stout hammer or mallet for driving those items into the ground. Such a tool qualifies as essential gear and is often overlooked until you reach your destination. Campers lacking such an item sometimes resort to trying to pound the pegs into the ground with a rock, stout tree limb, or heel of a shoe, all of which I have observed to be very ineffective substitutes for the proper implement.

Many outdoorspersons, in an attempt to cut down on the amount of gear hauled along on their expedition, omit a hammer and plan to use a hatchet or axe to drive their tent pegs. The heads of many such tools are seemingly designed for such dual use, with one edge being sharpened for cutting wood, and the opposite edge formed into a flat surface for convenient use as a striking rather than cutting instrument.

Such a dual-use tool seems at first glance to be a very efficient idea, but I would suggest you avoid falling prey to this trap, especially if you will be driving those pegs into some of that rocky ground. I propose here for perhaps the first time that this tool design can likely be traced to an early member of the Society for Full Employment of Emergency Room Physicians and Surgeons, since that sharp, ringing sound I mentioned earlier when you try to drive a metal peg into a rock will sooner or later be accompanied by the famous "rebound effect."

This phenomenon occurs when the peg is struck by the driving tool and refuses to penetrate that solid granite boulder just beneath the soil surface. If you stayed awake during physics class, you'll recall one of those basic laws of science, which went something like this: Every action is met by an equal and opposite reaction. In this case, when the tent peg contacts that rock and comes to an abrupt halt, the energy from your mighty blow with the hatchet is translated into an impressive bounce of the striking tool back toward the striker (that would be the person doing the striking).

The odds of the rebounding tool contacting a portion of the striker's body depend upon the stance taken to drive that tent peg, but since the striker is holding the stake with one hand and the striking tool with the other hand, about 99.99 percent of such individuals are in a kneeling position during this action. This makes the odds of a Painfully Melancholy Situation occurring infinitely higher than those of winning the lottery.

If the bouncing tool that contacts the striker's body is a hammer or mallet, the result is usually a serious owie, and with luck nothing worse than an impressive bruise. If, however, the back side of that tool is the sharp head of a hatchet or axe, the striker may become the strikee, with much more unpleasant results. The seriousness of the resulting injury is almost always in direct proportion to the number of miles to the nearest medical facility, multiplied by a factor based upon whether or not the strikee is covered by good medical insurance with little or no deductible for accidental injuries.

The final moral of this story: Don't use a tool with a sharp edge for driving tent pegs. There's a *lot* at stake.

In the Eye of the Beholder

A small percentage of park employees across the country actually live inside the park, where they usually occupy housing of some variety that is owned by the government. Living in a location such as a national park probably looks and sounds appealing, and while it does have some advantages, there is definitely more to this situation than meets the eye.

At least in the case of the National Park Service this lodging is not provided free of charge as a fringe benefit to the rangers or other staff members. They pay rent to Uncle Sam, based on a formula so complicated you know it could only have been developed by the government. The computation is supposed to take into account the rent for similar housing in the surrounding area, which is often a high-priced resort area, so in many cases these government quarters are far from a bargain. These staff members live there primarily to provide faster after-hours response to emergencies, and in most cases they are required to do so as part of the job.

Now that I've joined the ranks of retired rangers, I can put in a gentle plea on behalf of my peers who are still out there on the front lines. While a few of the larger parks have a dispatch center to take after-hours calls, in other cases that phone number you find listed for a ranger station or "in case of emergency call" is actually for a phone in the ranger's home. Many people aren't aware of that fact when they get a sudden urge to find out at midnight if the fish are biting, what the weather forecast is for tomorrow, or whether there are likely to be any vacant campsites weekend after next.

Dedicated as they are, rangers and their families do appreciate getting a little occasional rest, so now that you know the situation, hopefully you'll show a little mercy and make those calls at appropriate hours. John Milton wrote back in the seventeenth century, so he obviously wasn't disturbed by ringing telephones, but many a ranger living in government quarters has at times wondered with Milton, "What hath night to do with sleep?" For some people, apparently not very much!

If you live in a park, you'll soon find that there are an amazing variety of situations that prompt people to knock on your door or phone you at all hours of the day or night, and at times what constitutes an "emergency" is definitely in the eye of the beholder. There is a section in Title 4 of the Alaska State Statutes that reads, "It is the state policy that emergencies are held to a minimum and are rarely found to exist." Rangers don't mind helping out if there is a valid need, but I'll have to admit that there were times at about 2 A.M. during my career when I concluded the state of Alaska was on the right track, and its policy needed to be disseminated more widely among the general population.

In the other forty-nine states, where emergencies apparently exist more frequently, those dark-of-night knocks on our door included the expected missing children, pets, keys, wallets, and spouses—although there were a couple of times when I found a missing person and returned him to camp late at night, only to get the impression the other spouse was a little disappointed that I had been successful. Maybe the moral to this lesson for some folks is to be sure you don't carry so much life insurance that your spouse is tempted to secretly hope you *don't* return from that hike or fishing trip!

A good example of a situation that certainly *seemed* like an emergency to one man occurred during my assignment at Lake Mead National Recreation Area in northwestern Arizona. My duty station at the time was a place named Willow Beach, in the depths of Black Canyon about thirteen miles downstream from Hoover Dam. This area has some very pleasant weather from late fall to early spring, but during the summer months it's one of the hottest spots in the country. Daytime highs well above 120 degrees Fahrenheit are not uncommon—and that's measured in the shade.

This is serious desert country, and the landscape and climate sometimes come as a surprise to people making their first visit to the area. Returning to Lake Mead from a trip back East, I once found myself on a flight to Las Vegas with a large contingent of farmers from Illinois who were headed to a convention in that city. I was in the aisle seat, and two of the agriculturalists had the center and window spots. As we began our descent over southern Nevada one of them looked out the window and remarked, "Sure not much *green* down there."

His companion leaned over, took in the expanse of bare rock and sand, and ventured, "Yep, I hear it's been pretty dry out here this year."

Just for the record, dry years are the norm in that part of the world. Vegetation larger than small desert shrubs and cacti is pretty scarce except where there's irrigation, and down in the canyons around my duty station at Willow Beach there was plenty of dark rock to soak up the abundant sunshine during the day and release it slowly during the hours of darkness. It was a great natural demonstration of the principles of solar heating and, in this environment, the concept of the "minimum" temperature each night is definitely more relative than the humidity.

There is no longer a park service campground at Willow Beach, but back in the 1970s there was a large one that was very popular during the milder months of the year. Summer was a different story, and I often remarked that this was one of the few campgrounds I was aware of in a national park where you had absolutely no problem finding a vacant site on the Fourth of July weekend. In fact, if we had *any* tent campers at Willow Beach that time of the year, it was something of a surprise, and I was always tempted to perform an informal mental status check on those folks to determine if they realized what they had gotten themselves into.

With that background, you'll have a better understanding of the situation one midsummer's night when I was awakened by a knock on my door about 1 A.M. Our government quarters were located directly across from the entrance to the campground, so help from the rangers was easy to find if the need should arise.

I opened the door to find a middle-aged man standing outside and immediately noted that a matter of considerable urgency was weighing heavily upon his mind. In the driveway was what I presumed to be his car, with a roof rack piled high with camping equipment. The jumbled heap of gear on the roof clearly suggested that camp had been broken and gear loaded in considerable haste. The man had failed to close the driver's side car door completely, so the dome light was on and I could see a woman and two children, ages about eight and ten, inside.

One of the essential skills for a ranger is the ability to size up human nature, and based upon the expression on the woman's face, my

Any ranger who lives in a park will experience plenty of after-hours "Hey Ranger!" moments. This was the author's residence at Lake Mead National Recreation Area. (Jim Burnett)

sharply honed powers of observation told me that she was not a happy camper (and an apparent recent graduate to the status of *former* camper). It was pretty obvious that *this* lady's midsummer night's dream had not been very pleasant. As the expression goes, "If mama's not happy, ain't nobody happy," and this was definitely a very melancholy bunch.

This analysis took only a couple of seconds, and I turned my attention back to the man outside my door. "Hi, what can I do for you?"

With a look of pure desperation on his face, the man blurted out, "Mister, my wife says she has absolutely *no* idea why I brought us camping out here in the middle of nowhere in this heat. I don't care what it costs, but you have *got* to give me directions to the closest place that has air conditioning, a swimming pool, and cable TV!"

Based on his woeful expression, it wasn't entirely clear if he was willing to pay for directions, accommodations, or both, but of course the directions from his friendly ranger were free. That list of criteria for a lodging establishment doesn't sound especially challenging in today's world, but you need to remember that, as this gentleman said, we were "out here in the middle of nowhere." This was also before the widespread availability of satellite or cable television, so I didn't have an instant fix for his problem. There was a small motel at a fishing resort right down the road, but they only scored one for three on his list of amenities.

His mention of air conditioning reminded me to join the gentleman on my porch and pull the front door closed behind me as we continued our conversation. The ambient air temperature out there in Real Nature gave proof to the axiom that nature abhors a vacuum, and the (thankfully) cool air inside our house, obtained at the cost of ferociously high electric bills, was rapidly being sucked out into the nighttime heat.

My answer, therefore, was a mixture of good news and bad news. The good news was that there were a plethora of places that would meet his needs in Las Vegas, but unfortunately that was at least an hour and a half away. There were likely some possibilities a little closer in either Boulder City or Kingman, so I gave him directions, wished him well, and sent him on his way.

If I'm any judge of human nature, based on the glimpse I had of the expression on the faces of the rest of the family, I suspect the drive seemed longer than it really was. I hope the air conditioning in their car at least worked at peak efficiency during that trip back to civilization. If I were a betting man, I'd say that there were really good odds that a complete set of camping gear showed up in a garage sale in his neighborhood not long thereafter, probably with a sign that said something like "just make me an offer."

In many parks it's quite a drive to the nearest place for supplies, and more than one group of campers has experienced an uh-oh moment, often accompanied by a conversation that includes something like, "I thought *you* packed the. . . ." Jeremy Sullivan is a former park ranger who now authors an excellent blog on the Internet at www.parkremark .com that has lots of good information and commentary about the national parks. One of his assignments during his ranger career was at Hoh Rain Forest in Olympic National Park in Washington. I've visited there several times, and it's a fascinating spot, as long as you enjoy a setting that's both very green and often rather damp. It's also literally at the end of the road, and many miles from the nearest town, so the staff there had their share of after-hours knocks on the door.

Mr. Sullivan remarks that "our park housing was just in between the main parking lot and the campground, so it was pretty easy to find. We frequently had visitors knocking on our doors. These 'emergency' encounters typically involved being asked whether we had an extra can of soup or a can opener to borrow." I hope the rest of the group back at the campsite didn't have their hearts set on an old family recipe that required some exotic ingredients, but the lack of a can opener could pose a serious challenge.

Visitor requests for help weren't limited to knocks on the door, and that mixed blessing called a telephone offered almost boundless opportunities for conversations at all hours of the day and night. Although this situation is gradually changing in some areas with the advent of 911 numbers to report emergencies, in others the local ranger station is still the closest thing to Official Government Help. Sometimes this can lead to bizarre requests that aren't even remotely connected to national parks. The following story, shared by now-retired ranger Mike Greenfield, is a great example.

One of the scenic driving treats in the eastern United States is the 469-mile Blue Ridge Parkway. The long and narrow parkway follows the mountain ridgeline from Shenandoah National Park in Virginia to the Great Smoky Mountains National Park in North Carolina. Some beautiful views can be seen while navigating the winding roadway, especially if you obey the 45-mile-per-hour speed limit, and the three years Mike spent there in the mid-1970s still rank as his favorite tour of duty.

Mike's last assignment on the parkway was in the northernmost district that began at Rockfish Gap (Milepost 0) where the parkway connected to the southern end of the Skyline Drive in Shenandoah National Park. His assigned housing was near Milepost 16 in an area that once was named "Love." The rural community formerly had a post office, now long gone, that was popular in February when young men wanted to mail valentines postmarked from such an appropriate location.

As a condition of the job, most rangers at the parkway were required to live in government-owned quarters in the park in order to be readily available to provide emergency services to visitors. Rent for this required housing was deducted right up front from the employee's paycheck, a sure-fire way to ensure that your landlord never missed getting paid on time. Another great feature of required quarters was the government telephone that came with the house. The phone was technically free, as the occupants could use it for local calls; however, they had to use a telephone credit card or have another phone installed for long-distance service.

Every ranger who ever lived with a government telephone has plenty of tales about the unusual calls they received on those phones. The phones served an important purpose in the days before 911 as a relatively efficient way of calling for help. Rangers responding to calls for assistance after hours were sometimes rewarded with heartfelt thanks from visitors who had gotten themselves into some serious predicaments.

Although solving the real emergencies provided great job satisfaction, it was sometimes the unusual, not directly related to rangering, calls that provided some of the best memories. Mike took one such call one evening after work in February or March.

After politely and efficiently answering the phone, "Blue Ridge Parkway," he was rewarded with, "It's about time someone answered the phone up there!" Now "up there" immediately told our faithful ranger that the caller was from off the ridge, perhaps from the little town of Waynesboro located down in the nearby valley.

Mike's first step was to calmly answer the implied accusation that the Park Service doesn't answer its phones. He explained that the caller had reached a residence, not an office, and the occupant was often not home, out attending to the rangering duties that went along with his job. He was single at that time and, therefore, the park didn't have a "volunteer" at the house, otherwise known as a spouse, to handle government business as part of the required quarters benefit package. This was also before the days when answering machines were commonplace.

The gentleman seemed to accept Mike's explanation about why the phone had not been answered earlier, and after a couple of minutes of chatting it was obvious there was no emergency to report. Even so, Mike asked how he could help his after-hours caller.

Without hesitation the man said, "I need help with my taxes." *With* hesitation, Mike explained that the National Park Service was responsible for the Blue Ridge Parkway and really didn't have anything to do with collecting or filing taxes. He suggested the gentleman contact the Internal Revenue Service, as it was the government agency that handled such matters.

"Yeah, I know, but I thought you-all might be able to help me, being from the government and all." This statement is further confirmation in my mind of the wide-ranging scope of the Ranger Mystique and of the attitude of many people that if anybody would know the answer to *any* question, it must be a park ranger!

After a little further conversation, Mike finally learned the real reason the man had called him, or rather called the government number as it was listed in the local telephone directory. It turned out the ranger's number was the *only* government number listed that was a free local call. This man was willing to take tax advice from anyone connected with the government in order to save the cost of a long-distance call!

Well, sometimes things are meant to be. The irony here was that Mike actually had a great interest in tax law and fancied himself as pretty knowledgeable about the basics of income taxes for individuals. From the first time that he had to prepare taxes for a high school class, he reports that he always enjoyed reading and researching the tax manuals. Mike also volunteers that this "probably stems from the fact that I am cheap and don't want to pay any more than I have to in order to complete my own taxes."

It has often been said that rangers wear many hats, and they certainly have a wide variety of interests. At this point, Mike considered it fate that a government phone line had put this man in touch with him. He remarked as he related this story to me that in today's age of liability and lawsuits, he would never say now what he said at the time: "Tell me what your problem is. I might be able to help." Now there's some *real* service and proof that the old saying, "I'm from the government and I'm here to help you," really does have some validity.

The government phone line was tied up for quite a while that night, as the man had numerous questions. After a good bit of tax talk, Mike suggested that his "client" work on his forms with the new information he had gained and see if things fell into place. He thanked Mike and said, "Would it be all right to call back tomorrow if I come up with anything else?" Our all-purpose ranger told him that would be fine but reminded him that it might take several calls to catch Mike at home.

This last question brings up another fact of life about being a ranger: It is very hard to guarantee that you'll be home at any particular time. Even when schedules are all properly set down on paper, things have a way of happening that need tending to. Like most of his counterparts, Mike learned early on not to say things like, "I'll be home by six. I'll call you then." A promise like that seemed to ensure that something like a car wreck would happen and at six he would be waiting on a lonely stretch of road for the arrival of a wrecker. This was, of course, before the age of cell phones, so opportunities for communications on the road were limited to the park's two-way radio system. Rangers are also somewhat reluctant to give out their work schedules, since most parks have inadequate staff coverage and they don't want people who might have plans for less-than-honorable activities to know when rangers are on or off duty.

When he did get home the next night, Mike was actually hoping the government phone *would* ring, as he was anxious to know if his tax advice had helped. The man did indeed call, and his newfound unofficial tax adviser must have helped as he had just a couple of additional questions. These only took a short time and he again offered a big "thank-you" for the help.

Mike recounts that he thought about this off and on for a few days. Actually, he grew rather nervous thinking that if he was wrong or if the man used the information incorrectly, the taxpayer would be mad at both him and the National Park Service. Should that occur, he wondered how the Park Service would discipline a ranger for giving bad tax advice! Mike did make it clear to the man he had no connection to the IRS, but I suppose in this case that could also stand for **I**mplausible **R**anger **S**ervices.

Fortunately the man never called back, so Mike assumed the "real" IRS never audited him. If nothing else, Mike notes that this experience does confirm that from time to time a ranger's job can definitely be "taxing"! I'd add that his story is further proof that in the eyes of the public the duties of park rangers are wide-ranging indeed, and what constitutes an emergency is truly in the eye of the beholder.

"There You Are, Boys . . ."

Getting lost in the Great Outdoors can be a scary and sometimes dangerous situation. Fortunately, most people who end
up in such predicaments are found safely, although sometimes later
rather than sooner. The files of search and rescue teams are filled with
accounts of searches that involved huge numbers of people, lasted for
days, and cost a king's ransom, all because the lost person tried unsuc-
cessfully to find his or her way back to safety. In the process, the dis-
oriented victim kept getting further and further away from the area
where rescuers were looking. This is a situation where being a moving
target is definitely *not* a good idea, so if you realize you're lost, a good
rule of thumb is to stop moving, make yourself as comfortable and visible as possible, and wait for help.

If you should have the misfortune to become lost, even being
"found" can occasionally have a surprising outcome. When I was working at the Big Thicket National Preserve in southeast Texas, a hunter
became lost in a remote section of that area. This is a relatively new
addition to the National Park System, and many of you may not be
familiar with it. I'll just summarize the terrain by saying that the name
of the park says it all: The woods and swamps are big and the vegetation is thick, so getting lost doesn't require much effort.

In the case of the lost hunter, the man made some good choices by
staying put and occasionally firing off three rounds from his shotgun—

three of anything is the universal distress signal. A line from Shakespeare provides one other piece of good advice for such situations. In *Henry the Fourth* the character Falstaff notes, "For my voice, I have lost it with halloing and singing of anthems."

If you're lost in the wilderness, the quiet singing of anthems might not be a bad idea, but I'd suggest that you refrain from unproductive "halloing" and save your voice until it can prove useful—such as when you can actually see or hear other humans who might be able to help solve your problem.

Not long before darkness fell, the hapless hunter was greatly relieved to hear three distant shots fired in response to his signal. After several more exchanges of blasts, the hunter was finally out of ammo and decided it was safe to commence with the "hollering" phase. His loud "halloooooo . . ." was met with a similar response, and eventually the two men managed to join forces. I'm unable to report whether they celebrated this positive development with the singing of any anthems, but there was certainly considerable relief.

The following is a paraphrase of the conversation as I heard about it later:

Hunter #1: "Man, I'm sure glad to see you!"

Hunter #2: "Same here. It's a good thing you heard my signal."

Hunter #1: "Sure is. Hey, it's going to be dark real soon. You got a flashlight?"

Hunter #2: "Yep, but I figured I'd better come meet up with you instead of just wandering around."

Hunter #1: "Well, let's get started. Where'd you leave your truck?"

Hunter #2: "Out at the park boundary on the main road. I hope yours is closer, and you can give me a ride back to my rig after we get to yours. Where did you park?"

Hunter #1: "Sounds like about the same place as you did. Go ahead, I'll follow you since you've got the flashlight."

The second hunter looked a bit puzzled at this suggestion, and just a little more conversation got to the root of the problem. *Both* men were lost and each assumed the other had been sent to look for *him*. Finders may be keepers, but in this case, the only thing the finder could keep was company with his co-loser.

After realizing the irony of their situation the two men were at least wise enough to avoid wandering around all night in the dark. They built a fire, spent the night swapping hunting tales and probably a few legends about the "one that got away," and were safely located by real searchers the next morning.

This next story involves several lost canines rather than humans— and a found opportunity. It involves a woman who was a great example of the spirit of independence, fortitude, and resourcefulness that is often seen in lifelong residents of rural America. For reasons that will soon become apparent, she—and the specific location where this event occurred—will remain anonymous.

For purposes of the story, I'll call this lady Sally, and I'll remind you that for the sake of readability, I use the term *park* throughout this book to refer to any of the units of the national and state park systems and similar locations. That includes sites such as national recreation areas and national preserves, some of which allow hunting under specific guidelines included in the legislation that established the park.

It was about four days after the opening of deer season in the fall, and Sally's husband had joined a large group of friends and relatives at a hunting camp set up not far outside the park boundary. This location had been the scene of similar hunting camps for many of these same guys for years. Let's just say that the setting could be described as a bastion of good ol' boy culture, and I think you'll get the picture.

As previously arranged, Sally showed up at the camp in her four-wheel drive pickup with a supply of food and other essentials. She was greeted enthusiastically for several reasons in addition to the new stock of edibles for the pantry. One of those reasons was a serious shortage of clean pots and pans, since those items had been piling up next to the campfire for several days.

The patriarch of the group directed a couple of the boys to pile all of the dirty cookware into some open cardboard boxes and load them into the back of the pickup, so the "little woman" could take it all home, get it cleaned up, and then bring it back to camp in time to use for supper that night. (A note to all of you ladies reading this chapter: Please don't take offense at this narrative. I'm simply describing as accurately as possible a time, place, and culture from several decades ago that is understandably foreign to most of you today.)

If you've ever seen pots and pans used to cook over an open campfire, you can visualize the mess, and it was not a pretty picture. There was a thoroughly petrified residue of eggs, bacon, stew, and other culinary delights coating the inside and dribbling down the blackened outside of most of the cookware. In an apparent gesture of generosity, the guys explained that Sally didn't have to worry about "all that black stuff on the outside of the pots;" she only needed to get the insides cleaned up so they could use them again.

This idea was not exactly enthusiastically received by the lady, but she was wise enough to know when to keep her thoughts to herself. Just as she was ready to drive out of camp, one of the guys yelled to Sally to keep her eyes open for several of their hunting dogs, who hadn't been seen for a couple of days. (They were probably tired of the leftovers being offered by *that* bunch and had started for home in search of a good meal!)

With that parting admonition, our heroine headed for the house, the pots and pans rattling and banging in the back of the truck as the vehicle bounced over the rough gravel road. Sure enough, several miles away from camp, she came upon the four missing hunting dogs. They immediately recognized the truck and didn't require any coaxing to hop into the back of the pickup for a ride back to the house. The trip home across the back roads took over an hour, but Sally and her canine companions eventually arrived at their destination.

The lady climbed out of the vehicle, walked around to open the tailgate, and waited for the dogs to jump down so she could unload the dirty cookware and get to work. She had spent most of the ride home plotting her revenge for this unpleasant turn of events, but when she reached into the bed and started unloading the pans, her mood improved considerably.

Those big ol' dogs had been roaming the woods for the past two days and had apparently worked up a pretty good appetite. They were not especially discriminating when it came to their menu, and with their empty stomachs even the food residue sticking to those pots and pans must have looked and tasted pretty good. Given the opportunity and the proper incentive, it's amazing what can be accomplished by the busy tongues of four large, very hungry dogs in an hour's time.

Most of the items had been pulled out of the boxes for better access by the "cleaning crew," and a quick check of the cookware determined that it all looked pretty good. In fact, some of those pieces probably hadn't been that shiny in a long, long time!

With a smile on her face, the "little lady" tossed the now thoroughly "scrubbed" pots and pans back into the boxes, slid them into bed of the truck, slammed the tailgate, and went into the house for a snack and a nice nap. A couple of hours later, she figured enough time had passed to allow her to finish her "chores," so she headed back to the camp.

Upon her return, she found that most of the guys had stretched out for their own siesta after getting up early that morning to hunt. She

A meal skillfully prepared over a campfire can be
a tasty treat—but there's some serious cleanup
required later. (National Park Service)

eased the truck into a convenient parking spot, climbed out, and cheerfully unloaded the boxes of cookware. One of the group even started
to get up and give her a hand, but she told him stay put and just
stacked the clean pots and pans close to the campfire.

"There you are, boys, all nice and clean. Enjoy your supper."

With a friendly wave and a cheerful smile, Sally climbed back into
the truck and headed for home. As she backed out, she heard one of
the guys comment to her husband, "That's quite a woman you've got
there."

She was indeed!

Way Beyond the Call of Duty

Park rangers and their coworkers perform an amazing variety of duties, including search and rescue, emergency medical services, law enforcement, fire fighting, education, public relations, and too many others to list. Not every ranger performs all of these functions during his or her career, but one thing is certain—not a day goes by without some of these public servants going above and beyond the call of duty to help make someone's visit to a park safer or more enjoyable.

Occasionally those tasks are performed at great personal risk, and there is a very serious side to this profession. However, that aspect of the job has been nobly described by other writers, many of them former rangers themselves, so in this chapter we'll stick to a few examples of the lighter side of "other duties as assigned."

Mike Greenfield had a long and distinguished career as an NPS ranger and recently retired from Fredericksburg and Spotsylvania National Military Park in Virginia. He also worked in other parks around the country, and in the following story he shares an example of how there's often more to rangering than meets the eye—or is included in the official job description.

In the late seventies and early eighties Mike was assigned to the Virginia District at Assateague Island National Seashore and actually lived on the delightful Chincoteague Island. Assateague Island's dunes and beaches stretch for 37 miles along the coasts of Maryland and Virginia and include Assateague State Park and Chincoteague National Wildlife Refuge in addition to the National Seashore. You may recognize the name because the wild ponies that live on Assateague were made famous by Marguerite Henry's children's book *Misty of Chincoteague*.

As Mike describes the area, "During the summer months, Chincoteague and the recreational area of Assateague are awash in visitors. In the winter months, when the tourists are gone for the most part, these two islands are tranquil, and it is easy to understand why native Chincoteaguers think they live somewhere special. They do."

Along with the summer crowds come some occasional and unfortunate reminders that "getting away from it all" doesn't mean you've actually left behind all of the problems of day-to-day life. Parking areas at any public beach are a tempting target for "car clouters," a term for thieves who break into unoccupied vehicles in search of any valuables left there.

Most folks who are going to the beach don't want to carry any more than necessary with them, and they certainly don't want to lose anything of value while they are enjoying the sand and surf. As a result, they tend to leave a smorgasbord of items in vehicles, which the clouters know are ripe for picking.

Here's a little free Rangerly Advice: If you think your camera, purse, wallet, and other goodies are safe just because you hid them under the front seat or in the glove box of your vehicle, think again. Guess where a car clouter will look first after he gains entry to your four-wheel, not-so-safe deposit box?

Along with crowds and occasional car clouters, the summer months also brought the challenging ranger diversion known as "lock-outs." The scenario usually unfolded as follows:

Back at their motel, folks headed for the beach would often put a few clothes on over their swimsuits. This allowed them to save time at the beach by simply unloading their supplies, peeling off their outer garments, tossing those clothes into the car, locking the door, and heading for a day of fun in the sand, surf, and sun.

About four hours later, these vacationers would return to their vehicle, well-baked and ready for a nice, cool shower back at the motel. Let's see now, what did we do with the car keys? Oh, yeah, they were inside a pants pocket—and you already know where that pair of pants is located! This was a classic case of "so near and yet so far" and is one of those situations where you definitely don't want to be "on the outside looking in."

This situation occurred so frequently that the park staff became very adept at breaking into cars without damaging the vehicles, and the park had a great maintenance staff who worked these visitor assists along with the rangers. Unlike the car clouters, these break-ins were performed legally, at the plaintive request of the car's owner in an attempt to rescue those keys locked inside.

One of the best tools back then for these key rescue missions was the all-purpose metal coat hanger, and the rangers' vehicles were stocked with several of them. This was before the days when vehicles commonly came equipped with electric windows and locks and before auto manufacturers started protecting the lock mechanisms inside the doors from such fishing expeditions. While improved security measures don't do much to deter a skilled car clouter, they do make it much harder for Good Samaritans and amateurs such as the vehicle owner to get into a modern car with a simple coat hanger.

Some visitors actually thought ahead and were determined not to lock their keys inside their vehicle. Unfortunately, one of their solutions was simply to leave the family chariot unlocked, and this fear of being locked out played right into the hands of car clouters. It doesn't require much clout to break into an unlocked car. Hey, it doesn't even require a metal coat hanger!

During Mike's time at Assateague, the recreation area had two large parking lots with bathhouses and four smaller lots spread out along a two-and-one-quarter-mile road running parallel to the beach. That distance was great enough that the park brought in port-a-johns during the summer months to accommodate the needs of the crowds.

In some parts of the country, these basic fiberglass enclosures are called "port-a-lets," but a chemical toilet by any name is still the most basic of accommodations. I realize this sudden change of subject from car clouters, coat hangers, and car keys to port-a-johns may cause you to wonder if the editor took the day off, but hang in there, you'll soon see the connection between these wildly dissimilar items.

If you've ever had occasion to use one of these chemical toilets, it doesn't require much imagination to understand that during the hot summer months the port-a-johns were not always very pleasant. Regular cleaning and pumping were so important that the park had its own port-a-john pumper and holding tank mounted on a pickup truck. In many locations these rolling pump and tank arrangements are known euphemistically as "honey wagons," and their operation requires a fairly strong constitution—or a very numb sense of smell. See, you just *thought* you had the toughest job on the planet!

One day the maintenance worker assigned to the truck–honey wagon combo drove past Mike, who was going in the opposite direction on the roadway. A few minutes later, this same maintenance worker called Mike on the two-way radio and said, "There's something down here at Lot 4 that you need to take a look at."

Mike notes that he immediately had a bad feeling about this brief radio conversation. In the first place, he knew the task that was being performed by his coworker down the road. Second, Mike had been at Lot 4 only a short time earlier and had not seen anything amiss, so he reasonably suspected the matter at hand was connected to the maintenance work that was currently underway.

Arriving at Lot 4, Mike saw the maintenance employee standing next to the port-a-john and soon received additional, albeit melancholy, details. "As soon as I started pumping, the hose got stopped up," his coworker explained. "Look what came out," he continued, pointing to the ground.

Upon examination from a prudent distance, the item in question appeared to be a woman's wallet. I'm confident that Mike used the phrase *appeared to be* very accurately, because given the circumstances under which it had been recovered I think it's a safe bet that the article had recently suffered a rude and serious indignity.

There's an old cowboy expression used to describe a horse that's been given a hard workout and then returned to a stall or corral without proper care: "It looked like it was rode hard and put away wet." Even though I was (thankfully) not a witness to the scene in Mike's story, I'd venture the opinion that this phrase about a damp and dirty horse would also apply appropriately to the wallet lying there on the ground.

This was in the days before rangers routinely carried latex gloves for medical emergencies, so out came Mike's trusty coat hanger. (See, I promised you that all the seemingly disconnected elements of this story *were* going to come together.) Maneuvering the sodden object into the bed of his pickup truck/patrol vehicle, Mike was glad not to be driving a sedan that day. He then drove to the office where they had a garden hose and began hosing down the item and the bed of his pickup. Using the trusty coat hanger once again, he dumped his quarry into a bucket he had filled with a solution of bleach and water.

Mike wisely let the item soak for a good while before transferring it via coat hanger to a bucket of fresh water. After another good soak, he finally opened the wallet wearing a pair of protective gloves. It was no surprise that the leather billfold and the paper cards inside were rather badly stained. As expected, there was no cash or credit cards, but there was a Maryland driver's license.

This was before the days when licenses were laminated in plastic, and after taking one look Mike decided everything in the wallet needed another bleach soak. Once that step was completed and the drying process was underway, our ranger was able to make out the information on the driver's license and in short order he had a telephone number for the potential owner.

A phone call was made, and sure enough, the lady on the other end of the line had "lost" her purse while visiting the Eastern Shore of Virginia. She didn't discover it missing until she tried to buy something on the way home. Her last memory of her purse was placing it under the driver's seat of her car, but she couldn't be sure when and where she last saw it.

"Yes, I did visit Chincoteague and spent time on the beach at Assateague."

"Did you lock your car doors?" Mike inquired.

She couldn't remember. "Maybe not." Once she knew that it held no cash or credit cards, she accepted the fact that the "lost" wallet had in fact been stolen. Ah, enter the car clouters, and the final piece of our puzzle.

"At least I can get my wallet back. I really liked it; will you send it to me?" Mike told her it would have to dry first and then explained why it was wet. Upon delivering the details about the item's recent adventures, Mike sensed from the woman's tone of voice that the wallet would never be used again!

Not long thereafter the park received a thank-you letter commending the ranger for efforts above and beyond the call of duty. Although the sentiment was appreciated, Mike noted manfully that he would have had it all to do anyway. Since the wallet was considered probable evidence of a crime, it was his duty to learn as much as possible from it. However, he did note that the situation fit very nicely under that infamous catchall phrase usually found in position descriptions, those official documents that detail the duties for any government job: ". . . and other duties as assigned."

Those "other duties" can cover quite a range of tasks, especially in parks in very isolated parts of the country. Alaska's Noatak National Preserve, in the far northwestern corner of that state, certainly fits that description. Just to give you a little perspective, parts of this magnificent park are closer to Russia than to Fairbanks, Alaska, the nearest city of any size. A quick glance at a map of the area will also reveal a distinct scarcity of lines and dots indicating roads or human settlements of any significant size.

As is the case in much of Alaska, travel in this park is primarily conducted by small plane. On a mid-September day two park employees were conducting aerial patrols along the Noatak River and landed for the night at a spot named Kelly River Ranger Station. As savvy wilderness travelers they made sure their plane was properly secured before getting some well-deserved rest.

If you own a vehicle you probably have a ritual sometime before you turn in for the night that presumably includes making sure you've rolled up the windows and locked the car doors. I trust you also check to be sure there aren't any unattached valuables left inside the car, where they might tempt any less-than-honest persons who happen to pass by in the dark of night. If you're fortunate enough to have your own garage in which to park your vehicle, you can probably omit that last step—assuming that you are among the minority of individuals who have succeeded in keeping the amount of stuff stored there sufficiently under control to make it possible to actually get a vehicle inside the garage.

Those pre-bedtime steps are a little different in the wilds of Alaska. I've not had the opportunity to visit the Kelly River Ranger Station, but I think it's a safe bet it doesn't have a garage, at least not one big enough to accommodate even a small airplane. As a result, before they called it a night the park personnel in our story took prudent precautions to secure their aircraft. High on their list was ensuring that they didn't leave any food or other items in the plane that are known to be appealing to bears. See there, you thought you had problems with ruffians in *your* neighborhood.

There have probably been a few days when you've gotten up in the morning, enjoyed your cup of coffee and morning paper, and headed out to the car for your drive to work, only to find that a flat tire, dead battery, or other inconvenience suddenly got the day off to a bad start. Well, read on, because if your commute were by small plane from beyond the middle of nowhere in Alaska, it could be a lot worse.

Despite their precautions the previous evening, our Alaskan contingent started their day with the discovery that a bear had gone on an overnight rampage in and on the plane. It's not known whether the animal was bored, in a bad mood, or had something personal against airplanes, but the bruin had broken out the plane's left rear window, slashed the aircraft's fabric skin, chewed the rear seat, and slightly damaged the plywood floor. While all of this havoc would be a major annoyance, the damage to the plane's outer skin posed a particularly serious problem in terms of airworthiness. In short, this flying machine wasn't going to leave the ground in that condition.

Kelly River Ranger Station is not a location where you simply phone over to the main hangar and ask the airport mechanic to kindly come over and make the necessary repairs while you enjoy a snack and watch a couple of movies on the big-screen TV. Lacking that or any other options for outside help, some classic American ingenuity was required.

Fortunately these employees had the "right stuff," and I'm not talking about spare parts. Lacking a factory-authorized repair kit, former park pilot and regional aviation trainer Rich Kemp made temporary repairs to the plane with patches composed of plywood, a duffel bag, parachute cord, and—yep—duct tape.

Several books have been written about the almost countless uses for duct tape, but I don't know if any of them includes "repairing an airplane after a bear attack." These measures were probably just a bit outside of FAA guidelines, but they did the job, and Kemp successfully flew the plane back to park headquarters in Kotzebue, a distance of 110 miles. In recognition of his accomplishment, I'll give Mr. Kemp my award for the most unusual application of the world's best-known all-purpose fix-it stuff.

Small aircraft, such as this patrol plane in use during the author's assignment at Lake Mead, are invaluable tools in larger or more remote parks. (Jim Burnett)

Whatever you do from day to day, I suspect that situations come up occasionally at work, home, school, or on the road that require *you* to go above and beyond the call of duty. Just for good measure, maybe it would be a good idea if your stock of emergency supplies includes at least one wire coat hanger—and a roll of duct tape.

Going the extra mile—or a lot more—isn't limited to rangers, and some park visitors can also rise to the occasion when necessary. On a late September night, a fifty-six-year-old woman who was part of a group on an extended canoe trip in Utah's Canyonlands National Park became ill with symptoms resembling appendicitis. This could obviously be a serious situation, so two members of her party set out to report her condition and seek assistance. The closest point to begin a trip back to civilization was a spot with the rather unpromising name of Hardscrabble Bottom. From there it would be possible to access the White Rim Road, which led to the nearest government outpost where they could expect to contact the Proper Authorities.

The two Good Samaritans paddled their canoe upstream in the dark, and upon reaching their destination it initially appeared that they were in luck. They were relieved to find someone camped at Hardscrabble Bottom, a circumstance that provided hope that they could catch a ride to the Bureau of Land Management Ranger Station at Mineral Bottom.

Unfortunately, even in this remote corner of Utah, dire circumstances from the outside world had intruded, dashing the pair's hopes for a quick trip to civilization. There had been a recent fatal shooting in the vicinity, and before departing for his trip to the outback the camper at Hardscrabble Bottom had read that two fugitives who were suspects in that crime were still at large in the region. As a result, the camper was more than a little suspicious when two strangers suddenly appeared in the dark, seemingly out of nowhere in this isolated corner of the Wild West, and asked for a ride.

Although it is illegal to possess loaded firearms in the national park, the camper did claim to have a handgun. While he didn't actually point the weapon at the two would-be messengers, he apparently made it clear he was both armed and prepared to defend himself if necessary. No, he wouldn't give them a ride, thank you very much, but he *was* at least willing to point the way to their intended destination.

The duo's options were certainly limited, so they set out in the dark on a ten-mile hike to the ranger station. This outpost of civilization must have been a welcome sight when they finally arrived in the dawn's early light, but their joy was short-lived. To the pair's dismay, the station at Mineral Bottom was unoccupied. Whatever their political position might have been on government spending, I suspect at that particular moment they would have supported increased staffing for the various agencies of the Department of the Interior.

These folks were undoubtedly somewhat weary by this time, and lacking other alternatives they decided to sit down for a bit and hope for more positive developments. The report doesn't say how much time elapsed, but eventually they heard what must have been the very welcome sound of an approaching vehicle. Soon a pickup truck towing a horse trailer pulled into view. Things were finally looking up!

Our weary heroes must have been greatly relieved when the occupants of the truck agreed to give them a ride to the next closest bastion of the Proper Authorities, the National Park Service ranger station at Island in the Sky. There was, unfortunately, one small snag. The cab and bed of the truck were already full, so there was no room in the in(side) for two more passengers. They were, however, welcome to ride in the trailer with the horses.

The abbreviated official report didn't elaborate on the relationship between the two messengers and the lady with the suspected appendicitis, but it is evident that the pair was seriously committed to seeing their mission to its completion. The report is also thankfully silent on any further details about this leg of their journey, but if you've ever been around horse trailers you'll know that after they've been occupied for only a short period of time by their usual passengers (i.e., horses), they tend to acquire a rather distinctive aroma.

This fragrance arises from several sources, including the horses themselves and certain material of an organic nature that accumulates on the floor of the trailer while it's occupied. I will simply refer to this substance as "equine exhaust emissions," and while it makes great fertilizer for a garden, it's not necessarily desirable underfoot for humans. Basic models of horse trailers are also somewhat lacking in creature comforts for human passengers, especially while they are in motion, so I can only surmise that it was a rather rough and pungent ride to our heroes' destination.

In due time the pair finally arrived at the National Park ranger station and reported the emergency down on the river. A helicopter was dispatched to pick up the patient and transport her to a hospital, and our two messengers were finally rewarded for their efforts when the National Park Service employees gave them a ride back down the road to Hardscrabble Bottom so they could resume their river expedition. There was no mention of a horse trailer for this journey, so presumably they were able to ride in a more conventional and comfortable manner on their trip back to the riverbank.

When all was said and done, this was a case of "all's well that ends well," and one hopes that the pair in this tale could look back on their rather difficult quest for help and say philosophically that "this too shall pass." That would be a fitting commentary, since that's also what their lady friend with the suspected appendicitis did back in the hospital in town—with several kidney stones. I trust that she was thankful that her friends went way above and beyond the call of duty to make it possible for her to end her misadventure in the comfort of a modern hospital, a place where I trust they have minimal need for duct tape.

29

Upon Further Review . . .

Activities in the Great Outdoors provide plenty of opportunities for people to look back later and think, "I sure wish I had-
n't said (or done) that," along with some situations they're simply glad
to have escaped at least relatively unscathed. These miscues frequently
confirm the clarity of hindsight, although most of them prove (thankfully) to be an inconvenience rather than a disaster. Once the dust has
settled and everyone is safely back home they also often provide some
great stories.

A good example occurred at Padre Island National Seashore on the
lower Texas coast. Incidentally, my attorney, if I had one, would
undoubtedly advise me to include a disclaimer that I am not advocat-
ing anyone try the activity I'm about to describe!

This situation took place shortly before I began my Park Service
career, and I was visiting the area with a group of friends when we
noticed a very unusual sight. A tanned, athletic-looking man about 30
years old was wading into the water carrying a surfboard—a pretty routine activity for a beach on the Gulf Coast, except this guy had a huge
chunk of what appeared to be raw meat tucked securely under his other
arm. It therefore seems appropriate that I'll just refer to him in this tale
as "Hunk."

Closer observation revealed that this rather unappetizing mega-
morsel was connected by a stout line to the mother of all fishing rods,

247

which was in turn secured to a stout piece of pipe that had been driven into the sand. Some situations simply cry out for an explanation, and a member of my group couldn't resist the obvious question.

"Hey!" he yelled to Hunk. "What are you doing?"

The man stopped, turned around, and we were just close enough to catch his reply over the sound of the waves. His tone suggested the answer should be obvious. "I'm fishing for sharks," he shouted back.

"Sharks?" I think it's safe to say that everyone within earshot was stunned, but after a brief pause our self-designated interviewer asked the follow-up question.

"So where are you going with that—whatever it is you're carrying?"

If we'd been close enough, I suspect we would have detected a disgusted sigh. Didn't we know *anything* about fishing?

"I'm taking the bait out past the breakers. I sure can't cast it that far. Soon as I get the bait out to where the sharks are likely to be hanging out, I'll come back to the beach and wait for a strike."

Even though our group was scheduled to meet someone a couple of miles away, we felt a vague obligation (or perhaps simply morbid curiosity) to wait until we saw Hunk safely begin his trip back to shore. He must have been in incredible physical condition to paddle that surfboard with one arm while dragging the weight of that heavy fishing line behind him. I regret that I can't tell you the outcome of his angling adventure, but in the process of writing this book I discovered that shore fishing for sharks has attracted something of a following around the country.

Many shark fishing fans practice a "catch and release" approach, since this activity is not so much about fish for the grill as it is a chance to match wits and endurance with an exotic catch that sometimes outweighs the angler. Once the shark is successfully brought close to the shore, it's photographed with the fisherman, measured, and then often released to swim again another day.

While shark fishing is more easily (and safely) accomplished from a boat or pier, some practitioners such as Hunk fish from the beach and use surfboards or kayaks to transport the bait to a promising location offshore. As you fans of the movie *Jaws* will recognize, this approach is not without its risks, but based upon his demeanor Hunk didn't seem to be concerned. However, fishermen who are successful in bringing one of these impressive creatures close to land can certainly create an incentive for *other* beachgoers to reconsider their plans for the day.

Mike Edwards shared a great example of that fact in the following excerpt from his article "Shark Fishing in a Kayak," which appeared in

Unlike the fisherman in this chapter, these anglers at Cape Hatteras National Seashore in North Carolina are presumably hoping to catch something other than sharks! (National Park Service)

the *New England Sportsman* (www.nesportsman.com). He describes how a kayak can be used to transport a baited hook and tackle offshore to prime shark territory. His story takes place in a location where there had been a series of shark attacks against swimmers, and authorities were making a concerted but only partially successful effort to keep people out of the water—until a shark fisherman brought home the beast instead of the bacon.

Mr. Edwards notes, "If luck, skill and the gear all hold out a large shark is brought in to shore for pictures and bewildered viewing by fellow vacationers, some who have been swimming despite the shark warnings. After a few pictures the shark is turned towards the ocean and is let free to swim back to his environment. After viewing the sharks, many amazed swimmers often say that they are done swimming and are ready to retire to town to enjoy some dryer forms of entertainment."

I can certainly understand how viewing a shark at close range could cause more than one swimmer to conclude that his body has absorbed its Recommended Daily Allowance of salt from the surf and call it a day!

Upon Further Review . . .

Viewing a captured shark from a safe distance is one thing, but it's definitely best to avoid sharing *some* out-of-the-ordinary items or experiences with others. One of those situations occurred at California's Golden Gate National Recreation Area, when a hiker in the Marin Headlands area of that park spotted what appeared to be a "bomb-like device" in the vegetation. Proving that cell phones are a great tool but are not infallible, the man tried to call 911. Unfortunately, this was one of those spots where cell phone coverage was poor, so the answer to "Can you hear me now?" was a resounding silence.

This was clearly a serious situation, and I want to make the point that under such circumstances, the *last* thing anyone should do if they spot a suspected explosive device is to touch it, much less pick it up. Make a mental note of the exact location so authorities can find it, mark the spot with something conspicuous such as a brightly colored object you might have available, get away from the immediate area, and send for help. In the best of all possible worlds, one person could remain at a safe distance to warn others to stay clear while a second person goes to summon the experts.

The man who spotted the suspicious device certainly had good intentions, and since he was alone, could not reach anyone by cell phone, and was concerned that someone else might be endangered by the item, he decided to take matters—literally—into his own hands. He picked up the possible bomb, took it to his vehicle, and drove to the Coast Guard facility at Fort Baker, arriving at about 7 P.M.

Details about the exact conversation that ensued when this gentleman arrived at the Coast Guard station are not available. However, I think it's a safe bet that a good way to ruin someone's perfectly good evening would be to show up at their door and say something like, "Hi there, I've found what I think might be a bomb and I brought it to you to take care of. It's in my car, which is parked right here in your driveway."

For most people, this would register in the red zone on the Tums-O-Meter, since this form of "show and tell" would certainly qualify as a Truly Unsettling Melancholy Situation.

A park ranger and U.S. Park Police officers were summoned, and they in turn requested assistance from a nearby bomb squad. Those experts arrived a couple of hours later, which was probably not a case of "Time flies when you're having fun." After careful examination the specialists determined that the mystery item was a homemade fireworks device. It was subsequently dismantled and destroyed, and the situation thankfully had a successful ending.

As we leave this particular scene, I offer a sincere salute to the brave folks who serve on bomb squads everywhere. I once saw a photo of a man wearing a black T-shirt with the following legend emblazoned in large white letters on the back: "I am a bomb technician. If you see me running, try to keep up." Good advice, and I refer you to another popular slogan that I feel sure this gentleman would support when it comes to handling suspected explosives: "These are professionals; don't try this at home"—or anywhere else.

Whether it's at home or on the job, most of us at one time or another will tackle a job that's outside our realm of experience. Although thankfully those situations are much less serious than disposing of suspected bombs, they can still create some interesting opportunities for a look back with the thought, "I wish I'd done that just a little differently."

Greg Gnesios from Grand Junction, Colorado, recently completed a long career with the NPS, and he shared the following great illustration of the hindsight factor. Rangers have traditionally been adept at a lot of different tasks, but Greg's tale of the great doorknob caper certainly qualifies as unique. I'll let him tell the story in his own words:

> When I was a young park ranger in Canyonlands National Park back in the mid-1970s, the budget finally allowed for replacement of the old and quite smelly pit toilets that had graced the campground for many a year. Maintenance crews were called in to remove the outhouses and build, in their place, three brand-new, cinderblock vault toilets. As the work neared completion, the season drew to a close and the maintenance guys were directed elsewhere.
>
> All that remained to complete the toilet job was to put door knobs on them. My boss called me to his office one morning, handed me the doorknobs and told me to put them on the new vault toilets. I knew absolutely nothing about installing doorknobs but, not wanting to admit that, I took them and headed for the campground.
>
> Things went relatively well until I got to the third and final toilet. I was inside, making the final adjustments to the doorknob. My screw driver, park radio, and other items were outside. I shut the door to test it, then realized I had put the knob and lock on backwards and was thus trapped inside the vault toilet! It was a winter day and no one else was in the campground, and I was too embarrassed to shout for help anyway.
>
> I spent several minutes trying to figure out how to extricate myself from this dilemma. Then I noticed a small, triangular area at the peak of the toilet where screening had been put in to allow for ventilation.

It looked like, if I stepped onto the toilet seat and really stretched myself, I might just be able to cut the screen and squeeze through the opening. After much struggling, I did just that—cut a slit into the screen, squirmed my way out the opening and dropped to the ground and back to freedom.

Once outside, I immediately reinstalled the doorknob the proper way, collected my tools, and left the area. No one ever knew what had happened, but the slit in that screen remained there for several years as a reminder of my big adventure.

Greg's experience proves once again that agility and the ability to improvise are very useful attributes for a good park ranger. His situation certainly required some "thinking outside the box" to *get* outside that box!

Some "upon further review" situations involve words rather than deeds, and I observed a good example during my assignment at Lake Mead National Recreation Area. This one occurred while I was working at Willow Beach, in the far northwestern corner of Arizona. That's a rather sparsely populated part of the country, so more of our visitors came from the Las Vegas area and even Southern California than from Arizona. We also had a pretty high percentage of repeat visitors, some of whom had been coming to that area for many years.

Irrespective of where they lived, some of these regular customers gradually developed a sense of ownership of the area, and the fact that they viewed it as "my park" wasn't necessarily bad. Such attitudes can encourage some people to take a little better care of the features and facilities in the park. In this particular case, however, proprietary interest caused a classic case of foot-in-mouth disease.

It was a beautiful Saturday morning, the sun shone brightly from cloudless skies, a gentle breeze helped cool the desert air, and the sparkling blue water of the lake beckoned to a host of boaters lined up for their turn at the launch ramp. Parking spaces near the ramp were filled to capacity, and latecomers were relegated to an overflow lot some distance away. One of our regulars had arrived early and had a prime parking space, immediately adjacent to the marina. His spot afforded a good view of the hustle and bustle and occasional entertainment that occurs when too many people are in a hurry to launch their boats at the same time.

The man in question was well known to other locals for his rather grouchy disposition, so I'll just call him Oscar in honor of a famous character on the children's television program *Sesame Street*. Oscar was slouched against his pickup truck and surveying the busy scene on the ramp below when I happened to walk by. He spotted me and decided to offer a comment about the world in general and the crowded conditions in particular.

"Hey Ranger!"

I recognized him immediately, greeted him in return, and paused briefly in my appointed rounds to see if he just wanted to make conversation or actually needed some help.

"Looks like you've got your hands full today," Oscar observed astutely.

"Yes, sir, it's a typical Saturday for this time of the year."

Oscar scanned the sea of cars, trucks, and boat trailers in the jammed parking lot and the line of vehicles waiting their turn on the boat ramp and made the Comment of the Week: "Well, this place would be pretty nice if all these yahoos from out-of-state would just stay at home."

Since we happened to be standing in Arizona at the time, the irony of this remark wasn't lost on another group of visitors who overhead Oscar's remark as they strolled past. They had almost completed the hike back to the boat ramp from the overflow parking area and had worked up a respectable sweat in the process. One of them stopped, wiped his brow, glanced first at the Nevada license plate on Oscar's truck, and then back at our self-appointed philosopher.

"Man, you're exactly right! Maybe we ought to ask the park to reserve these prime parking spaces for people like us who live right here in Arizona." He paused briefly for effect, and then tossed the zinger. "What state are *you* from, by the way?"

I don't think the distinct reddish tinge that suddenly appeared on Oscar's face was entirely due to the abundant desert sunshine.

"Well," he huffed, "I'm from just up the road in Vegas. I was talking about all them *Californians*." Pointing across the water to the opposite cliffs, he wrapped up his defense. "That's Nevada, just right across the river. All the same here at Lake Mead, Nevada and Arizona."

"Oh, okay," concluded the new arrival as his group resumed their walk. "I thought maybe you were from the State of Confusion."

In his defense Oscar was in pretty exalted company when it came to muddled geography. A former high-ranking elected official whom I'll leave unnamed is reported to have once said, "I *love* California. I practically *grew up* in Phoenix!"

This view of Black Canyon and Lake Mohave is not far from Willow Beach in Lake Mead National Recreation Area. The boundary between Arizona and Nevada runs through the center of the canyon and follows the channel of the Colorado River, which now lies beneath the waters of the lake. (Phil Stoffer, USGS)

Regardless of where *you* grew up I hope you've had an opportunity to enjoy some of the scenic wonders and historical landmarks found in our parks and other public lands. Thanks for letting me share the stories in this book with you. I hope you've enjoyed them and perhaps even learned something during our time together that will help you avoid a visit to Oscar's "State of Confusion"—or the need to subject your recreational pursuits to any further review.

I wish for you safe and pleasant journeys and trust that you'll have some fun adventures—but no *mis*adventures—on any future trips to the Great Outdoors. Whenever you're out and about, if you encounter any rangers along the way, tell them "Hey" for me.

Sources of Additional Information

Books and Videos

There are numerous guidebooks about national parks and other public lands in the U.S. and abroad. To ensure you have current information, check with your favorite bookseller for recent editions or see the websites under the following listing for "Organizations and Government Agencies." Listed below are a few useful sources of additional information about the Great Outdoors.

Association of National Park Rangers. 2004. "Live the Adventure–Join the National Park Service." If you're interested in becoming a national park ranger, this short pamphlet does a fine job of explaining the kinds of opportunities that are available, the requirements that must be met to qualify for a position, and some key terms that help unravel the mysteries of applying for a government job. You can order a copy online at http://www.anpr.org/ or contact ANPR at 25958 Genesee Trail Rd., PMB 222, Golden, CO 80401.

———. 1999 "Lost ! . . . but Found, Safe and Sound." This is a twelve-minute, professionally produced video that is designed to show children, ages four to twelve, what to do if they become lost in remote areas such as parks or forests. It is available in DVD, VHS, or CD-ROM format. For ordering information, see the above entry for this same organization.

Farabee, Charles "Butch." 2005. *Death, Daring, and Disaster: Search and Rescue in the National Parks*. Rev. ed. Taylor Trade Publishing, 576 pages. A retired ranger who was a leader in the field of search and rescue, the author describes hundreds of exciting tales of heroism and tragedy drawn from the nearly 150,000 search-and-rescue missions carried out by the National Park Service since 1872.

———. 2003. *National Park Ranger: An American Icon*. Roberts Rinehart, 180 pages. Farabee traces the history of park rangers from the early days of Yellowstone National Park, when the army performed that role, through the establishment of the present-day National Park Service in 1916, and on to the modern era. The book describes some of the duties of early rangers, provides some interesting anecdotes from more contemporary times, and includes plenty of historic photos to illustrate the romance of this unique profession.

Whittlesey, Lee H. 1998. *Death in Yellowstone: Accidents and Foolhardiness in the First National Park*. Roberts Rinehart, 240 pages. A review from *Booklist* says, "Whittlesey believes that far too many people enter our national parks with 'a false sense of security'. . . He then goes on to chronicle the deaths in Yellowstone National Park of more than 250 people." In addition to a good history of incidents in Yellowstone, this book provides some excellent tips to help readers avoid encountering a similar fate anywhere in the out-of-doors.

Organizations and Government Agencies

The Association of National Park Rangers is a nonprofit organization "created to communicate for, about and with park rangers, and to promote and enhance the park ranger profession and its spirit. Membership of ANPR is comprised of individuals who are entrusted with and committed to the care, study, explanation and/or protection of those natural, cultural and recreational resources included in the National Park System, and persons who support these efforts." The organization publishes a quarterly magazine, *Ranger*. For more information, see its website, www.anpr.org/ or contact its business office at 25958 Genesee Trail Road, PMB 222, Golden, CO 80401.

The Association of Partners for Public Lands (APPL). Not-for-profit organizations known as "cooperating" or "interpretive" associations operate bookstores and conduct a variety of educational programs at many national parks, forests, wildlife refuges, and similar areas. A number of those groups are members of APPL, and you can find a directory of those organizations and links to their websites at www.appl.org/ Members_New/member_directory.htm.

Bureau of Land Management (BLM) is an agency within the U.S. Department of the Interior that administers millions of acres of America's public lands, located primarily in the western states. These areas provide a variety of recreational opportunities. More information is available at www.blm.gov/.

The **National Park Service** (NPS) website (www.nps.gov) has a wealth of information about any park in the system, as well as plenty of other details about the agency, including employment and volunteer opportunities. The site also has links to National Park Cooperating Associations, the not-for-profit partner organizations that operate bookstores in many parks and that offer a wide variety of publications, maps, audiovisual programs, and park-related merchandise.

National Parks Conservation Association is a nonpartisan, nonprofit organization that since 1919 has been the leading voice of the American people in the fight to safeguard our National Park System. NPCA, its members, and its partners work together to protect the park system and preserve our nation's natural, historical, and cultural heritage for future generations. Members receive the group's excellent magazine, *National Parks*. You can obtain information about the organization and learn about current national park issues at www.npca.org, by writing to NPCA at 1300 19th St., N.W., Suite 300, Washington, D.C. 20036, or by phoning 800-628-7275. Its website is also a great source of information to help you plan your next visit to a national park or take action to help protect these beloved places.

National Weather Service is a good source of weather information for any area of the country. Check the forecast prior to heading out on your next trip to a park—or anywhere else in the United States—on the website, www.nws.noaa.gov/.

U.S. Army Corps of Engineers operates recreational facilities including campgrounds and boat ramps at numerous locations across the country. See the website at www.corpslakes.us/ for more information.

U.S. Fish and Wildlife Service is the federal agency that operates wildlife refuges across the country. For details about its facilities and a wealth of information about wildlife, see the website at www.fws.gov/. You can also contact the agency by phone during weekday business hours at 1-800-344-WILD.

U.S. Forest Service is another federal agency that is a major provider of outdoor recreation opportunities. See the website at www.fs.fed.us/ for more information.

Acknowledgments

Appreciation is gratefully expressed to the following individuals, organizations, and agencies, who provided some of the photographs, stories, or information used in this book: American Ostrich Association; Deb Anderson; Scott Anderson; Pat Ballengee; Oakley Blair; Eric Blehm; Paul Boccadoro; Kevin Callan; John Chew; Dumb.com; Mike Edwards; Roderick Eime; Dee Renee Ericks; Myra Foster; Thom Gabrukiewicz; Greg Gnesios; Mike Greenfield; Kathryn Grogman; Susan Groth; Sam Hale; Bill Hayer; Neal Herbert; Mike Holmes; Neil Howk; Linda Kennedy; Chris Largent; Anders and Barbara Lock; Bob Marley; Michigan Lawsuit Abuse Watch; National Park Service; Leslie Paige; Brett Prettyman; Susan Conrad Ream; Kurt Repanshek; Charlie Rogers; Gordon Smith; Ken Smith; Phil Stoffer, USGS; Jeremy Sullivan; Terry Traywick; U.S. Army Corps of Engineers; Melinda Webster; Ed Winfrey; Slim Woodruff.

I would like to express my gratitude to the staff at Taylor Trade Publishing who were instrumental in making this book a reality. Special thanks go to Jehanne Schweitzer for her superb work in coordinating the whole project as production editor and to Jane McGarry for her skills as copyeditor. My local expert proofreader Edith V. Oates was once again a valuable ally in finalizing the manuscript. Most of all, thanks to Rick Rinehart, editorial director at Taylor Trade Publishing, for his expert advice and encouragement in this sequel to my first book.

As in the first *Hey Ranger!* I concluded that space would not allow me to mention by name all of the colleagues from the National Park Service who were part of the stories in this book or who were instrumental in shaping my career during 30 years with that agency. Rather than omit anyone, I offer an inadequate but heartfelt thanks to all of you—and your families—who served alongside me as coworkers, supervisors, mentors, and friends. Many of you truly gave meaning to the concept of the National Park Service family.

Thanks to all of you who have read and supported my first book—readers, booksellers, reviewers, and members of the media—without you, there would be no *Hey Ranger 2*.

Finally, my career as a ranger and completion of this book would not have been possible without the encouragement and support of my immediate and extended family. To my daughter Kathy and son David, I offer special thanks for your patience during those years you grew up in sometimes difficult places to live, during those moves to new duty stations that interrupted your lives, and for those times when weird work schedules, long hours, and those infamous emergencies intruded upon family life. Most of all, to my wife Velma—best friend, life partner, and literal in-house editor—thanks for your love, patience, and help throughout this project. This book is dedicated to all of you, with love and gratitude.

Sources Quoted

Appreciation is gratefully expressed to the following authors, publishers, and organizations for permission to quote selected passages from copyrighted material:

Introduction. Quote by a former vice president courtesy of www.dumb.com, used by permission.

Chapter 1, "It Seemed Like a Good Idea at the Time." Examples of product warning label text courtesy of www.dumb.com, used by permission.

Chapter 3, "Does the River Run Downstream?" Quoted material from Ken Smith, *Buffalo River Handbook*, Ozark Society Foundation, 2004, page 234, used by permission.

Chapter 7, "Monumental Mix-ups." Stories about historical reenactors courtesy of Paul Boccadoro, "The Civil War Fife and Drum Page," www.geocities .com/cwfifedrum/duh.html, used by permission.

Chapter 8, "The Bear Facts—and a Little Fun." Headlines from news stories about bears are from the website for the "Genesis Brighton Bears Basketball Club" and are used courtesy of the editor of that site, Sam Hale, www.seriouswebsupport.com.

Chapter 10, "Sadder but Wiser?" Story about feeding kangaroos by Roderick Eime, editor of the travel website www.traveloscopy.com, used by permission.

Chapter 11, "Assumption Junction." Descriptions of the term *assumption* from *Roget's Super Thesaurus*, copyright © 2004 by Marc McCutcheon. Used with the kind permission of Writer's Digest Books, a division of F+W Publications, Inc., Cincinnati, Ohio. All rights reserved.

Chapter 17, "Skip These Tips." Quote from Kevin Callan from his article, "Bow Paddlers Are People Too," published at www.paddling.net/guidelines/ showArticle.html?176, used by permission.

Chapter 17, "Skip These Tips." Quote about kids on river trip from the September 1992 issue of the newsletter posted on www.kwagunt.net/, used by permission of Bob Marley and Susan Groth.

Chapter 20, "Don't Believe Everything You Read." Information from the annual "Wacky Warning Label Contest" is used by permission of The Michigan Lawsuit Abuse Watch (www.mlaw.org/).

Chapter 23, "Old MacDonald Had a Farm—But Not a Park." Information about ostriches is from the website for the American Ostrich Association (http://www.ostriches.org/faq.html) and is used with permission.

Chapter 29, "Upon Further Review . . ." Quotation from Mike Edwards from his article, "Shark Fishing in a Kayak," which appeared in the *New England Sportsman* (www.nesportsman.com), used by permission.

Chapter 29, "Upon Further Review . . ." Quotation by former elected official about California courtesy of www.dumb.com, used by permission.

How to Contact the Author or Order Additional Copies of the *Hey Ranger* Books

If you'd like to contact the author concerning a speaking engagement, media appearance, book signing, or similar event, my mail and e-mail addresses are provided below. A complete media kit is available upon request.

If you have questions or comments for the author about this book, my contact information is shown below. Perhaps you know about an outdoor "misadventure" you'd like to share for possible use in a sequel to this book, on our website, or for other educational purposes. Your stories don't have to be limited to national parks—such situations can occur virtually anywhere in the out-of-doors. If so, I'd enjoy hearing from you. Along with your information, just let me know how I can contact you in case I need to clarify any details. If I use your story, you can remain anonymous if you prefer!

Need additional copies of this book or the original *Hey Ranger!* for yourself or friends? If your local bookstore didn't stock enough copies, it should be able to obtain them for you. If you'd rather order them yourself from one of the many booksellers on the Internet, you'll find all the necessary details on our website (www.heyranger.com). Just be sure you order one of the two *Hey Ranger!* books by Jim Burnett.

Several other books using that same title have also been published recently.

Still need help finding a copy or don't have access to the Internet? You're welcome to contact me at the following address, and I'll be glad to help you locate a bookseller.

Jim Burnett
P.O. Box 1519
Athens, TX 75751
e-mail: heyranger@earthlink.net
on the Internet at: www.heyranger.com